Intelligent Data-Driven Modelling and Optimization in Power and Energy Applications

This book provides a comprehensive understanding of how intelligent data-driven techniques can be used for modelling, controlling, and optimizing various power and energy applications. It aims to develop multiple data-driven models for forecasting renewable energy sources and to interpret the benefits of these techniques in line with first-principles modelling approaches. By doing so, the book aims to stimulate deep insights into computational intelligence approaches in data-driven models and to promote their potential applications in the power and energy sectors. Its key features include:

- an exclusive section on essential preprocessing approaches for the data-driven model,
- a detailed overview of data-driven model applications to power system planning and operational activities,
- specific focus on developing forecasting models for renewable generations such as solar PV and wind power, and
- showcasing the judicious amalgamation of allied mathematical treatments such as optimization and fractional calculus in data-driven model-based frameworks.

This book presents novel concepts for applying data-driven models, mainly in the power and energy sectors, and is intended for graduate students, industry professionals, research, and academic personnel.

Intelligent Data-Driven Systems and Artificial Intelligence

Series Editor: *Harish Garg*

Data-Driven Technologies and Artificial Intelligence in Supply Chain: Tools and Techniques
Mahesh Chand, Vineet Jain and Puneeta Ajmera

Intelligent Data-Driven Modelling and Optimization in Power and Energy Applications

Edited by
B Rajanarayan Prusty, Neeraj Gupta, Kishore Bingi, and Rakesh Sehgal

CRC Press
Taylor & Francis Group
Boca Raton London New York

CRC Press is an imprint of the
Taylor & Francis Group, an **informa** business

Designed cover image: Shutterstock

MATLAB® and Simulink® are trademarks of The MathWorks, Inc. and are used with permission. The MathWorks does not warrant the accuracy of the text or exercises in this book. This book's use or discussion of MATLAB® or Simulink® software or related products does not constitute endorsement or sponsorship by The MathWorks of a particular pedagogical approach or particular use of the MATLAB® and Simulink® software.

First edition published 2024

by CRC Press
2385 NW Executive Center Drive, Suite 320, Boca Raton FL 33431

and by CRC Press
4 Park Square, Milton Park, Abingdon, Oxon, OX14 4RN

CRC Press is an imprint of Taylor & Francis Group, LLC

ISBN: 978-1-032-47206-5 (hbk)
ISBN: 978-1-032-70790-7 (pbk)
ISBN: 978-1-003-47027-4 (ebk)

DOI: 10.1201/9781003470274

Typeset in Sabon
by Deanta Global Publishing Services, Chennai, India

Contents

Preface

In engineering, model development is a common practice used to understand and solve complex problems, particularly non-linear ones. Recently, there has been a surge of interest in data-driven models for modern engineering systems due to their accuracy and ease in modelling highly non-linear systems and their uncertainties. These models extract critical information from the data that characterize a strategy and establish relationships among input, internal, and output variables without requiring knowledge of their physical behaviour. To develop these models, it is imperative to have a deep understanding of statistics, computational intelligence, optimization, signal processing, and data analytics. Among data-driven modelling frameworks, machine learning/deep learning models are fundamental and they have been impressively used in the literature. In addition, fractional calculus is a dominating research area that adds another dimension to enrich existing data-driven models. Novel fractional calculus-based activation functions and training algorithms have been proven to be potential candidates for boosting the performance of data-driven modelling frameworks. Recent research has also utilized optimization concepts to develop elegant models that facilitate the execution of feasible decisions.

Data-driven models have tremendous applications in allied engineering, particularly in power and energy applications. These models can be used for load/renewable generation forecasting, energy consumption estimation, smart energy assessment, smart building energy prediction, smart grid stability prediction, cyber security of power systems, and more. With growing concerns regarding climate change, environmental protection, and sustainable development, power and energy generation and its applications have become essential for the economical and safe operation of traditional and sustainable energy. However, more than traditional first-principles modelling approaches are required due to the ever-growing system scale and uncertainties. This is where machine learning, data-driven modelling, and optimization techniques come into play, offering an improved alternative to traditional methods. In light of this, this book provides a detailed understanding of the application of intelligent data-driven techniques for modelling, control, and optimization in various power and energy applications. The book also aims to develop multiple data-driven models for forecasting renewable energy sources. In all cases, the benefits of intelligent data-driven techniques are interpreted according to first-principles modelling approaches. Ultimately, the book aims to stimulate deep insights into computational intelligence approaches in data-driven models and to promote their potential applications in the power and energy sectors.

MATLAB® is a registered trademark of The MathWorks, Inc. For product information, please contact:

The MathWorks, Inc.
3 Apple Hill Drive
Natick, MA 01760-2098 USA
Tel: 508 647 7000
Fax: 508-647-7001
E-mail: info@mathworks.com
Web: www.mathworks.com

Editors

B Rajanarayan Prusty (Senior Member, IEEE) is a Professor and Dean (Research) at Galgotias University, Greater Noida, India. He obtained his Ph.D. from the National Institute of Technology Karnataka, Surathkal. His exceptional research work during his Ph.D. has led him to win the prestigious POSOCO Power System Awards for 2019 by Power System Operation Corporation Limited in partnership with IIT Delhi. In recognition of his publications from 2017 to 2019, he was awarded the University Foundation Day Research Award 2019 from BPUT, Rourkela, Odisha. He has 30 SCI journal publications and 50 international conference publications. He has authored 10 book chapters. He has co-authored a textbook entitled *Power System Analysis: Operation and Control* in I. K. International Publishing House Pvt. Ltd. He has also edited two books for CRC Press. He has been an active reviewer and has reviewed more than 500 manuscripts. He is the Associate Editor of the *Journal of Electrical Engineering & Technology* and the *International Journal of Power and Energy Systems*. He is also the Academic Editor for the journals (i) *Mathematical Problems in Engineering*, (ii) *International Transactions on Electrical Energy Systems*, and (iii) *Journal of Electrical and Computer Engineering*. He has handled more than 200 manuscripts in the capacity of Journal Editor. His research interests include data preprocessing, time series forecasting, high-dimensional dependence modelling, and applying machine learning and probabilistic methods to power system problems.

Neeraj Gupta obtained his Ph.D. in power systems from the Indian Institute of Technology Roorkee, Roorkee, India. He is a senior member of IEEE. He was a faculty with Thapar University, from 2008 to 2009, Adani Institute of Infrastructure Engineering, Ahmedabad, India, in 2015 and NIT Hamirpur from 2015 to 2018, and presently, he has been working as Assistant Professor with the Electrical Engineering Department, National Institute of Technology, Srinagar, J&K, India. His work has been published in Q-1 international journals of repute like IEEE, Elsevier, etc. He is presently guiding four Ph.D. scholars in the area of power systems. He has also supervised eight M.Tech. and four B.Tech. dissertations. He has more than 40 SCI journal publications/conference publications/book chapters to his credit. He has edited three books titled *Control of Standalone Microgrid* (Elsevier 2021), *Renewable Energy Integration to the Grid: A Probabilistic Perspective* (CRC Press 2022), and *Smart Electrical and Mechanical Systems: An Application Publisher* (Elsevier 2022). He has been an active reviewer since 2015 and has reviewed 200 manuscripts submitted to repute SCI-indexed journals/conferences. He has delivered 15 invited expert talks in various organizations in India. He is also the scientific advisory/organizing secretary of many reputed conferences in the country. He is a referee of reputed journals of IEEE, Elsevier, Taylor and Francis, IET, and so on. He has been included in the list of top 2% highly cited scientists by Stanford University working in power in 2021. His research interests include the uncertainty quantification of power system; probabilistic power system; solar, wind, and electric vehicle technologies; artificial intelligence; machine learning; prediction; and so on.

Kishore Bingi received his B.Tech. degree in Electrical and Electronics Engineering from Acharya Nagarjuna University, Guntur, Andhra Pradesh, India, in 2012. He received his M.Tech. degree in Instrumentation and Control Systems from the National Institute of Technology Calicut, India, in 2014, and a Ph.D. in Electrical and Electronic Engineering from Universiti Teknologi PETRONAS, Malaysia, in 2019. From 2014 to 2015, he worked as Assistant Systems Engineer at TATA Consultancy Services Limited, India. From 2019 to 2020, he worked as Research Scientist and Post-Doctoral Researcher at the Universiti Teknologi PETRONAS, Malaysia. From 2020 to 2022, he served as Assistant Professor at the Process Control Laboratory, School of Electrical Engineering, Vellore Institute of Technology, Vellore, India. Since 2022, he has been working as a faculty member at the Department of Electrical and Electronic Engineering at Universiti Teknologi PETRONAS, Seri Iskandar, Perak, Malaysia. His research area is developing fractional-order neural networks, including fractional-order systems and controllers, chaos prediction and forecasting, and advanced hybrid optimization techniques. He is an IEEE and IET Member and a registered Chartered Engineer (CEng) from the Engineering Council, UK.

Rakesh Sehgal is currently working as Professor (HAG) at the National Institute of Technology, Hamirpur (H.P.), after serving as Director of the National Institute of Technology for more than five years. Prof. Sehgal received his B.E. degree in Mechanical Engineering with distinction from the Faculty of Engineering & Technology, Annamalai University (T.N.), M.Tech. in Design of Mechanical Equipment from IIT Delhi with 9.75 CGPA securing the first position in Design stream and Ph.D. in Tribology from R.E.C. Kurukshetra, Kurukshetra University. He pursued Post-Doctorate in the area of thermal behaviour of non-circular hydrodynamic journal bearings under the UGC Fellowship Award between 2009 and 2011 and developed film thickness equations for elliptical and off-set halves hydrodynamic journal bearings. Prof. Sehgal has a distinguished career of 38 years in the field, teaching, research, and administration. Prof. Sehgal has supervised 11 Ph.D. scholars and 1 post-doctoral scholar in the area of tribo-materials, active vibration control, and thermal analysis of non-circular journal bearings for various industrial applications in automobile, aerospace, and metal rolling sectors. He is presently guiding seven Ph.D. scholars in the area of material's tribology. He has published 178 research papers in international/national journals and international/national conference proceedings, 6 reference books, 3 patents, and 22 high-quality book chapters. Prof. Sehgal has completed 6 high-value research projects (5 national and 1 international) and is currently handling 3 (1 national and 2 international) projects. He has attended more than 35 international/national conferences in India and abroad.

Contributors

Pihu Agarwal
Dayalbagh Educational Institute
Dayalbagh, Agra,
Uttar Pradesh, India

Arshaque Ali
School of Information Technology,
   Engineering, Mathematics and
   Physics (STEMP)
The University of the South
   Pacific (USP)
Laucala Campus, Suva, Fiji

Tania Arora
Dayalbagh Educational Institute
Dayalbagh, Agra,
Uttar Pradesh, India

Mohamed Atef
School of Engineering and
   Technology
Central Queensland University
Gladstone, QLD, Australia

Kishore Bingi
Department of Electrical and
   Electronics Engineering
Universiti Teknologi PETRONAS
Seri Iskandar, Malaysia

Maurizio Cirrincione
School of Information Technology,
   Engineering, Mathematics and
   Physics (STEMP)

The University of the South Pacific
   (USP)
Laucala Campus, Suva, Fiji

Neeraj Gupta
Department of Electrical
   Engineering
National Institute of Technology
Srinagar, India

Rosdiazli Ibrahim
Department of Electrical and
   Electronics Engineering
Universiti Teknologi PETRONAS
Seri Iskandar, Malaysia

Sujith Jacob
School of Computer Science
   Engineering
Vellore Institute of Technology
Vellore, Tamil Nadu, India

Ramani Kannan
Department of Electrical and
   Electronics Engineering
Universiti Teknologi PETRONAS
Seri Iskandar, Malaysia

Purna Prakash Kasaraneni
Department of Computer Science
   and Engineering
Koneru Lakshmaiah Education
   Foundation

Vaddeswaram, Andhra Pradesh,
   India

Venkata Ramana Kasi
School of Electrical Engineering
Vellore Institute of Technology
Vellore, Tamil Nadu, India

Ashneel Kumar
School of Information Technology
   Engineering, Mathematics and
   Physics (STEMP)
The University of the South Pacific
   (USP)
Laucala Campus, Suva, Fiji

Gaurav Kumar
Department of Electronics and
   Engineering
Alliance College of Engineering
   and Design
Alliance University
Bengaluru, Karnataka, India

Yellapragada Venkata Pavan Kumar
School of Electronics Engineering
VIT-AP University
Amaravati, Andhra Pradesh, India

Utkal Mehta
School of Information Technology
   Engineering, Mathematics and
   Physics (STEMP)
The University of the South Pacific
   (USP)
Laucala Campus, Suva, Fiji

Madiah Omar
Department of Chemical
   Engineering
Universiti Teknologi PETRONAS
Seri Iskandar, Malaysia

B Rajanarayan Prusty
Department of Electrical, Electronics
   and Communication Engineering
School of Engineering, Galgotias
   University
Greater Noida, Uttar Pradesh, India

Bhukya Ramadevi
School of Electrical Engineering
Vellore Institute of Technology
Vellore, Tamil Nadu, India

Md Masud Rana
School of Engineering &
   Information Technology
The University of New South Wales
Canberra, ACT, Australia

Challa Pradeep Reddy
School of Computer Science and
   Engineering
VIT-AP University
Amaravati, Andhra Pradesh, India

Md Rasel Sarkar
School of Engineering &
   Information Technology
The University of New South Wales
Canberra, ACT, Australia

K. Pritam Satsangi
Dayalbagh Educational Institute
   Dayalbagh, Agra,
Uttar Pradesh, India

G. M. Shafiullah
Discipline of Engineering
   and Energy
Murdoch University
Perth, WA, Australia

Moslem Uddin
School of Engineering &
   Information Technology
The University of New South Wales
Canberra, ACT, Australia

Prem Prakash Vuppuluri
Dayalbagh Educational Institute
Dayalbagh, Agra,
Uttar Pradesh, India

Chapter 1

Preprocessing approaches for data-driven modelling

Kishore Bingi, B Rajanarayan Prusty,
and Neeraj Gupta

1.1 INTRODUCTION

Time series data which refers to a chronologically ordered sample at regular time intervals is enormously used in research that involves data-driven models [1, 2, 3, 4]. Real-world raw time series needs an extra preprocessing step, after which it can be used for data-driven model development based on the application. This preprocessing step may involve one or several steps. In the literature, few notable data preprocessing activities are performed. They are (i) missing value updation, (ii) outlier detection and correction, (iii) characterization of predictable variation in data, (iv) data decomposition, etc. More than one of the above activities is performed in specific applications before data-driven model development. This chapter considers outlier detection and correction as preprocessing. In a time series dataset, an observation (or a set of observations) that appears inconsistent, i.e., deviates notably from the remaining samples, is referred to as an outlier. An outlier is alternatively termed an anomaly, outlying observation, etc. [1]. Overwhelming research interest has recently been observed in time series forecasting, where the prediction accuracy depends on data quality often affected by outlying data samples [5]. Therefore, the detection of outliers is of paramount importance and serves as the first stage of data preprocessing. Although most of the research excludes the detected outliers from the dataset, research that deals with time series and accounts for the autocorrelation and cross-correlation effects demands an additional stage termed outliers' correction (an appropriate replacement of the corrupted data). Hence, data preprocessing, which performs outliers' detection and their apt correction, is vital in building precise forecasting models [1, 2]. Besides, the application of outlier detection and correction algorithm is also indispensable in the following applications, to name a few but not limited to.

- Sensor networks,
- Image processing,
- Healthcare analysis and medical diagnosis,
- Data logs and process logs,

DOI: 10.1201/9781003470274-1   1

- Fraud detection,
- Intrusion detection, etc.

It is always expected that a preprocessing method's detection and correction performances are ideal. The objective of ideal outlier detection is to (i) spot true positives (TPs) and (ii) ensure zero false positive (FP) and false negative (FN) counts. Whereas ideal outlier correction aims to (i) bring back the TP(s) to their corresponding clean data value(s) and (ii) leave FP(s) unaffected [6]. Here, TP refers to a data point correctly detected as an outlier, whereas FP corresponds to a data point incorrectly detected as an outlier. The indicator FN is an undetected outlier. In general, to check whether a preprocessing method perform ideal, the following points may be checked.

1. When there are no outliers, the preprocessing method should not detect any outliers.
2. If p_i, $i = 1, 2, \ldots, p$ is the number of times a given data is preprocessed by "p" methods and stops once no outliers are detected, then the method with the lesser value of p indicates better preprocessing accuracy.

A great deal of literature addresses the importance of data preprocessing. The outlier data points' position in the raw time series being unknown prior, a preprocessing method's performance evaluation via graphical interpretation is a way to highlight a method's success or failure [5, 7]. It is important to highlight that the performance comparison among various methods with numeric values can only be possible if the information about outliers is known prior. This can be done if outlier correction is performed on a polluted dataset formed by introducing outliers in a synthetically generated clean dataset. Further, complex trends, seasonality, and volatility effects may be synthetically embedded in the clean dataset to investigate preprocessing methods' ability to detect and correct outliers in these facets' presence. In this chapter, x, y, and z represent clean, polluted, and corrected data. The calculation of the F-score using TP, FP and FN helps evaluate the detection performance of a set of methods [1, 3, 4, 6, 8]. The nonzero FP and FN count by a preprocessing method indicates the method's failure to distinguish outliers and exactness.

While mammoth research interest in recent times is focused on proposing a new preprocessing method, it has been literally overlooked in formulating a new set of reliable performance metrics for impartial preprocessing result comparison. Not much research has focused on developing suitable metrics for assessing outlier correction performance. Overall preprocessing performance assessment uses metrics such as Mean Absolute Error (MAE) [5] and Root Mean Square Error (RMSE) [9]. The error metrics' values were calculated between clean data and preprocessed data by a method. On the contrary, the accuracy of the preprocessing in [2] and [5] is based on the obtained forecasting result. Forecasting accuracy depends on several factors, including data preprocessing; therefore, it is not wise to comment on the preprocessing performance of a set of methods solely based on forecasting accuracy. The above approaches must signify the level to which a method is suitable. The authors in [6] overcome the above-highlighted lacunae by proposing a new metric named Complemented Normalized Sum of Absolute Deviations (CNSAD) to compare several methods' correction abilities numerically. With the help of a detailed result analysis, it is revealed that the overall preprocessing performance assessment using an error-calculation-based metric (e.g., MAE) underweights the detection performance [6]. Since the detection performance using the F-score is directly affected by TP and FP counts, a new unbiased metric, OPP, equally weighing detection and correction performances, was suggested by Jain et al. [6] to combine F-score and CNSAD.

The ensuing sections in this chapter are planned as mentioned below. Firstly, the challenges for a preprocessing method to preprocess a seasonal time series used in power and energy application is discussed. A few well-established techniques in the present context are cited, followed by a comprehensive performance comparison. The available metrics for outlier detection and correction are thoroughly explained, highlighting each one's merits and demerits. A special interest is devoted to highlighting their significance. This chapter further proposes new outlier correction metrics to envisage how the correction performance of a preprocessing method against each characteristic of ideal outlier correction. A detailed case study and result validation section is included to provide a better understanding of the discussed concepts via numeric quantification. Finally, the concluding remarks, along with future scopes, are enlisted.

1.2 PREPROCESSING OF SEASONAL TIME SERIES

Time series used in power and energy application are seasonal and have inherent trend and volatility effects. The presence of the above facets in the time series makes it hard for a preprocessing method to effectively preprocess as each of the above aspects has its categories, and it is challenging to build a generic algorithm that can effectively fit a particular application. Although a great deal of literature has proposed various preprocessing methods, selecting a suitable method for data preprocessing for a particular application requires a performance comparison among existing methods [1, 5, 6]. Outlier detection and correction methods can be designed to preprocess univariate and multivariate datasets. While a univariate outlier represents a variable's extreme value, a multivariate outlier, on the other hand, is the combination of unusual values of at least two variables. Methods based on statistics and distance are applied for the preprocessing of univariate outliers. On the other hand, for a multivariate dataset, methods based on density and clustering concepts are used. Each approach highlighted above has limitations while dealing with seasonal time series Embodying different time series facets. Further challenges arise when the length of the time series is increased. A mammoth research interest is devoted to preprocessing univariate time series in the literature.

Univariate methods such as Improved Sliding Window Prediction (ISWP), Portrait dataset-based (PDB), k-nearest neighbor (kNN), and B-spline are a few well-established methods extensively used for seasonal time series in power and energy applications. As detection and correction are two crucial stages of data preprocessing, the overall performance depends on each stage's recital. Additionally, a preprocessing method's performance is affected by time series length. A method may not develop/adjust a proper relational model for a shorter time series. In contrast, the challenge for more extended time series is the system's processing power computing the calculations (e.g., B-spline and kNN) [6]. A thorough comparison of well-established methods considering several attributes is elucidated in Table 1.1. For each feature, the performance level and the corresponding reason highlighted in the table help a novice researcher get enough experience about a method's performance, shortcomings, and possible improvements needed while proposing a new method.

1.3 PERFORMANCE EVALUATION METRICS

Identifying unbiased performance evaluation metrics is necessary to compare the preprocessing performance of several methods applied to a given data. Most of the research uses metrics for outlier detection, and there are hardly any metrics for outlier correction. Various outlier detection metrics are portrayed in Figure 1.1. The figure provides the formulations of the detection indicators Precision (P), Recall (R), and F, along with their range values. The significance of the basic indicators TP, FP, and FN are comprehended. Outlier correction is an equally important concern, like detection. Accurate outlier correction adds to a method's enhanced overall accuracy. A preprocessing method's correction capability strictly depends on the data characteristics, which often vary while dealing with outliers on the upper and lower extreme sides, i.e., Upper Extreme Outlier (UEO) and Lower Extreme Outlier (LEO). Focusing on extreme outliers is based on the belief that if a method can accurately handle them, it can undoubtedly deal with the other outliers [6]. The following terminologies are frequently used in the ensuing sections.

> Upper side – Data points above the time-varying mean line.
> Lower side – Data points below the time-varying mean line.
> Extreme side – The one-third portion towards the time series edge.

If outliers' information in a polluted dataset is known prior, a metric ranging between 0 and 1 can be designed using (i) averaging absolute relative

Table 1.1 Comparison of methods' preprocessing performance while handling a seasonal time series

No.	Attribute	Performance	ISWP	PDB	kNN	B-Spline
1	Detection of TP(s)	Level	Average	Good	Poor	Poor
		Reason	Local neighbourhood is used for prediction	Analyses the data in portrait view.	Depends on similarity/dissimilarity between data segments/windows.	Fits a curve using all data points including outliers results in detection of low number of TPs.
2	Correction of TP(s)	Level	Average	Poor	NA	Poor
		Reason	Calculates average of seasonally periodic values.	Considers median value of a portrait dataset.		Replaces outliers with their fitted curve value, which itself is affected by outliers.
3	Detection of FP(s)	Level	Good	Poor	Very poor	Good
		Reason	Local neighbourhood is used for prediction.	Detection performance depends on stability of the portrait dataset.	Declares entire window as outlier	Fits a curve that follows the periodic pattern in the raw data.
4	Correction of FP(s)	Level	Good	Very poor	NA	Poor
		Reason	Calculates average of seasonally periodic values.	Considers median value of a portrait dataset.		Replaces outliers with their fitted curve value, which itself is affected by outliers.
5	Overall detection accuracy	Level	Good	Average	Very poor	Poor
		Reason	Prediction using local points results in high TP counts and very low FP counts.	Portrait mechanism results in high TP counts and high FP counts.	Similarity/dissimilarity check between data segments results in low TP counts and high FP counts.	Curve fitting using raw data points results in low TP counts and low FP counts.

Continued

Table 1.1 Continued

No.	Attribute	Performance	ISWP	PDB	kNN	B-Spline
6	Overall correction accuracy	Level	Good	Very poor	NA	Poor
		Reason	Replacing an outlier with average of its periodic values results in low deviation from clean data value, for both TPs and FPs.	Replacing outliers with median of a portrait dataset often results in very high deviation from clean data value, for both TPs and FPs.		Depends on the magnitude of outliers and results in a high deviation of corrected data from the clean data.
7	Effectiveness to tackle any time resolution	Level	Average	Average	Poor	Very poor
		Reason	Works better for high-resolution data due to the use of local neighbourhood for prediction and periodic values for correction.	High-resolution portrait datasets are more unstable, which affects the performance.	High-resolution data segments are more dissimilar which downgrades the performance.	High-resolution data affects curve-fitting process and hence lowers the entire performance.
8	Effectiveness to tackle any time series length	Level	Good	Average	Very poor	Poor
		Reason	It only uses the local neighbourhood of a point, hence can process any length of data.	Data within a portrait dataset are unstable for longer time series, affecting the overall performance.	Longer the data, lesser is the similarity between data segments which affects the overall performance.	Curve fitting becomes difficult with increase in length of the time series, degrading the overall performance.

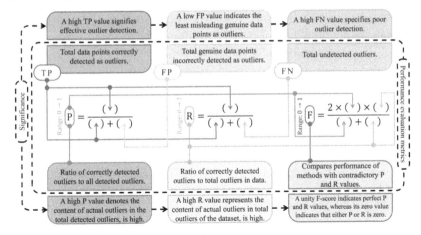

Figure 1.1 Outlier detection metrics and their significances.

deviations and (ii) normalizing the sum of absolute deviations. The metric Average Absolute Relative Deviations (AARD) is expressed as,

$$\text{AARD} = \frac{1}{\text{TP} + \text{FP}} \sum_{i=1}^{\text{TP+FP}} \frac{|z_{j_i} - x_{j_i}|}{|x_{j_i}|},$$ (1.1)

where:
  i – Counting variable for detected outliers,
  j_i – Index of ith outlier,
  x_{j_i} – j_ith value of x, and
  z_{j_i} – j_ith value of z.

In Equation (1.1), the summands corresponding to extreme outliers may exceed one. It is explained with an example in Section 1.3.1. The existence of most of such cases leads AARD value greater than one. This scenario more likely to happen for LEOs compared to UEOs. This clearly indicates AARD fails to compare correction performance unbiased. Outlier correction is affected by positioning of outliers and the total number of outliers present. The above aspects must be taken into account while designing a stable correction metric. On this note, normalization, i.e., the second approach seems befitting where the method's correction ability is quantified by the SAD. In this case, the metric value always lies in the interval [0, 1]; therefore, it is fit for numeric comparison among methods. For ideal outlier correction, the SAD value becomes zero, i.e., the lowest, whereas its value is maximum, i.e., SAD^M for the worst-case outlier correction. Normalized Sum of Absolute Deviations (NSAD) is expressed as,

$$\text{NSAD} = \frac{\text{SAD}}{\text{SAD}^M}.$$ (1.2)

A typical correction method corrects an outlier either based on an estimation using polluted data or based on polluted data's mean, or median. In either of the cases, the corrected data lies within the limits $y_{L_{Lim}}$ and $y_{U_{Lim}}$ of the polluted dataset. Therefore, SAD^M is expressed as,

$$\text{SAD}^M = \sum_{i=1}^{\text{TP+FP}} \max(|y_{U_{Lim}} - x_{j_i}|, |y_{L_{Lim}} - x_{j_i}|). \tag{1.3}$$

NSAD $= 0$ denotes the best correction performance, whereas NSAD $= 1$ indicates worst correction performance. To match the limiting values of NSAD with that of F, Complemented Normalized Sum of Absolute Deviations (CNSAD) is calculated as CNSAD $= 1 - $ NSAD. So, the scores F and CNSAD combined can effectively compare the overall performance of multiple preprocessing methods. Further, both the scores should be given equal weightage while deciding the overall preprocessing performance because if a method performs excellent detection performance but performs poor correction or vice versa, the overall preprocessing is not considered good. The metric Overall Preprocessing Performance (OPP) calculated as the harmonic mean of F and CNSAD values is suitable when the outcomes of the latter two scores are contradictory. The metric OPP is expressed as

$$\text{OPP} = \frac{2 \times F \times \text{CNSAD}}{F + \text{CNSAD}} \tag{1.4}$$

The value of OPP lies in the interval [0, 1]. If F is zero, the correction doesn't make any sense; thus, OPP $= 0$ indicating worst-case. While a preprocessing method's better performance is expected irrespective of outliers' positions, the chance of unequal performance while handling outliers at different parts arises because of the inaccurate outlier region computation. F and CNSAD cannot evaluate a particular method's specific performance while dealing with extreme outliers. In that case, the derived metrics $F_U - F_L$ and $\text{CNSAD}_U - \text{CNSAD}_L$ can be used. The calculation for (F_U, F_L) and $(\text{CNSAD}_U, \text{CNSAD}_L)$, respectively, use the formulations of F-score and CNSAD, considering the true and false outliers of the respective sides. The significance of the derived detection metrics is listed in Table 1.2. Similar set of significances can also be written for derived correction metrics CNSAD_U, CNSAD_L, and $\text{CNSAD}_U - \text{CNSAD}_L$. An ideal method would detect all the outliers in the upper and lower envelopes without detecting any false outlier in any of the two envelopes. It should return the detected outliers (TPs) to their original values. Based on this assumption, the values for the above metric for an ideal preprocessing method are as follows:

$$F_U = 1, F_L = 1, F_U - F_L = 0, \text{CNSAD}_U = 1,$$
$$\text{CNSAD}_L = 1, \text{CNSAD}_U - \text{CNSAD}_L = 0.$$

Table 1.2 Significance of metrics $F_U, F_L, F_U - F_L$

Metric	Significance
F_U, F_L	• These metrics demonstrate a method's outlier detection performance in upper/lower envelope, respectively. • These metrics give a comprehensive view of a method's outlier detection performance which generally gets neglected while observing the metrics which show overall performance (such as F-score). • These metrics can even help in selecting a method suitable for certain scenarios, e.g., when a dataset has most outliers in the lower envelope. Then a method with the highest F_L value should be selected, even though its overall F-score is not the best compared to other methods.
$F_U - F_L$	• This difference shows the inclination of a method's outlier detection performance towards a particular envelope. • If this difference is positive/negative, then the inclination of the outlier detection performance is towards upper/lower envelope. • For a good method, this difference should be close to zero, and for an ideal method, this difference should be exactly zero, which shows the envelope effect is not prominent/absent, and the method is performing equally good or bad in both the envelopes.

1.3.1 An example case to compare AARD and CNSAD performance

As highlighted above, AARD and CNSAD can be two possible metrics (whose value can range between 0 and 1) for assessing outlier correction performance. Compared to CNSAD, AARD is unreliable. An example case highlighting AARD's unreliable calculation of metric value is elaborated below. Consider the time series shown in Figure 2.4 as an example case where the outliers detected and corrected at 2nd, 6th, and 10th samples. For the given values of clean, polluted, and corrected data, the metrics AARD and CNSAD are calculated as follows:

$$\text{AARD} = \frac{1}{\text{TP} + \text{FP}} \sum_{i=1}^{\text{TP+FP}} \frac{|z_{j_i} - x_{j_i}|}{|x_{j_i}|}$$

$$= \frac{1}{3}\left[\frac{|6.8 - 8|}{8} + \frac{|2.5 - 1|}{1} + \frac{|8 - 9|}{9}\right] = 0.5995$$

$$\text{SAD} = \sum_{i=1}^{\text{TP+FP}} |z_{j_i} - x_{j_i}| = |6.8 - 8| + |2.5 - 1| + |8 - 9| = 4$$

$$\text{SAD}^{\text{M}} = \sum_{i=1}^{\text{TP+FP}} \max(|y_{U_{\text{Lim}}} - x_{j_i}|, |y_{L_{\text{Lim}}} - x_{j_i}|)$$

$$= \max(|10 - 8|, |3 - 8|) + \max(|10 - 1|, |3 - 1|)$$

$$+ \max(|10 - 9|, |3 - 9|) = 20$$

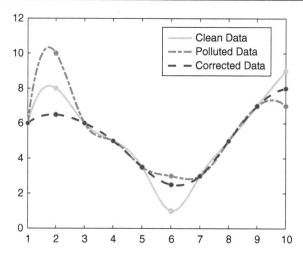

Figure 1.2   An example case to compare the effectiveness of AARD and CNSAD.

$$\text{NSAD} = \frac{\text{SAD}}{\text{SAD}^{\text{M}}} = \frac{4}{20} = 0.2$$

$$\text{CNSAD} = 1 - \text{NSAD} = 1 - 0.2 = 0.8$$

In the above calculation of AARD, the second summand value, i.e., 2.5, is greater than one. Although the value of AARD is less than one, the existence of a summand value greater than one is unrealistic, making the use of the metric AARD unsuitable for the fair comparison of outlier correction performance.

1.4 NEW METRICS TO JUDGE INDIVIDUAL CHARACTERISTIC'S PERFORMANCE

The new metrics are based on judging the correction performance against each characteristic of the ideal correction mechanism. Like P and R, one can examine the correction performance of a method while dealing with TP(s) and FP(s).

Let CNSAD_{TP} and CNSAD_{FP} represent the correction performance of a method while dealing with TP(s) and FP(s). They are given as,

$$\text{CNSAD}_{\text{TP}} = 1 - \text{NSAD}_{\text{TP}} = 1 - \frac{\text{SAD}_{\text{TP}}}{\text{SAD}_{\text{TP}}^{\text{M}}} \qquad (1.5)$$

where

$$\text{SAD}_{\text{TP}}^{\text{M}} = \sum_{i=1}^{\text{TP}} \max(|y_{U_{\text{Lim}}} - x_{j_i}|, |y_{L_{\text{Lim}}} - x_{j_i}|) \text{ and}$$

$$\text{CNSAD}_{\text{FP}} = 1 - \text{NSAD}_{\text{FP}} = 1 - \frac{\text{SAD}_{\text{FP}}}{\text{SAD}_{\text{FP}}^M} \tag{1.6}$$

where

$$\text{SAD}_{\text{FP}}^M = \sum_{i=1}^{\text{FP}} \max(|y_{U_{\text{Lim}}} - x_{j_i}|, |y_{L_{\text{Lim}}} - x_{j_i}|).$$

The metrics CNSAD_{TP} and CNSAD_{FP} can be combined to come up with a new outlier correction metric (say $\text{CNSAD}_{\text{New}}$) which will incorporate the two characteristics of the ideal correction mechanism, just like the F-score includes the attributes of perfect detection by taking the harmonic mean of P and R. Still, it is to highlight that correction is followed by detection and hence dependent on detection. Therefore, harmonic mean won't work in the present case. A weighted average would be an appropriate choice, which is proposed as,

$$\text{CNSAD}_{\text{New}} = \frac{w_1 \text{CNSAD}_{\text{TP}} + w_2 \text{CNSAD}_{\text{FP}}}{w_1 + w_2} \tag{1.7}$$

where

$$w_1 = \frac{\text{TP}}{\text{TP} + \text{FP}}, \quad w_2 = \frac{\text{FP}}{\text{TP} + \text{FP}}, \quad \text{and } w_1 + w_2 = 1.$$

Therefore,

$$\text{CNSAD}_{\text{New}} = \frac{\text{TP}}{\text{TP} + \text{FP}} \text{CNSAD}_{\text{TP}} + \frac{\text{FP}}{\text{TP} + \text{FP}} \text{CNSAD}_{\text{FP}}. \tag{1.8}$$

The limiting values of $\text{CNSAD}_{\text{New}}$ are $[0, 1]$, "0" being the worst case and "1" being the best-case scenario, respectively. Further, $\text{CNSAD}_{\text{New}}$ should not be calculated when TP = 0 and FP = 0, which is evident as correction performance doesn't make sense if no outliers are detected. Therefore, a new formula for overall preprocessing performance is proposed, i.e., OPP_{New}, where

$$\text{OPP}_{\text{New}} = \frac{2 \times F \times \text{CNSAD}_{\text{New}}}{F + \text{CNSAD}_{\text{New}}}. \tag{1.9}$$

In the summary, there are several possible ways to examine a preprocessing method's correction capability: (i) graphical approach and (ii) metric-based approach. The metric-based approach is well established and more realistic. While proposing a new metric for outlier correction, the metric must be devised strictly based on the objectives of ideal outlier correction.

- *Assume ideal outlier detection and check the correction capability:* In this approach, a complete unbiased estimate of how good or bad a method's outlier correction is not possible as the evaluation accounts for the performance only in bringing TP(s) closer to their corresponding clean data values.

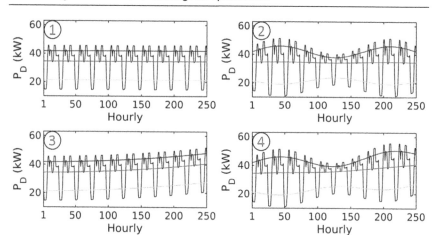

Figure 1.3 The clean datasets under consideration.

- *Assume actual outlier detection and check the correction capability:* Outlier correction performance being detection performance dependent, this approach effectively characterizes a preprocessing method's correction capability.

1.5 RESULT ANALYSIS AND VALIDATION

This section compares various metrics suitable for outlier detection and correction and exposes their merits and limitations. Since metric-based data preprocessing can only be done with synthetic data, the required data for the study is synthetically generated, keeping in mind that the data to be used mimics the time series facets of the real-world raw data used in power and energy applications. The primary dataset for result analysis is the load power data collected from [9]. Three new datasets are generated with the synthetically embedded trend and volatility effects in the dataset of [11] (refer to Figure 2.5) to validate the proposed metrics' significance. The time-varying mean line in red and lower and upper boundary lines (to highlight extreme one-third portions) respectively in green and blue are highlighted in the figure for all the cases. The width of the extreme region set to one-third is a random selection considered for this study. The chapter's objective is twofold. They are as under:

Objective 1: The importance of $F_U - F_L$ and $CNSAD_U - CNSAD_L$ is critically studied; further, the level to which the inclination of methods' performance to a particular side is affected by time series effects is investigated.

Objective 2: The unbiased overall performance of OPP is compared with MAE.

For a dataset of n samples, the metric MAE is calculated as

$$\text{MAE} = \frac{\sum_{i=1}^{n} |z_i - x_i|}{n}$$

where i is a counting variable.

An ideal method's equilibrium performance indicates how consistently it deals with extreme outliers. Methods, such as the PDB [4] and the ISWP [5], have a likely chance to inconsistently deal with extreme outliers as they compute confidence interval or outlier region for outlier detection, hence are considered in this chapter. The algorithmic steps for PDB and ISWP methods are portrayed in Figure 1.4. The inconsistencies arise from inaccurately estimating a data point's value by a method across various datasets (with different trend and seasonality effects) that further computes incorrect confidence interval/outlier regions.

To investigate the methods' performance, two pollution introducing mechanisms, M_1 and M_2, which can bring appreciable deviation, are discussed underneath.

1. M_1: Dissimilar deviation in terms of magnitude

   - A sample value randomly altered by 50% of the clean data magnitude.

2. M_2: Similar deviation in terms of magnitude

   - A sample value randomly altered by a fixed magnitude.

The pollution level is set at 10% of the whole dataset, i.e., 50 outliers seem a reasonable fraction to carry out this investigation and can be suggested for any other preprocessing analysis. The outliers on the extreme sides are proportional to the sample size on those sides to maintain the standard condition for analyses. The indices of the outliers are kept the same throughout the investigation for realistic comparison of results on case-to-case basis.

The hypotheses for the first objective are:

(i) While dealing with UEOs, a method's detection for M_1 is better,
(ii) While dealing with true LEOs, a method's correction for M_1 is better, and
(iii) Both performances shift towards the equilibrium for M_2.

For M_1, the chance is high that a preprocessing method detects an extreme outlier at a significant distance from the corresponding clean data value compared to an outlier with a lower distance deviation. Further, the corrected values of upper extreme true outliers also deviated with a higher value from the corresponding clean data value. On the other hand, for M_2, extreme

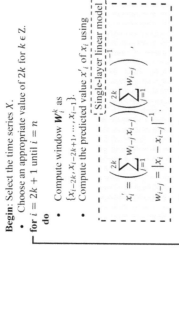

ISWP Method

Begin: Select the time series X.
- Choose an appropriate value of $2k$ for $k \in Z$.

for $i = 2k + 1$ until $i = n$

do
- Compute window W_i^k as $\{x_{i-2k}, x_{i-2k+1}, \ldots, x_{i-1}\}$.
- Compute the predicted value x'_i of x_i using

  Single-layer linear model:

$$x'_i = \left(\sum_{j=1}^{2k} w_{i-j} x_{i-j}\right)\left(\sum_{j=1}^{2k} w_{i-j}\right)^{-1},$$

$$w_{i-j} = |x_i - x_{i-j}|^{-1}.$$

- Compute the PCI for x_i using

$$\mathrm{PCI} = x'_i \pm \left(q_{\frac{\alpha}{2}, 2k-1} \times s \sqrt{1 - \frac{1}{2k}}\right).$$

  Note: $q_{\frac{\alpha}{2}, 2k-1}$ is the $100 \times (1 - \alpha)\%$ percentile critical value for the Student's t-distribution with $2k - 1$ degrees of freedom and s is the standard deviation of the corresponding window.

if x_i does not lie within PCI

  Outlier correction
- Replace x_i with the average of x_i and selected seasonal periodic values of x_i.

end if
end for

PDB Method

Begin: Select the time series X.
- Calculate the fundamental period T.
- Construct BPDs as follows

$$\mathrm{BPD}_j = \{x_i \mid i = j + gT\}, \begin{cases} j = 1,2,\ldots,\mathrm{T} \\ g = 0,1,\ldots,\frac{n}{\mathrm{T}} - 1 \end{cases}.$$

- Construct characteristic vector $v = [\theta, \mathrm{MAD}]$ for each BPD.

for $j = 1$ until $j = \mathrm{T}$

do
- Calculate the α outlier region of jth BPD as

$$\mathrm{out}\{\alpha, (\mu, \sigma^2)\} = \left\{x: |x - \mu| > Z_{1-\frac{\alpha}{2}}\sigma\right\}.$$

  Note: The value of μ and σ are set to θ_j and MAD_j respectively; $Z_{1-\frac{\alpha}{2}}$ is the $100 \times (1 - \alpha/2)\%$ percentile of $N(0,1)$.

for $g = 1$ until $g = \frac{n}{\mathrm{T}}$

do

if g^{th} data point lies in the α outlier region

  Outlier correction
- Replace the data point with an acceptable value of gth BPD.

end if
end for
end for

Figure 1.4 Algorithms of PDB and ISWP methods.

outliers being deviated nearly the same magnitude have the same chance of being detected as outliers. Further, a method is more likely to perform identical corrections.

In the PDB method, a data point is considered an outlier if its absolute deviation from the median of the portrait dataset is greater than the product of mean absolute deviation and α. The median value and mean absolute deviation are constant for a portrait dataset. In case 1, the portrait datasets consist of clean data points with similar magnitude; therefore, if one clean data point is detected as FP, then there is a high possibility that others will be seen as outliers in that portrait dataset. In case 2, the data has a volatility effect due to which the clean data points have a different magnitude in portrait datasets. So, if a data point is marked as FP, then there is a low possibility that nearby data points will be seen as outliers since their magnitude is comparatively different.

For both the mechanisms, a detailed comparison of various metrics' values for all four cases is carried out in Table 1.3. In the table, "U" and "L" indicate upper and lower. The upper and lower counts for TP, FP, and FN are also highlighted for better interpretation of results. Further, a summarization of preprocessing performance for objective 1 is compared in Table 1.4. It compares the preprocessing performance using the suggested metrics. Due to the absence of time series effects in case 1, computing the outlier region accurately by the methods is relatively high irrespective of the used mechanism. For the remaining cases, the observations are as per the hypothesis. The metric $F_U - F_L$ helps to reveal that both preprocessing methods have a significant average value of $F_U - F_L$ for M_1. The value inclines towards the equilibrium performance for M_2 (Figure 1.5).

The comparison of mechanism-wise correction of outliers is highlighted in Table 1.4. In both the tables and in ensuing sections, "C" stands for CNSAD. It is worth observing from the table that the correction performance comparison is near the hypothesis. The shift in correction performance's inclination towards equilibrium for M_2 is indicated in all cases except for the third and fourth cases using the PDB method. It is due to the presence of a trend effect in the data. It is to highlight that $C_U - C_L$ helps envisage the impact of the position of the outlier on the correction. $F_U - F_L$ and $C_U - C_L$ are mainly helpful in indicating a method's sensitivity to a specific data characteristic, pollution mechanism, and pollution level. Although this study considers a specific pollution mechanism and pollution level, for a more comprehensive analysis of results and the judgement of a preprocessing method's stable performance, different other pollution mechanisms and pollution cases (with different pollution levels) as highlighted in Figure 1.6 may be considered. In the figure, μ_C is the time-varying mean value line. Using synthetic datasets, the two metrics can reveal the sensitivity of the inclination of a method to a particular side concerning time series effects. Since outliers can be of any magnitude, irrespective of the mechanism, a method should have stable performance.

Table 1.3 Detailed comparison of metrics' values for all cases

Mechanism 1

Case	Method	Data points		Outliers		TP_U+TP_L	FP_U+FP_L	FN_U+FN_L	F_U	F_L	F_U-F_L	F	C_U	C_L	C_U-C_L	C
		U	L	U	L											
1	PDB	322	178	31	19	31 + 19	85 + 40	00 + 00	0.422	0.487	−0.065	0.444	0.995	0.997	−0.002	0.996
	ISWP	322	178	31	19	15 + 08	00 + 00	16 + 11	0.652	0.593	0.059	0.630	0.881	0.958	−0.077	0.915
2	PDB	322	178	31	19	31 + 11	07 + 04	00 + 08	0.899	0.647	0.252	0.816	0.888	0.941	−0.053	0.908
	ISWP	322	178	31	19	15 + 05	00 + 01	16 + 14	0.652	0.400	0.252	0.563	0.902	0.956	−0.054	0.923
3	PDB	322	178	31	19	28 + 10	40 + 29	03 + 09	0.566	0.345	0.221	0.484	0.792	0.780	0.012	0.787
	ISWP	322	178	31	19	16 + 08	00 + 00	15 + 11	0.681	0.593	0.088	0.649	0.907	0.971	−0.064	0.934
4	PDB	322	178	31	19	29 + 08	48 + 24	02 + 11	0.537	0.314	0.223	0.465	0.793	0.731	0.062	0.773
	ISWP	322	178	31	19	17 + 06	00 + 00	14 + 13	0.708	0.480	0.228	0.630	0.919	0.954	−0.035	0.930

Mechanism 2

Case	Method	Data points		Outliers		TP_U+TP_L	FP_U+FP_L	FN_U+FN_L	F_U	F_L	F_U-F_L	F	C_U	C_L	C_U-C_L	C
		U	L	U	L											
1	PDB	322	178	31	19	31 + 19	85 + 40	00 + 00	0.422	0.487	−0.065	0.444	0.997	0.997	0.000	0.997
	ISWP	322	178	31	19	15 + 08	00 + 00	16 + 11	0.652	0.593	0.059	0.630	0.919	0.940	−0.021	0.926
2	PDB	322	178	31	19	31 + 19	07 + 00	00 + 00	0.899	1.000	−0.101	0.935	0.915	0.944	−0.029	0.925
	ISWP	322	178	31	19	15 + 08	00 + 01	16 + 11	0.652	0.571	0.081	0.622	0.933	0.956	−0.023	0.942
3	PDB	322	178	31	19	23 + 17	41 + 30	08 + 02	0.484	0.515	−0.031	0.497	0.821	0.792	0.029	0.809
	ISWP	322	178	31	19	15 + 08	00 + 00	16 + 11	0.652	0.593	0.059	0.630	0.929	0.954	−0.025	0.938
4	PDB	322	178	31	19	19 + 12	48 + 20	12 + 07	0.388	0.471	−0.083	0.416	0.814	0.758	0.056	0.797
	ISWP	322	178	31	19	15 + 08	00 + 00	16 + 11	0.652	0.593	0.059	0.630	0.935	0.952	−0.017	0.941

Table 1.4 Comparison of preprocessing performance for objective 1

Method	PDB				ISWP			
Case no.	1	2	3	4	1	2	3	4
M_1	Avg. $F_U - F_L$=0.158				Avg. $F_U - F_L$=0.157			
	Avg. $C_U - C_L$=0.002				Avg. $C_U - C_L$=-0.058			
M_2	Avg. $F_U - F_L$=0.070				Avg. $F_U - F_L$=0.064			
	Avg. $C_U - C_L$=0.009				Avg. $C_U - C_L$=-0.022			

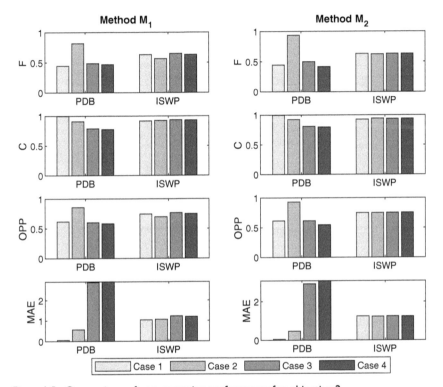

Figure 1.5 Comparison of preprocessing performance for objective 2.

Finally, with few critical observations, the OPP's suitability over MAE is justified. For case 1, although the detection performance of the ISWP method is better than the PDB method with nearly the same correction, the value of MAE for PDB is less, indicating its superior performance (refer to Figure 1.5). The ISWP detects many true outliers and significantly smaller false outlier counts. In contrast, a comparatively higher number of true outliers are detected by PDB, along with a sizeable false outlier count. Hence, ISWP's detection performance is much better than that of PDB. During outlier correction, both perform similarly, as indicated by the CNSAD score.

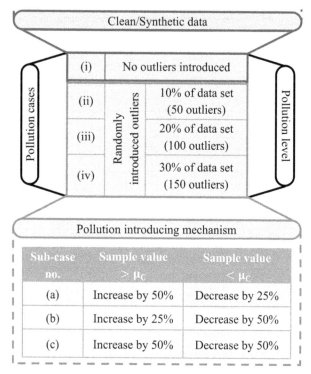

Sub-case no.	Sample value $> \mu_c$	Sample value $< \mu_c$
(a)	Increase by 50%	Decrease by 25%
(b)	Increase by 25%	Decrease by 50%
(c)	Increase by 50%	Decrease by 50%

Figure 1.6 Various pollution cases and pollution levels for comprehensive result analysis.

Also, ISWP doesn't correct a fraction of undetected true outliers. On the contrary, the PDB method corrects both true and false outliers. As the MAE score is sensitive to outlier correction, the score is low for PDB, irrespective of poor detection.

Further, for case 3, PDB performs better preprocessing for M_2 than in M_1, as indicated by F-score and CNSAD value. The MAE value is still high in M_2, implying a decrease in overall performance. The same observation is also seen with ISWP for case 4, which is contradictory. The increase in individual detection and correction performances improves the overall performance comprehended by the metric OPP better (refer to Figure 1.5). Based on the above observations, a biased MAE result is inferred as it weakens a method's detection performance, gives higher weight to the correction performance, and sometimes offers contradictory results. Comparison based on MAE is unbiased only when methods with unlike correction performance have F-score = 1. Finally, OPP equally weighs detection and correction and, therefore, finally provides fair results in all cases. Further, OPP gives a meaningful comparison between any two methods. In the present study, ISWP performs better than PDB by 13.1% in case 1.

1.6 CONCLUSION AND FUTURE SCOPES

The importance of time series preprocessing is enlightened. The need for metrics for data preprocessing is comprehensively discussed, and existing metrics for time series preprocessing and derived metrics, along with a new set of metrics, are discussed. The capability of metrics to successfully handle extreme outliers with different magnitude deviations is verified. The validity of the metrics is elaborated via thorough result analysis considering various polluted datasets and pollution mechanisms. The motivation was also to investigate whether the position of the outliers, data's specific characteristics, pollution mechanism, and pollution level impacts a method's outlier correction performance. The suggested metrics' role would be vital while devising a new preprocessing method applicable to the seasonal time series of power and energy systems.

The research scopes for interested researchers are proposing a suitable approach to preprocessing the first "2k" data points while using the ISWP method and deciding an appropriate value of α for a particular application.

REFERENCES

1. Kumar Gaurav Ranjan, B Rajanarayan Prusty, and Debashisha Jena. Review of preprocessing methods for univariate volatile time-series in power system applications. *Electric Power Systems Research*, 191:106885, 2021.
2. Hermine N Akouemo and Richard J Povinelli. Data improving in time series using arx and ann models. *IEEE Transactions on Power Systems*, 32(5):3352–3359, 2017.
3. Jiyi Chen, Wenyuan Li, Adriel Lau, Jiguo Cao, and Ke Wang. Automated load curve data cleansing in power systems. *IEEE Transactions on Smart Grid*, 1(2):213–221, 2010.
4. Guoming Tang, Kui Wu, Jingsheng Lei, Zhongqin Bi, and Jiuyang Tang. From landscape to portrait: a new approach for outlier detection in load curve data. *IEEE Transactions on Smart Grid*, 5(4):1764–1773, 2014.
5. Kumar G Ranjan, Debesh S Tripathy, B Rajanarayan Prusty, and Debashisha Jena. An improved sliding window prediction-based outlier detection and correction for volatile time-series. *International Journal of Numerical Modelling: Electronic Networks, Devices and Fields*, 34(1):e2816, 2021.
6. Nimish Jain, Shraddha Suman, and B Rajanarayan Prusty. Performance comparison of two statistical parametric methods for outlier detection and correction. *IFAC-PapersOnLine*, 54(16):168–174, 2021.
7. Kumar Gaurav Ranjan, B Rajanarayan Prusty, and Debashisha Jena. Comparison of two data cleaning methods as applied to volatile time-series. In *2019 International Conference on Power Electronics Applications and Technology in Present Energy Scenario (PETPES)*, pages 1–6. IEEE, 2019.
8. You Lin and Jianhui Wang. Probabilistic deep autoencoder for power system measurement outlier detection and reconstruction. *IEEE Transactions on Smart Grid*, 11(2):1796–1798, 2019.

9. Li Ma, Xiaodu Gu, and Baowei Wang. Correction of outliers in temperature time series based on sliding window prediction in meteorological sensor network. *Information*, 8(2):60, 2017.

10. Hourly Load Consumption. 2021. https://openei.org/ datasets/files/961/pub.

11. B Rajanarayan Prusty, Nimish Jain, Kumar Gaurav Ranjan, Kishore Bingi, and Debashisha Jena. New performance evaluation metrics for outlier detection and correction. In *Sustainable Energy and Technological Advancements: Proceedings of ISSETA 2021*, pages 837–845. Springer, 2022.

Chapter 2

Power system planning using data-driven models

B Rajanarayan Prusty, Sujith Jacob, and Kishore Bingi

2.1 INTRODUCTION

Power system analyses must account for the uncertainty factors via suitable characterization into the modelling framework to ensure sufficient reliability during power system planning. A detailed modelling framework and data requirement are elucidated by Li and Zhou (2008) and Prusty and Jena (2019) [1, 2]. Based on the study's requirement, the time horizon, time-scale, and time-step of uncertain inputs change. A detailed elaboration is indicated in Figure 2.1. For precise uncertainty management, knowledge of the time horizon and time-scale based on the study's interest plays a vital role. Time horizon may broadly be classified as short-term, mid-term, and long-term. Further, typical time-scales commonly used include minutes, hours, days, months, years, several years, etc. Besides, the degree of uncertainty varies significantly from one time-scale to the other, e.g., it substantially increases from an operational study's short time-scale to a planning-based study's large time-scale. Time resolution, e.g., low-resolution, and high-resolution data, also affects uncertainty management.

In recent times, power system studies have used temperature-dependent data-driven models (refer to Figure 2.2) [3, 4]. These models are based on the electro-thermal coupling, as explained in the figure. T_{Ref} and R_{Ref} are the reference values of T and R. T_{Amb} refers to ambient temperature. T_F is the temperature constant, and R_θ is the thermal resistance. During power system planning using the abovementioned models, daily time-step data of power system inputs for several years are essential [2, 5]. Daily temperature data have several other applications. Daily minimum and maximum temperatures are necessary for scenarios such as devices that function in a particular temperature range. Daily average temperatures are critical to analyzing a specific location's increasing or decreasing temperature trend. The average temperature trends are considered for forecasting rains, snowfall, and climatic phenomena. The clear seasonality is also observed in average temperature variations, visible in normal daily temperature datasets. The average temperature data can be used to analyze temperature variations over time. It is used to study phenomena like global warming and climate

DOI: 10.1201/9781003470274-2

Expansion planning	Long-term	Years-to-decade(s)	Yearly	Grid expansion plans, capacity credit assessment, etc.
	Medium-term	Years	Daily	Infrastructural investment plans
	Short-term	Months	Daily	Installation of protection systems, phase shifters, etc.
Operational planning	Long-term	Year(s)	Daily	Release of transmission equipment(s) for maintenance and scheduled repair
	Medium-term	Month(s)	Daily	Delaying or anticipating the commitment of transmission facilities
	Short-term	Day(s)-to-week	Hourly/daily	Modifying the operational strategy, postponing scheduled outages, etc.
Real-time operation	Long-term	Day-to-day(s)	Hourly	Unit commitment
	Medium-term	Minute(s)-to-day	15 min-to-1 hour	Economic dispatch
	Short-term	Second(s)-to-minute(s)	30 sec-to-5 min	Automatic generation control, storage control, assessment of ramping events, etc.

Figure 2.1   Power system studies and applications.

change. The development of data-driven models in the above context is well established. And the research demands apt regressor set identification that mimics the actual variation in data [6, 7, 8]. A brief block-diagrammatic representation for predictable variation modelling is shown in Figure 2.3. Identification of reliable sources for relevant data is vital. Unfortunately, the raw data cannot be directly used for further processing based on the study's requirements. Here comes the preprocessing step to update missing sample values, further ensuring the time series basic properties are intact. It additionally corrects the outliers in the dataset to a possible reasonable value. The seasonal dataset must have a variation, i.e., periodic, and therefore must be carefully captured by selecting a set of apt regressors using a data-driven regression type modelling framework. Finally, removing this deterministic model of the periodic pattern from the ambient temperature time series yields the time series' uncertainty content.

   This chapter envisages the apt regressor set selection for ambient temperature time series. The variation of ambient temperature has an impact on numerous natural processes like rainfall patterns, evaporation, melting of glaciers, heat waves. It has applications in meteorological studies, energy management, climate change studies, and many more [9, 10]. Hence, modelling predictable variations in ambient temperature becomes extremely important and valuable. In-sample predictions in a dataset may help fill in missing values. Out-of-sample forecasting, on the other hand, helps in all the above applications. Modelling predictable variations implies identifying the factors responsible for repetitive patterns in ambient temperature over several years. Such modelling would be tedious, particularly in a country like India, with climatic diversity and geographical expanse.

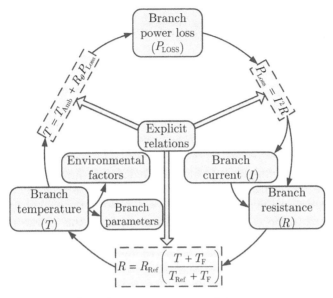

Figure 2.2   Temperature-dependent power system model.

Figure 2.3   Predictable variation modelling steps.

The modelling of ambient temperature's predictable variation using a Fourier-term-based model [8, 11], however, can only sometimes be a pre-eminent model as it cannot be generic as no fixed set of Fourier terms can precisely model the predictable variation at different time instants [8]. On the other hand, a model comprising the set of theoretically relevant regressors can change their variation plot at different time instants; thus, a fixed group can help capture varying predictable variation at multiple time instants [7]. Furthermore, in the former case, the number of regressors may be more, requiring the dominant frequency extraction technique to select the potential regressors for the model [3]. Judicious selection of time trend order in the model has successfully captured the trend effect and accurately captured the recurrent pattern in data without sufficient theoretically relevant regressors. In the latter case, the time trend terms act as adjusting/smoothing function(s) [8]. Multiple time trend terms may be necessary to compensate for the absence of a single potential regressor, which will unnecessarily increase the model order and the simulation time for a prediction application. This emphasizes the necessity of proper regressor set selection. Also, overfitting is a significant concern in all regression techniques, predominantly due to considering redundant or irrelevant regressors in the regressor set. In other words, the model loses its ability to generalize the data's underlying patterns and instead characterizes the noise in the time series. Also, the issue of underfitting may arise if important regressors are eliminated from the regressor set. Another study has given a regressor set consisting of only three regressors. However, it is only potent for region-specific modelling [8]. Hence, genericity or location independence of the regressor set and minimizing the dimensionality of the model are key factors in accurately modelling ambient temperature variation patterns. A common regression-based modelling technique must also be fixed along with a generic regressor since having similar techniques is imperative for comparative analysis.

This chapter aims to provide a generic regressor set for modelling ambient temperature variations across India. It also discusses the various modelling techniques and ways to choose the most optimal one. The chapter attempts to build upon the regressor set proposed by Shyamsukha et al. [8] and includes atmospheric and other solar position-inspired regressors to find the best possible regressor set and, thereby, the best viable model and accuracy. Different comparative analyses have been performed based on location and time of the day.

2.2 PREDICTABLE VARIATION MODELLING FRAMEWORKS

Regression-based modelling techniques better model the predictable variation in ambient temperature [6, 7, 8]; they include multiple linear regression (MLR), non-linear regression (NLR), feed-forward neural network (FNN), hybrid models. However, MLR and FNN are the most potent options for most applications. NLR allocates different functions to each regressor of the model and tries to characterize the dependent variable's actual variation precisely. However, it is time-consuming to identify efficient hypothesis functions for a given application. Although non-linearity can be characterized adequately using the NLR model, with the same or reduced number of regressors compared to MLR, the difficulty in identifying an apt function for each regressor suppresses its application. Adopting a non-linear activation function in FNN helps it learn the non-linear patterns better. Further, the FNN-based modelling framework eliminates regressors with specific redundancy characteristics without compromising modelling accuracy. Additionally, a backpropagation-assisted FNN enhances model superiority in mimicking the periodic pattern.

While choosing an appropriate modelling framework, the following factors must be considered:

1. Dimensionality of the model: A common problem in machine learning models is the curse of dimensionality. An increase in the number of

model's regressors increases the model's complexity. Dimensionality reduction is often used to lessen the number of regressors by retaining only the apt set. Feature selection and feature extraction are two well-established dimensionality reduction techniques.

2. Sensitivity to outliers: Outliers in a data set significantly impact the fitted machine learning model's performance. The inaccurate model that is created due to the presence of outliers in the dataset leads to prediction inaccuracy. A significant deviation from the true line may be noticed even for in-sample prediction. Outlier detection and their apt correction is one of the best approaches to improve the machine learning model's prediction accuracy.

3. Interpretability: The interpretability of a machine learning model refers to how easy it is to comprehend the model, primarily concerning the prediction performance of the model. The sensibility of an interpretable model's prediction results can be quickly commented on.

In a nutshell, MLR seems the better option when conserving resources are considered; however, in terms of efficiency, a more complex model like FNN is the more optimal choice.

2.3 DATA ANALYSIS AND PREPROCESSING

The study considers daily ambient temperature data from 24 locations across India (refer to Figure 2.4) with diverse climate and temperature variation patterns from 2016 to 2020 [12]. An effort has been made to cover all different climatic regions across the country while choosing these locations. A deep analysis of the daily temperature at different time instants helps observe the relevance of various factors at a particular time of day. For example, the main factor driving ambient temperature at 7 am (morning) may differ from the one at 5 pm (evening) or noon. It helps pinpoint the behaviour of temperature patterns at a particular location and the different factors driving them at other times.

Although the temperature is predominantly affected only by the solar radiation received, which in turn is dependent upon the latitude of the region, proximity to the oceans also plays a crucial role. It helps distinguish the regions of India into separate climatic zones [13]. In the coastal areas, because nearby bodies of water can transfer heat energy to or from the surrounding air through evaporation and condensation, the coastal areas' proximity to water has a moderate impact on temperature. In contrast, thermal energy is released into the air when water condenses, increasing the temperature of the air around it. This is because the water acts as a buffer, absorbing and releasing heat energy as needed to keep the temperature relatively constant. In contrast, areas far from water bodies tend to have more extreme temperature fluctuations between seasons.

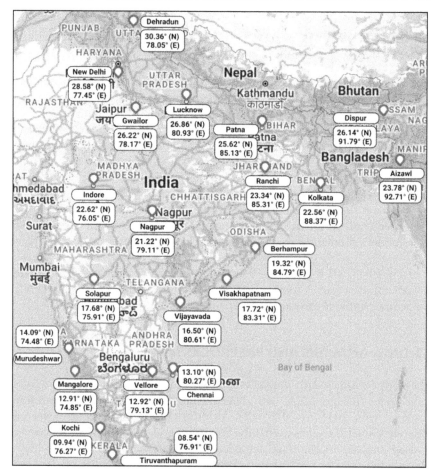

Figure 2.4 Ambient temperature data collection locations across India.

The temperature data and regressors are scaled to lie between zero and one. Normalization is performed to remove the bias that regressors with a greater numerical value have over those with smaller values [11]. As each regressor characterizes a particular aspect of the predictable variation in ambient temperature, the regressors must be normalized before modelling.

2.3.1 Observations from ambient temperature time series

By considering the time series plots of 24 places across India (refer to Figure 2.5) and considering various climatic factors, the following points are worth highlighting:

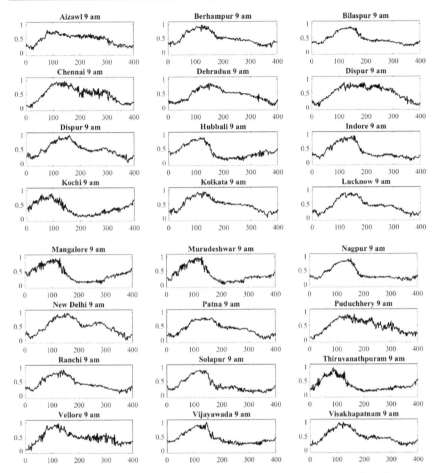

Figure 2.5 Ambient temperature time series plots for 24 locations. Note: For all the plots, x-axis: day number; y-axis: normalized ambient temperature.

1. Day-time temperature regulation: Insolation is the primary factor regulating day-time ambient temperature at different times across locations in India. Further, two characteristics affecting insolation are as under:

   (i) Positional effect: Geographically closer sites, i.e., the areas with similar latitude and longitude, show remarkably identical ambient temperature variation patterns.

   (ii) Atmospheric effects: The atmosphere absorbs or reflects a certain amount of solar radiation received from the Sun and thereby affects the overall net insolation; hence it could characterize certain variations in ambient temperature across locations in India. At a particular place on a given day, atmospheric effects are negligible around noon as the Sun is perpendicular to the Earth's surface. Hence, the amount of radiation absorbed by the atmosphere becomes insignificant compared to the total insolation.

2. Night-time temperature regulation: The temperature variation pattern at night-time is like the day-time ambient temperature patterns even in the absence of solar radiation. The regulation of temperature at night-time is the result of the greenhouse effect. The surface absorbs solar radiation or some greenhouse gases in the atmosphere during the day. These gases emit this absorbed radiation at night in thermal energy, which warms the location and maintains a similar temperature variation pattern at night.

Note: There is a significant difference in ambient temperature variation patterns in north and south India. The two main reasons are mentioned below:

• India's latitudinal expanse is vast; hence, from south India to north India, the climatic temperature shifts from tropical to temperate, which highly influences the temperature variation patterns.
• The aerosol optical depth (AOD) is higher in north India than in south India, directly affecting the atmospheric transmissivity and insolation. Generally, aerosols have a cooling influence on climate, e.g., sulphate and nitrate produce a cooling effect on the globe by scattering and reflecting incoming solar radiations.

2.3.2 Selection of model predictor variables

Solar radiation and its circulation through the atmosphere are the most critical factors governing ambient temperature variations – mainly influenced by the Sun's relative position with respect to the Earth at a given location and time as it decides the intensity of solar radiation. Hence, the factors dependent on parameters that describe the Sun's relative position with respect to the Earth are very potent for the analysis of ambient temperature patterns. Also, resistance and absorption of the atmosphere are key factors driving total insolation and are necessary factors to be considered to model the ambient temperature variations.

The points cited below are significant challenges when selecting a regressor set for a particular application.

• A critical analysis is paramount as it is not predefined about the regressor set's size for any given application.
• It is tedious to remove redundant regressor(s).

- The choice of a metric(s) for accuracy measurement is complex. It is essential as any unsuitable metric(s) may decide to eliminate a potent regressor from the set.

While selecting the optimal regressor set, considering a pool of multiple possible regressors, which are functions of parameters associated with the solar position, is the first step. The next step is to plot the regressors and observe to find which characteristic of the data, like skewness, multimodality, etc., a particular regressor(s) from the pool is identifying. This process discards the least relevant regressors from the list, selecting the most justifying optimal regressor set for a particular application. The above-suggested steps are applied, and the most potent list is enlisted by highlighting their theoretical relevance.

1. An extremely influential parameter is the solar elevation angle denoted by θ_S. It gives the apparent altitude of the Sun with respect to the Earth. Hence, the factors listed below which are functions of θ_S are ideal for the analysis of ambient temperature patterns.

    (i) $\sin\theta_S$: It gives the perpendicular component of incident solar radiation and hence determines intensity at a particular regulation, thereby influencing ambient temperature variation patterns.
    (ii) Solar radiation pressure: It is also a measure of solar intensity at a particular location and time, hence, crucial for ambient temperature variation analysis. Solar radiation pressure is expressed as

    $$P = 2E_f \sin^2\theta_S \qquad (2.1)$$

    where E_f: solar radiation constant = 1362 kW; c = speed of light.
    (iii) Transmittance by air molecules and water vapour (T_M): This considers the effect of the different molecules in the atmosphere and water vapour, respectively, on the incident solar radiation. It is given as

    $$T_M = 1.041 - 0.15\big[M(949 \times 10^{-6}p + 0.051)\big]^{0.5} \qquad (2.2)$$

    where $M = 35/[(1224(\sin\theta_S)^2 + 1)]^{0.5}$; $p = 101.3 \times \big[\frac{293-0.0065\times h}{293}\big]^{5.26}$; h = altitude from sea level of the location.
    (iv) Direct solar radiation: It accounts for the impact of air mass which is another atmospheric factor which influences insolation.

2. The sine of the solar azimuthal angle ($\sin\gamma_S$) measures the relative horizontal position of the Sun with respect to the Earth. The farther the Sun is from the Earth, there is a decrease in solar intensity. Hence, it becomes an essential factor influencing ambient temperature variations.

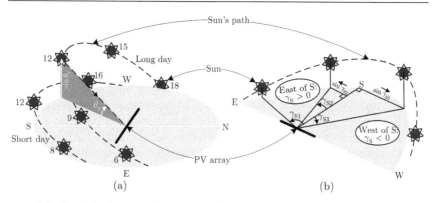

Figure 2.6   Physical relevance of regressors: (a) $\sin\theta_S$ and (b) $\sin\gamma_S$.

3. The time of sunrise directly determines the total sunshine hours every day. It gives us a relative idea of the total insolation and the amount of evaporation of water bodies releasing water vapor âŁ" the most potent greenhouse gas that regulates night-time temperature due to the greenhouse effect [8].

The physical relevance of the regressors $\sin\theta_S$ and $\sin\gamma_S$ is pictorially indicated in Figure 2.6.

2.4 PREDICTABLE VARIATION MODELS AND COMPARISON OF RESULTS

The proposed methodology for predicting ambient temperature has been implemented using the dataset [12]. 80% of the data has been considered for model training and optimization, whereas 20% of data (2020) has been used for out-of-sample forecasting. Three new regressors, namely solar radiation pressure, transmittance due to the atmosphere, and direct solar radiation, are added to the regressor set by Shyamsukha et al. [8]. Along with proximity to the sea, which is constant at a particular location, at one place at different times, the atmospheric effects are decisive factors driving the variation in the ambient temperature time series [14]. Two regression-based models, namely the MLR and FNN, are applied using the regressor set, and their performance is further compared and analysed.

First, the relevance of the regressor selection in mimicking the actual temperature pattern is closely examined in Figure 2.7 for a few randomly selected cases. It is to be noted that the temperature data and regressors have been scaled to lie between 0 and 1. Feature scaling is done for a more straightforward interpretation of results. It is evident that all the regressors have some way of mimicking the corresponding ambient temperature

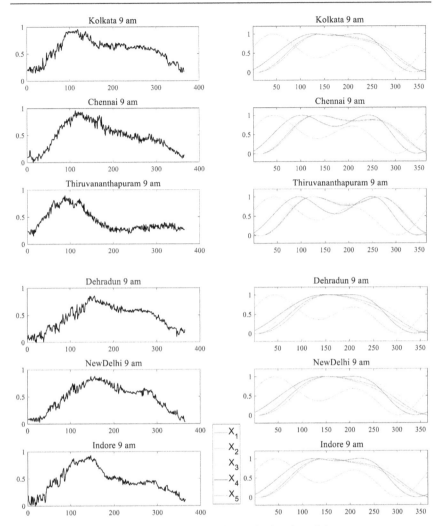

Figure 2.7 Plots of actual temperature data alongside the plot of dominant regressors; $X_1 = \sin(\theta_s)$, X_2 = solar radiation pressure, X_3 = transmittance by water vapour, $X_4 = \sin(\gamma_s)$, and X_5 = time of sunrise.

variation pattern. In this case, the daily ambient temperature time series of different locations corresponding to a fixed time instant, 9 am, have varying variation patterns. The pattern is characterized by a combination of facets, like skewness, multimodality. These patterns repeat each year, indicating the presence of natural factors responsible for the same. When those factors, considered here as regressors, are plotted, it could be clear that, although a single element is not able to mimic the entire pattern in the data, individually, the regressors mimic the pattern in ambient temperature data; therefore, they all needed to be encompassed in a data-driven regression model.

2.4.1 Models under consideration

The MLR is a linear mapping between the six regressors and ambient temperature data. However, the following issues were encountered while using MLR:

1. Being a linear model, MLR cannot characterize non-linear relationships in data, predominantly seen in places near the oceans; hence this needs a non-linear approach to modelling.
2. Also, in most ambient temperature-related applications, the regressors have a high correlation and cannot be discarded, as each regressor characterizes a particular feature of the variation. And since an assumption of MLR is that the regressors are independent, the results may prove inaccurate.
3. MLR is also poor at handling high-dimensional data; hence the increased number of regressors may lead to further complexity.

An FNN model has been chosen to resolve the issues encountered in MLR. Being a simpler neural network, FNNs are very useful for ambient temperature-related applications [11].

The scaled dataset for the MLR is also used for the FNN model. The implemented FNN model consists of one hidden layer and has five neurons in the hidden layer. As there is no specific rule to determine the number of neurons for one application, trial and error methods are followed. However, a general rule of thumb is that the number of neurons in the hidden layer is equal to two-third times the number in the input layer plus the number in the output layer [15], which has been followed in this study, too, for most optimal results. The dataset is divided into the training, validation, and testing data, of which 60% is considered for training and validation, and the rest is taken for out-of-sample forecasting (testing). The above 60% of the data was divided randomly for training and validation. The hyperbolic tangent sigmoid transfer function "tansig" is the activation function used in the hidden layer. A linear transfer function "purelin" is used in the output layer for the best possible results. The optimizer "trainbr" from the MATLAB® deep learning toolbox has been used for hyperparameter optimization. The Bayesian regularization "trainbr" optimizer is preferred due to its faster computation rate than standard optimizers like ADAM and SGD and its adaptive learning, wherein the learning rate is varied based on the present neural network performance. For performance analysis, the RMSE and R^2 are again considered. The entire process of modelling using MLR and FNN is shown in Figure 2.8.

First, ambient temperature data and the chosen regressors are normalized. Using these data, an MLR model is developed. Upon MLR assumption check, possible redundant regressor(s) are identified. Then, a revised model is developed, excluding the redundant regressor(s). Using the revised model,

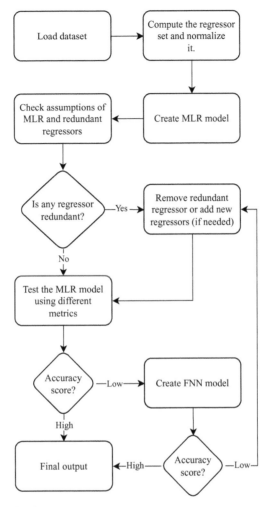

Figure 2.8 Model development steps.

accuracy scores are determined using various metrics. For any obtained low value of accuracy score, an FNN model is created using the revised set of normalized regressors. The accuracy score is again calculated using the FNN model. Based on the score, either new regressor(s) are added or existing least relevant regressors are removed.

2.4.2 Proposed model's performance comparison

A comparative analysis of MLR and FNN models:

The model selection depends solely on the characteristics and relationships observed in the regressor set and the regressand. The linear relationship between the regressor set and the regressand is measured by using statistical tools like the correlation coefficient or by measuring the score R^2 of a linear regressor model.

1. If the dependent variable shows a highly linear relationship with the regressor set, it is highly recommended to opt for a linear regressor model like the MLR over neural networks or other complicated models due to the following reasons:

   (i) Less computational cost: MLR is a simpler model than the FNN, making the computation faster. The MLR is also more efficient in terms of memory usage.
   (ii) Handling missing data: Missing values from a dataset can be assigned easily using mean, median, etc., while using an MLR model, the FNN calls for more complex techniques for the same.
   (iii) Overfitting: There is a lower chance of overfitting in the MLR compared to the FNN.
   (iv) Interpretability: The MLR model is more interpretable due to its simple architecture which is helpful for tuning and enhancement of pre-existing models.

However, the relationships are not always linear. FNN is preferred over other regression counterparts in such locations due to the following reasons:

1. The FNN is a highly efficient methodology to characterize non-linear patterns and complex patterns in time series data. It is suited for modelling highly complex and high-dimensional data.
2. The FNN model is also more robust to outliers due to the use of non-linear activation functions used in the model when compared to the MLR.
3. It is important to note that the FNN model does characterize highly linear relationships, however not recommended for the same always due to its higher computational costs and risk of overfitting.

Table 2.1 shows a comparison of the performances of both models using RMSE values and R^2 values as the performance metrics. The optimal method of model selection must be to check the extent of linear relationships between regressors and regressand, and if the linear relationship is high, MLR is worth opting, else FNN is the optimal choice. In coastal regions, the MLR model is ineffective in characterizing the patterns in time series with even less than 50% accuracy at certain places, demanding a non-linear approach, e.g., the FNN model. Due to its high computational power and ability to characterize complex non-linear variations, the FNN model's accuracy increased drastically. The FNN performs exceptionally better than the MLR

Table 2.1 Comparison of model performance at 9 am

Location	RMSE		R^2	
	MLR	FNN	MLR	FNN
Aizawl	0.0957	0.0660	0.897171	0.896542
Berhampur	0.1130	0.0691	0.857686	0.934342
Bilaspur	0.1005	0.0722	0.818736	0.868992
Chennai	0.1783	0.0783	0.85326	0.958063
Dehradun	0.0934	0.0538	0.916626	0.907919
Dispur	0.0921	0.0715	0.923012	0.918102
Gwalior	0.0811	0.0593	0.944863	0.955325
Hubbali	0.1606	0.0719	0.60881	0.942995
Indore	0.1679	0.0727	0.8266	0.923017
Kochi	0.1442	0.0664	0.417723	0.892718
Kolkata	0.1019	0.0783	0.833509	0.888563
Lucknow	0.1094	0.0591	0.92474	0.94147
Mangalore	0.1507	0.0532	0.562454	0.939549
Murudeshwar	0.0851	0.0697	0.570639	0.912102
Nagpur	0.0499	0.0515	0.801155	0.909043
New Delhi	0.0564	0.0537	0.958408	0.955594
Patna	0.0672	0.0603	0.843244	0.830692
Puducherry	0.0887	0.0954	0.822802	0.922158
Ranchi	0.0957	0.0660	0.826674	0.882224
Solapur	0.0897	0.0753	0.752893	0.929045
Thiruvananthapuram	0.0971	0.0833	0.406388	0.939801
Vellore	0.0624	0.0644	0.757167	0.917182
Vijayawada	0.0726	0.0748	0.710594	0.938712
Vishakhapatnam	0.0648	0.0654	0.842221	0.940763

model in these coastal locations. It stays on par with the MLR model in the other two regions. The main issue in these regions is the risk of overfitting the FNN. In a nutshell, FNN is the most optimal modelling technique in this application. At different time instants, in the same location, the performance of the model is compared in Table 2.2.

MLR model performs efficiently in locations across northern Indian sites with reasonable accuracy. However, at the same location at different times, the model performs worst around noon (refer to Figure 2.9). The change in model accuracy can be visualized roughly as a parabola with minima during noon. This may be attributed to the non-linearity induced by the insolation peaks at noon, and the model cannot characterize this non-linearity. On the other hand, FNN model overcomes this issue and gives improved predictions throughout the day. Hence, to identify a generic location-independent model, FNN model is the better choice if the computational cost is not the most significant concern in the application. Ambient temperature data can be highly non-linear, as seen in the two climatic regions in India, and this further reinstates the need for a non-linear model.

Table 2.2 Comparison of R^2 value

Location	9 am		noon		3 pm	
	MLR	*FNN*	*MLR*	*FNN*	*MLR*	*FNN*
Aizawl	0.897	0.896	0.833	0.854	0.905	0.918
Berhampur	0.858	0.934	0.671	0.925	0.802	0.936
Bilaspur	0.819	0.869	0.628	0.822	0.731	0.823
Chennai	0.853	0.958	0.744	0.920	0.894	0.938
Dehradun	0.917	0.908	0.878	0.853	0.939	0.932
Dispur	0.923	0.918	0.911	0.908	0.945	0.959
Gwalior	0.945	0.955	0.849	0.926	0.905	0.931
Hubbali	0.609	0.943	0.455	0.893	0.518	0.946
Indore	0.827	0.923	0.510	0.938	0.688	0.947
Kochi	0.418	0.893	0.275	0.899	0.574	0.910
Kolkata	0.833	0.889	0.677	0.882	0.834	0.926
Lucknow	0.925	0.941	0.793	0.877	0.885	0.904
Mangalore	0.562	0.939	0.371	0.917	0.537	0.941
Murudeshwar	0.571	0.912	0.359	0.890	0.464	0.941
Nagpur	0.801	0.909	0.458	0.913	0.666	0.910
New Delhi	0.958	0.956	0.925	0.915	0.936	0.924
Patna	0.843	0.831	0.800	0.918	0.894	0.943
Puducherry	0.823	0.922	0.798	0.921	0.911	0.908
Ranchi	0.827	0.882	0.633	0.885	0.732	0.807
Solapur	0.753	0.929	0.564	0.912	0.550	0.899
Thiruvananthapuram	0.406	0.940	0.243	0.928	0.486	0.909
Vellore	0.757	0.917	0.516	0.815	0.649	0.837
Vijayawada	0.711	0.939	0.419	0.920	0.613	0.896
Vishakhapatnam	0.842	0.941	0.669	0.940	0.810	0.934

2.5 CONCLUSION

A generic and optimal regressor set for modelling ambient temperature across locations in India is identified. This chapter identifies an optimal way to opt for a linear modelling technique like MLR or a non-linear one like FNN. Comparative analysis at different locations and time instants is performed, and an accuracy improvement of approximately 14% is observed because of the newly added regressors. Future research may focus on working with more complex climate systems of other countries. Further, to explore other viable modelling techniques which consider the temporal characteristics of the time series data. This research can also be extended into different nature-related time series data, as most are solar position dependent.

This chapter further opens opportunities for novice researchers to perform the following analysis.

- Merits of including regressors in the model having nearly the similar shape.
- Quantification of each selected regressor's ability to capture the skewness/multimodality effects in ambient temperature data.

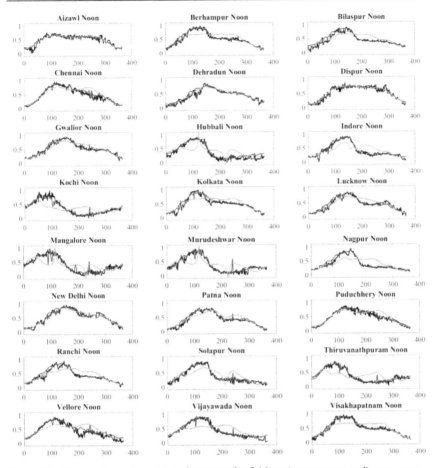

Figure 2.9 Comparison of model performance for 24 locations corresponding to noon.

REFERENCES

1. B Rajanarayan Prusty and Debashisha Jena. Uncertainty modeling steps for probabilistic steady-state analysis. In *Applications of Computing, Automation and Wireless Systems in Electrical Engineering: Proceedings of MARC 2018*, pages 1169–1177. Springer, 2019.
2. Wenyuan Li and Jiaqi Zhou. Probabilistic reliability assessment of power system operations. *Electric Power Components and Systems*, 36(10):1102–1114, 2008.
3. B Rajanarayan Prusty and Debashisha Jena. A spatiotemporal probabilistic model-based temperature-augmented probabilistic load flow considering PV generations. *International Transactions on Electrical Energy Systems*, 29(5):e2819, 2019.
4. B Rajanarayan Prusty and Debashisha Jena. An over-limit risk assessment of PV integrated power system using probabilistic load flow based on multi-time

instant uncertainty modeling. *Renewable Energy*, 116:367–383, 2018.

5. Miao Fan, Vijay Vittal, Gerald Thomas Heydt, and Raja Ayyanar. Probabilistic power flow studies for transmission systems with photovoltaic generation using cumulants. *IEEE Transactions on Power Systems*, 27(4):2251–2261, 2012.

6. Miao Fan, Vijay Vittal, Gerald Thomas Heydt, and Raja Ayyanar. Preprocessing uncertain photovoltaic data. *IEEE Transactions on Sustainable Energy*, 5(1):351–352, 2013.

7. B Rajanarayan Prusty and Debashisha Jena. Preprocessing of multi-time instant PV generation data. *IEEE Transactions on Power Systems*, 33(3):3189–3191, 2018.

8. Udith Shyamsukha, Nimish Jain, Tirthankar Chakraborty, B Rajanarayan Prusty, and Kishore Bingi. Modeling of predictable variations in multi-time instant ambient temperature time series. In *2020 3rd International Conference on Energy, Power and Environment: Towards Clean Energy Technologies*, pages 1–6. IEEE, 2021.

9. AJ Iseh and TY Woma. Weather forecasting models, methods and applications. *International Journal of Engineering Research & Technology*, 2, 2013.

10. Xuefei Liu, Chao Zhang, Pingzeng Liu, Maoling Yan, Baojia Wang, Jianyong Zhang, and Russell Higgs. Application of temperature prediction based on neural network in intrusion detection of IoT. *Security and Communication Networks*, 2018:1–10, 2018.

11. Francisco J Diez, Adriana Correa-Guimaraes, Leticia Chico-Santamarta, Andrés Martínez-Rodríguez, Diana A Murcia-Velasco, Renato Andara, and Luis M Navas-Gracia. Prediction of daily ambient temperature and its hourly estimation using artificial neural networks in an agrometeorological station in castile and león, spain. *Sensors*, 22(13):4850, 2022.

12. Manajit Sengupta, Yu Xie, Anthony Lopez, Aron Habte, Galen Maclaurin, and James Shelby. The national solar radiation data base (NSRDB). *Renewable and Sustainable Energy Reviews*, 89:51–60, 2018.

13. Amarendra Pamarthi. The recent trend of the temperature in major cities of India: A difference between inland areas and coastal areas in the climate change scenario. *Atmospheric Science*, 1:1, 2019.

14. G Myhre, CEL Myhre, BH Samset, and T Storelvmo. Aerosols and their relation to global climate and climate sensitivity. *Nature Education Knowledge*, 4(5):7, 2013.

15. B Rajanarayan Prusty, Kishore Bingi, G Arunkumar, C Dhanamjayulu, Neeraj Gupta, Anuradha Tomar, and Rakesh Sehgal. Machine learning application to power system forecasting. In *Smart Electrical and Mechanical Systems*, pages 225–236. Elsevier, 2022.

Chapter 3

Data-driven analytics for power system stability assessment

Purna Prakash Kasaraneni, Yellapragada Venkata Pavan Kumar, and Ramani Kannan

3.1 INTRODUCTION

Electricity has become a very essential commodity to modern civilizations. Consumers of electricity are always looking for an uninterrupted power supply according to their needs [1]. Data-driven analytics plays a crucial role in power system stability assessment by providing insights into the system's behaviour subjected to diverse operating/test scenarios. The stability of a power system is its ability to maintain its operating state after a disturbance. A stability assessment is critical to ensure the security and reliability of the power system. Some key ways of data analytics for power system stability assessment are predictive modelling, fault detection and diagnosis, real-time monitoring, and control, and scenario analysis can be used to analyse large volumes of data collected from the power system. This data can include measurements of voltage, current, and frequency at different points in the system, as well as other relevant parameters such as load demand and weather conditions. The data-driven models can be built to predict system stability based on historical data. These models can use machine learning (ML) methods to ascertain patterns and trends in the collected large volumes of data and use this information to make predictions about future system stability. These predictive models can be used to identify potential stability issues before they occur, allowing engineers to take proactive measures to prevent them. In this regard, a thorough review of numerous ML techniques was conducted by Alimi et al. [2]. By analysing data from sensors and other sources, engineers can identify abnormal behaviour in the system and pinpoint the source of the problem. This can help engineers for analysing real-time data to quickly identify stability issues and take corrective actions to maintain system stability. Besides, data analytics can be used to simulate various scenarios and assess their impact on system stability, and develop strategies to mitigate any negative effects. The fast progress of data analytics especially in power systems scenarios has raised the importance of learning the characteristics of energy data analytics and enhanced the service to customers [3, 4].

DOI: 10.1201/9781003470274-3

3.1.1 Importance of power system stability assessment

Power system stability assessment is important because it ensures the secure and reliable operation of the electric power system. Power system stability denotes the capacity of the power system to maintain its operational state after being influenced by disturbances. These disturbances can include sudden changes in load, loss of generation, or faults in the transmission system. If the power system is not stable, it can lead to voltage instability, frequency instability, or even collapse, which can result in power outages and damage to the equipment. This can have serious consequences, including loss of life, economic losses, and damage to the environment. Therefore, power system stability assessment is essential for power system planning, operation, and maintenance.

The stability assessment of the grid was executed using the stabilization method which uses a virtual impedance method [5]. A comprehensive review of the assessment methods, namely, equal area criterion, steady state, quasi-static, and so on, for stability analysis was conducted by Taul et al. [6]. A model was developed to assess the impact and the transient stability (TS) behaviour [7]. A spatio-temporal feature learning approach was discussed to assess short-term voltage stability [8]. A data mining method decision tree was implemented to get insights into the data in decentralized power systems for solving stability issues [9]. The addressing of grid stability issues in a decentralized generation is discussed by Schäfer et al. [10]. The abovementioned works discussed the significance of data analytics and stability assessment in power systems. Further, the literature works that discuss several methods implemented to examine the power system's stability are discussed as follows.

3.1.2 State-of-the-art literature review

To assess the TS in power systems, the ML-based quantum method was implemented [11]. A framework that relied on supervised and unsupervised ML techniques was implemented for the assessment of power systems [12]. A support vector machine-based convolutional neural network was proposed to assess the TS of the power system [13]. An ML model was discussed for the analysis of the vulnerability, verification of robustness, and mitigation strategies in the power system under adversarial examples [14]. A deep learning-based framework and hierarchical dynamic graph pooling technique were implemented to assess the TS in modern power systems [15, 16]. The TS of the power system was assessed by the techniques of the Teager Kaiser energy changes, empirical wavelet transform, and random forest [17]. An active learning-based approach was implemented to assess the power system stability [18]. A stacked ensemble model which uses the wide-area synchrophasor measurements was proposed to assess whether the power is stable or unstable [19]. The voltage instability detection index algorithm was proposed to detect voltage instability in a doubly-fed induction generator [20]. A feedforward neural network was developed for stability studies in smart cyber-physical grids [21]. A deep imbalanced-learning framework was discussed in assessing the TS of the power systems [22]. A deep belief network model was proposed for evaluating the TS [23]. A recurrent graph convolutional network-based framework was developed for TS assessment [24]. A spatio-temporal adaptive approach was discussed for assessing the TS assessment [25]. An improved support vector machine technique was implemented to better interpret the stability of a power system [26]. A stratified process that relied on artificial intelligence and mutual information theory was implemented for power system stability assessment [27]. A self-adaptive hierarchical data analytics technique was implemented to evaluate the short-term voltage stability in the power system [28]. A data analytics model was suggested to examine the stability of the power system that contains incomplete phasor measurement unit data [29].

The above literature works discussed various methods and models to evaluate the stability of the power system. To the best of the authors' knowledge, there is no such work to identify the correlation between the parameters of the power system, which influences the system's stability. This correlation analysis helps in identifying the parameters that impact the stability of the power system. This is the major contribution of this chapter.

3.1.3 Dataset description

The dataset "smart grid stability" [30] is available on Kaggle. The dataset contains 14 attributes and 60,000 records, including one target variable (stabf) with two classes: stable and unstable. The dataset was generated using a dynamic simulator for a smart grid system, and the goal is to predict the stable/unstable behaviour of the system. The attributes tau1 to tau4 represent the reaction time of the systems. The tau values are the real values ranging [0.5, 10] s. The attribute tau1 represents the reaction time for energy producers and the attributes tau2 to tau4 represent the reaction time for energy consumers. The attributes p1 to p4 represent the power balance. A negative value in power balance represents energy consumption and a positive value represents energy production. The attribute p1 represents the power balance for energy producer and the attributes p2 to p4 represent the power balance for energy consumer. The p1 value is the absolute value obtained by the summing of p2, p3, and p4 whose range is 1.58–5.86. The range for the p2, p3, and p4 is $[-0.5, -2]$ s$^-2$. The attributes g1 to g4 represent the price elasticity coefficient (gamma). The attribute g1 represents the price elasticity coefficient for energy producers and g2–g4 represents the price elasticity coefficient for energy consumers. The gamma values range is [0.05, 1] s$^-1$. The attribute stab represents the maximum real part of the eigenvalue of the power system matrix whose value is positive

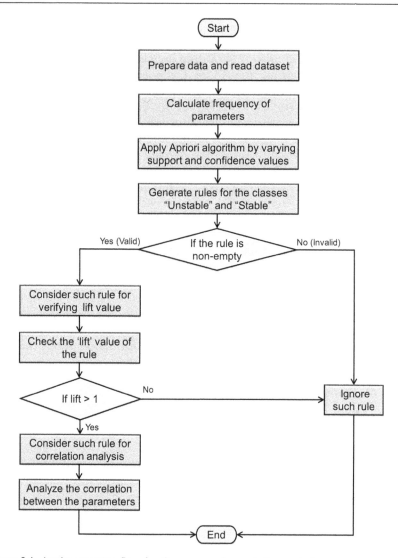

Figure 3.1 Implementation flow for the proposed correlation analysis.

which indicates the system is linearly unstable. The attribute stabf represents the stability label (stable/unstable) of the system. To perform the proposed analysis, out of 14 attributes, 13 attributes except stab and all 60,000 records are considered.

3.2 METHODOLOGY

The implementation flow for the proposed correlation analysis is given in Figure 3.1. The procedure starts with the data preparation and reading of the dataset. The preprocessing of the dataset is carried out by verifying the existence of garbage values and incomplete data. During the preprocessing step, it is noticed that the dataset is free from such issues and suitable for implementing the proposed method. Once the data are ready calculate the frequency of parameters (items) in the dataset. Then apply the Apriori algorithm to the dataset by varying support and confidence values. For every support and confidence value, generate the rules for classes "Unstable" and "Stable." If the rule is non-empty, then consider the rule for the analysis. If the rule is empty, then ignore such a rule. A rule with an empty antecedent is not a valid association rule.

In association rule mining, the antecedent and the consequent are both non-empty itemsets. An empty antecedent means that there is no condition to satisfy, so the rule becomes trivially true for all transactions in the dataset. This does not provide any useful information for analysing the association between items in the dataset. Therefore, a rule with an empty antecedent is usually not considered in association rule mining. Further, the support and confidence values are not valid for a rule obtained with an empty antecedent. Next, observe the lift value in each rule. Identify the rules with a lift value greater than 1 which are said to be strong association rules. If the lift value is greater than 1 for a rule then consider such a rule for correlation analysis, otherwise ignore it. Finally, analyse the correlation between the parameters. The details of the Apriori algorithm are discussed in Section 3.2.1 and support, confidence, and lift are discussed in Section 3.2.2.

3.2.1 Apriori algorithm

The Apriori algorithm is a popular algorithm used in association rule mining. The steps involved in the Apriori algorithm are given in Table 3.1. All these steps are repeated until no more frequent itemsets or association rules can be obtained. The Apriori algorithm's output is a set of frequent itemsets and association rules that meet the minimum support and confidence thresholds specified by the user.

3.2.2 Support, confidence, and lift

Support (supp) is a measure of the frequency of the itemset's occurrence in a dataset, while confidence (conf) is a degree of the strength of association between two items in the itemset. These values range from 0 to 1, with 1 indicating a strong association. Both "supp" and "conf" are calculated based on the occurrence of the items in the dataset, and if an itemset or rule never occurs in the dataset, their "supp" and "conf" values will be 0. However, it is important to note that having a "supp" or "conf" value of 0 may not be very informative for association rule mining. A supp of 0 indicates that the itemset is not present in the dataset at all, while a "conf" of 0 indicates that

Table 3.1 Steps involved in the Apriori algorithm

Step	Description
Data preparation	Prepare the data by converting it into a suitable format
Item frequency calculation	Calculate the frequency of each item in the dataset
Setting minimum support threshold	This threshold is the minimum frequency that is necessary for an itemset to be recognized as frequent. It is set by the user.
Generating candidate itemsets	Generates candidate itemsets by combining frequent items to form larger itemsets. The algorithm produces k-itemsets by combining k-1 itemsets that satisfy the minimum support threshold.
Pruning candidate itemsets	Prunes the candidate itemsets, which don't obey the minimum support threshold. It reduces the number of itemsets that need to be considered in subsequent iterations.
Generating association rules	Generates association rules, which obey the minimum confidence threshold. The confidence of a rule is the conditional probability that a transaction containing the antecedent of the rule also contains the consequent of the rule.
Pruning association rules	The algorithm prunes the association rules that do not satisfy the minimum confidence threshold. This reduces the number of rules that need to be considered in subsequent iterations.

the rule has no predictive power. In most cases, the researchers are interested in finding frequent itemsets or strong rules, so having a "supp" or "conf" value of 0 is not very useful.

The "supp" and "conf" can be equal to 1 in association rule mining, but it would be rare and only occur in specific cases. If the "supp" and "conf" values are equal to 1, it means that the itemset or rule appears in every transaction in the dataset, which is a rare occurrence in real-world datasets. It may indicate that the dataset is too small or that the rules obtained are too general and not informative. In most cases, a "supp" or "conf" value close to 1 indicates a strong association between items, and this is what we aim for in association rule mining. However, it is important to remember that a high "supp" or "conf" value does not always imply causation or a meaningful relationship between the items, and further analysis is required to determine the significance of the results.

Lift is a quantity of the strength of association between two items in a dataset. Specifically, lift measures how much more often two items occur together than would be estimated if they were statistically independent. Lift is calculated by dividing the observed frequency of co-occurrence of two items by the expected frequency of co-occurrence if the two items were statistically independent. A lift value higher than 1 denotes a positive association between the two items, while a lift value lower than 1 represents a negative association. However, it is important to note that lift alone is not sufficient to make causal inferences or predictions about future behaviour.

3.3 RESULTS AND DISCUSSION

The implementation of the proposed approach has provided the following results. The result of the frequency of parameters in the dataset is shown in Figure 3.2. The results of varying confidence value, varying support value, and the correlation analysis between the parameters using association rules are presented in Sections 3.1–3.3, respectively. From Figure 3.2, it is observed that the relative frequency of the parameters tau1, tau2, tau3, tau4, p1, p2, p3, p4, g1, g2, g3, and g4 is 0.33. Similarly, the relative frequency of the class "stable" is 0.36 and the class "unstable" is 0.64 in the "stabf" attribute.

3.3.1 Results of varying confidence values

The results of varying conf values are shown in Figure 3.3(a) through Figure 3.3(j). In this, the total rules were obtained at varying conf values 0.1, 0.2, 0.3, 0.4, 0.5, 0.6, 0.7, 0.8, 0.9, and 1. In Figure 3.3(a), the rules are obtained at supp = 0.1 and varying conf value. From this figure, it is observed that the total rules obtained at conf = 0.1 for the classes unstable and stable are 47 and 25, respectively. At conf = 0.2, the total rules obtained for the classes unstable and stable are 47 and 25, respectively. At conf = 0.3, the total rules obtained for the classes unstable and stable are 47 and 25, respectively. At conf = 0.4, the total rules obtained for the classes unstable and stable are 47 and 8, respectively. At conf = 0.5, the total rules obtained for the classes unstable and stable are 43 and 4, respectively. At conf = 0.6, the total rules obtained for the classes unstable and stable are 39 and 0, respectively. At conf = 0.7, the total rules obtained for the classes unstable and stable are 16 and 0, respectively. At conf = 0.8, the total rules obtained for the classes unstable and stable are 4 and 0, respectively. At conf = 0.9, the total rules obtained for the classes unstable and stable are 0. At conf = 1, the total rules obtained for the classes unstable and stable are 0.

The summary of the rules obtained at supp = 0.1 is given in Table 3.2. In this table, the status of the obtained rules is given in two cases such as "Invalid" and "Valid." The rules that contain the status "Invalid" represent that there is an empty set. When there is an empty set, it means that any condition is acceptable. But this is not useful to interpret the impact of the parameters on the stability of the power system. The rules that contain the status "Valid" represent that there is no empty set and the lift value is also greater than 1 in such rules. From the table, it is observed that the number of rules 16 and 4 at Unstable with conf values 0.7 and 0.8, respectively, are Valid. Similarly, the number of rules 8 and 4 at Stable with conf values 0.4

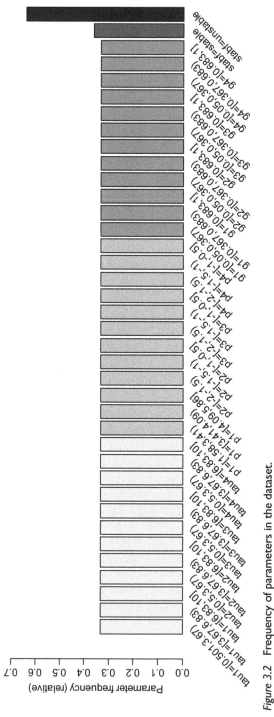

Figure 3.2 Frequency of parameters in the dataset.

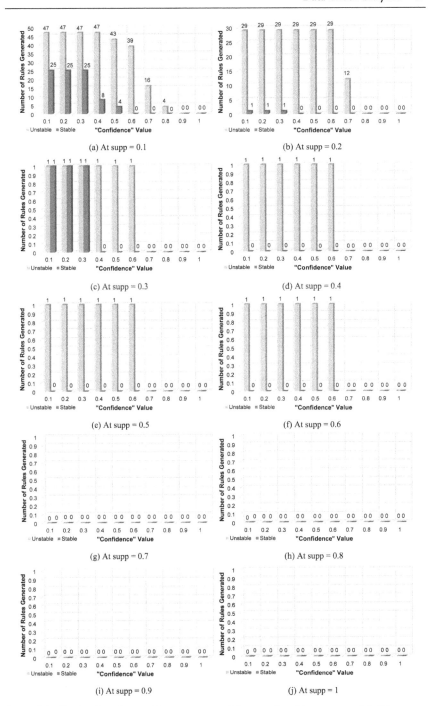

Figure 3.3 Total rules obtained for varying confidence value: (a) at supp = 0.1; (b) at supp = 0.2; (c) at supp = 0.3; (d) at supp = 0.4; (e) at supp = 0.5; (f) at supp = 0.6; (g) at supp = 0.7; (h) at supp = 0.8; (i) at supp = 0.9; and (j) at supp = 1.

Table 3.2 Summary of rules obtained at supp = 0.1

Conf	Unstable		Stable	
0.1	47	Invalid	25	Invalid
0.2	47	Invalid	25	Invalid
0.3	47	Invalid	25	Invalid
0.4	47	Invalid	8	Valid
0.5	43	Invalid	4	Valid
0.6	39	Invalid	0	Invalid
0.7	16	Valid	0	Invalid
0.8	4	Valid	0	Invalid
0.9	0	Invalid	0	Invalid
1	0	Invalid	0	Invalid

Table 3.3 Summary of rules obtained at supp = 0.2

Conf	Unstable		Stable	
0.1	29	Invalid	1	Invalid
0.2	29	Invalid	1	Invalid
0.3	29	Invalid	1	Invalid
0.4	29	Invalid	0	Invalid
0.5	29	Invalid	0	Invalid
0.6	29	Invalid	0	Invalid
0.7	12	Valid	0	Invalid
0.8	0	Invalid	0	Invalid
0.9	0	Invalid	0	Invalid
1	0	Invalid	0	Invalid

and 0.5 are Valid. All the remaining rules in both Unstable and Stable are Invalid.

In Figure 3.3(b), the rules are obtained at supp = 0.2 and varying conf value. From this figure, it is observed that the total rules obtained at conf = 0.1 for the classes unstable and stable are 29 and 1, respectively. At conf = 0.2, the total rules obtained for the classes unstable and stable are 29 and 1, respectively. At conf = 0.3, the total rules obtained for the classes unstable and stable are 29 and 1, respectively. At conf = 0.4, the total rules obtained for the classes unstable and stable are 29 and 0, respectively. At conf = 0.5, the total rules obtained for the classes unstable and stable are 29 and 0, respectively. At conf = 0.6, the total rules obtained for the classes unstable and stable are 29 and 0, respectively. At conf = 0.7, the total rules obtained for the classes unstable and stable are 12 and 0, respectively. At conf = 0.8, the total rules obtained for the classes unstable and stable are 0. At conf = 0.9, the total rules obtained for the classes unstable and stable are 0. At conf = 1, the total rules obtained for the classes unstable and stable are 0. The summary of the rules obtained at supp = 0.2 is given in Table 3.3. From the table, it is observed that the number of rule 12 at Unstable with conf value 0.7 is Valid. All the remaining is Invalid.

Table 3.4 Summary of rules obtained at supp = 0.3

Conf	Unstable		Stable	
0.1	1	Invalid	1	Invalid
0.2	1	Invalid	1	Invalid
0.3	1	Invalid	1	Invalid
0.4	1	Invalid	0	Invalid
0.5	1	Invalid	0	Invalid
0.6	1	Invalid	0	Invalid
0.7	0	Invalid	0	Invalid
0.8	0	Invalid	0	Invalid
0.9	0	Invalid	0	Invalid
1	0	Invalid	0	Invalid

In Figure 3.3(c), the rules are obtained at supp = 0.3 and varying conf value. From this figure, it is observed that the total rules obtained at conf = 0.1 for the classes unstable and stable are 1 and 1, respectively. At conf = 0.2, the total rules obtained for the classes unstable and stable are 1 and 1, respectively. At conf = 0.3, the total rules obtained for the classes unstable and stable are 1 and 1, respectively. At conf = 0.4, the total rules obtained for the classes unstable and stable are 1 and 0, respectively. At conf = 0.5, the total rules obtained for the classes unstable and stable are 1 and 0, respectively. At conf = 0.6, the total rules obtained for the classes unstable and stable are 1 and 0, respectively. At conf = 0.7, the total rules obtained for the classes unstable and stable are 0. At conf = 0.8, the total rules obtained for the classes unstable and stable are 0. At conf = 0.9, the total rules obtained for the classes unstable and stable are 0. At conf = 1, the total rules obtained for the classes unstable and stable are 0. The summary of the rules obtained at supp = 0.3 is given in Table 3.4. From this table, it is observed that all rules are Invalid.

In Figure 3.3(d), the rules are obtained at supp = 0.4 and varying conf value. From this figure, it is observed that the total rules obtained at conf = 0.1 for the classes unstable and stable are 1 and 0, respectively. At conf = 0.2, the total rules obtained for the classes unstable and stable are 1 and 0, respectively. At conf = 0.3, the total rules obtained for the classes unstable and stable are 1 and 0, respectively. At conf = 0.4, the total rules obtained for the classes unstable and stable are 1 and 0, respectively. At conf = 0.5, the total rules obtained for the classes unstable and stable are 1 and 0, respectively. At conf = 0.6, the total rules obtained for the classes unstable and stable are 1 and 0, respectively. At conf = 0.7, the total rules obtained for the classes unstable and stable are 0. At conf = 0.8, the total rules obtained for the classes unstable and stable are 0. At conf = 0.9, the total rules obtained for the classes unstable and stable are 0. At conf = 1, the total rules obtained for the classes unstable and stable are 0. The summary of the rules obtained at supp = 0.4 is given in Table 3.5. From this table, it is observed that all rules are Invalid.

Table 3.5 Summary of rules obtained at supp = 0.4

Conf	Unstable		Stable	
0.1	1	Invalid	0	Invalid
0.2	1	Invalid	0	Invalid
0.3	1	Invalid	0	Invalid
0.4	1	Invalid	0	Invalid
0.5	1	Invalid	0	Invalid
0.6	1	Invalid	0	Invalid
0.7	0	Invalid	0	Invalid
0.8	0	Invalid	0	Invalid
0.9	0	Invalid	0	Invalid
1	0	Invalid	0	Invalid

Table 3.6 Summary of rules obtained at supp = 0.5

Conf	Unstable		Stable	
0.1	1	Invalid	0	Invalid
0.2	1	Invalid	0	Invalid
0.3	1	Invalid	0	Invalid
0.4	1	Invalid	0	Invalid
0.5	1	Invalid	0	Invalid
0.6	1	Invalid	0	Invalid
0.7	0	Invalid	0	Invalid
0.8	0	Invalid	0	Invalid
0.9	0	Invalid	0	Invalid
1	0	Invalid	0	Invalid

In Figure 3.3(e), the rules are obtained at supp = 0.5 and varying conf value. From this figure, it is observed that the total rules obtained at conf = 0.1 for the classes unstable and stable are 1 and 1, respectively. At conf = 0.2, the total rules obtained for the classes unstable and stable are 1 and 1, respectively. At conf = 0.3, the total rules obtained for the classes unstable and stable are 1 and 1, respectively. At conf = 0.4, the total rules obtained for the classes unstable and stable are 1 and 0, respectively. At conf = 0.5, the total rules obtained for the classes unstable and stable are 1 and 0, respectively. At conf = 0.6, the total rules obtained for the classes unstable and stable are 1 and 0, respectively. At conf = 0.7, the total rules obtained for the classes unstable and stable are 0. At conf = 0.8, the total rules obtained for the classes unstable and stable are 0. At conf = 0.9, the total rules obtained for the classes unstable and stable are 0. At conf = 1, the total rules obtained for the classes unstable and stable are 0. The summary of the rules obtained at supp = 0.5 is given in Table 3.6. From this table, it is observed that all rules are Invalid.

In Figure 3.3(f), the rules are obtained at supp = 0.6 and varying conf value. From this figure, it is observed that the total rules obtained at conf = 0.1 for the classes unstable and stable are 1 and 1, respectively. At conf =

Table 3.7   Summary of rules obtained at supp = 0.6

Conf	Unstable		Stable	
0.1	1	Invalid	0	Invalid
0.2	1	Invalid	0	Invalid
0.3	1	Invalid	0	Invalid
0.4	1	Invalid	0	Invalid
0.5	1	Invalid	0	Invalid
0.6	1	Invalid	0	Invalid
0.7	0	Invalid	0	Invalid
0.8	0	Invalid	0	Invalid
0.9	0	Invalid	0	Invalid
1	0	Invalid	0	Invalid

0.2, the total rules obtained for the classes unstable and stable are 1 and 1, respectively. At conf = 0.3, the total rules obtained for the classes unstable and stable are 1 and 1, respectively. At conf = 0.4, the total rules obtained for the classes unstable and stable are 1 and 0, respectively. At conf = 0.5, the total rules obtained for the classes unstable and stable are 1 and 0, respectively. At conf = 0.6, the total rules obtained for the classes unstable and stable are 1 and 0, respectively. At conf = 0.7, the total rules obtained for the classes unstable and stable are 0. At conf = 0.8, the total rules obtained for the classes unstable and stable are 0. At conf = 0.9, the total rules obtained for the classes unstable and stable are 0. At conf = 1, the total rules obtained for the classes unstable and stable are 0. The summary of the rules obtained at supp = 0.6 is given in Table 3.7. From this table, it is observed that all rules are Invalid.

In Figure 3.3(g), the rules are obtained at supp = 0.7 and varying conf value. From this figure, it is observed that the total rules obtained at conf = 0.1 for the classes unstable and stable are 0. At conf = 0.2, the total rules obtained for the classes unstable and stable are 0. At conf = 0.3, the total rules obtained for the classes unstable and stable are 0. At conf = 0.4, the total rules obtained for the classes unstable and stable are 0. At conf = 0.5, the total rules obtained for the classes unstable and stable are 0. At conf = 0.6, the total rules obtained for the classes unstable and stable are 0. At conf = 0.7, the total rules obtained for the classes unstable and stable are 0. At conf = 0.8, the total rules obtained for the classes unstable and stable are 0. At conf = 0.9, the total rules obtained for the classes unstable and stable are 0. At conf = 1, the total rules obtained for the classes unstable and stable are 0. The summary of the rules obtained at supp = 0.7 is given in Table 3.9. From this table, it is observed that all rules are Invalid.

In Figure 3.3(h), the rules are obtained at supp = 0.8 and varying conf value. From this figure, it is observed that the total rules obtained at conf = 0.1 for the classes unstable and stable are 0. At conf = 0.2, the total rules obtained for the classes unstable and stable are 0. At conf = 0.3, the total

Table 3.8 Summary of rules obtained at supp = 0.8

Conf	Unstable		Stable	
0.1	0	Invalid	0	Invalid
0.2	0	Invalid	0	Invalid
0.3	0	Invalid	0	Invalid
0.4	0	Invalid	0	Invalid
0.5	0	Invalid	0	Invalid
0.6	0	Invalid	0	Invalid
0.7	0	Invalid	0	Invalid
0.8	0	Invalid	0	Invalid
0.9	0	Invalid	0	Invalid
I	0	Invalid	0	Invalid

Table 3.9 Summary of rules obtained at supp = 0.7

Conf	Unstable		Stable	
0.1	0	Invalid	0	Invalid
0.2	0	Invalid	0	Invalid
0.3	0	Invalid	0	Invalid
0.4	0	Invalid	0	Invalid
0.5	0	Invalid	0	Invalid
0.6	0	Invalid	0	Invalid
0.7	0	Invalid	0	Invalid
0.8	0	Invalid	0	Invalid
0.9	0	Invalid	0	Invalid
I	0	Invalid	0	Invalid

rules obtained for the classes unstable and stable are 0. At conf = 0.4, the total rules obtained for the classes unstable and stable are 0. At conf = 0.5, the total rules obtained for the classes unstable and stable are 0. At conf = 0.6, the total rules obtained for the classes unstable and stable are 0. At conf = 0.7, the total rules obtained for the classes unstable and stable are 0. At conf = 0.8, the total rules obtained for the classes unstable and stable are 0. At conf = 0.9, the total rules obtained for the classes unstable and stable are 0. At conf = 1, the total rules obtained for the classes unstable and stable are 0. The summary of the rules obtained at supp = 0.8 is given in Table 3.8. From this table, it is observed that all rules are Invalid.

In Figure 3.3(i), the rules are obtained at supp = 0.9 and varying conf value. From this figure, it is observed that the total rules obtained at conf = 0.1 for the classes unstable and stable are 0. At conf = 0.2, the total rules obtained for the classes unstable and stable are 0. At conf = 0.3, the total rules obtained for the classes unstable and stable are 0. At conf = 0.4, the total rules obtained for the classes unstable and stable are 0. At conf = 0.5, the total rules obtained for the classes unstable and stable are 0. At conf = 0.6, the total rules obtained for the classes unstable and stable are 0. At conf = 0.7, the total rules obtained for the classes unstable and stable are 0. At

Table 3.10 Summary of rules obtained at supp = 0.9

Conf	Unstable		Stable	
0.1	0	Invalid	0	Invalid
0.2	0	Invalid	0	Invalid
0.3	0	Invalid	0	Invalid
0.4	0	Invalid	0	Invalid
0.5	0	Invalid	0	Invalid
0.6	0	Invalid	0	Invalid
0.7	0	Invalid	0	Invalid
0.8	0	Invalid	0	Invalid
0.9	0	Invalid	0	Invalid
1	0	Invalid	0	Invalid

Table 3.11 Summary of rules obtained at supp = 1

Conf	Unstable		Stable	
0.1	0	Invalid	0	Invalid
0.2	0	Invalid	0	Invalid
0.3	0	Invalid	0	Invalid
0.4	0	Invalid	0	Invalid
0.5	0	Invalid	0	Invalid
0.6	0	Invalid	0	Invalid
0.7	0	Invalid	0	Invalid
0.8	0	Invalid	0	Invalid
0.9	0	Invalid	0	Invalid
1	0	Invalid	0	Invalid

conf = 0.8, the total rules obtained for the classes unstable and stable are 0. At conf = 0.9, the total rules obtained for the classes unstable and stable are 0. At conf = 1, the total rules obtained for the classes unstable and stable are 0. The summary of the rules obtained at supp = 0.9 is given in Table 3.10. From this table, it is observed that all rules are Invalid.

In Figure 3.3(j), the rules are obtained at supp = 1 and varying conf value. From this figure, it is observed that the total rules obtained at conf = 0.1 for the classes unstable and stable are 0. At conf = 0.2, the total rules obtained for the classes unstable and stable are 0. At conf = 0.3, the total rules obtained for the classes unstable and stable are 0. At conf = 0.4, the total rules obtained for the classes unstable and stable are 0. At conf = 0.5, the total rules obtained for the classes unstable and stable are 0. At conf = 0.6, the total rules obtained for the classes unstable and stable are 0. At conf = 0.7, the total rules obtained for the classes unstable and stable are 0. At conf = 0.8, the total rules obtained for the classes unstable and stable are 0. At conf = 0.9, the total rules obtained for the classes unstable and stable are 0. At conf = 1, the total rules obtained for the classes unstable and stable are 0. The summary of the rules obtained at supp = 1 is given in Table 3.11. From this table, it is observed that all rules are Invalid.

Table 3.12 Summary of rules obtained at conf = 0.1

Supp	Unstable		Stable	
0.1	47	Invalid	25	Invalid
0.2	29	Invalid	1	Invalid
0.3	1	Invalid	1	Invalid
0.4	1	Invalid	0	Invalid
0.5	1	Invalid	0	Invalid
0.6	1	Invalid	0	Invalid
0.7	0	Invalid	0	Invalid
0.8	0	Invalid	0	Invalid
0.9	0	Invalid	0	Invalid
1	0	Invalid	0	Invalid

3.4 RESULTS OF VARYING SUPPORT VALUE

The results of varying "supp" values are shown in Figure 3.4(a) through Figure 3.4(j). In this, the total rules were obtained at varying supp values 0.1, 0.2, 0.3, 0.4, 0.5, 0.6, 0.7, 0.8, 0.9, and 1.

In Figure 3.4(a), the rules are obtained at conf = 0.1 and varying supp value. From this figure, it is observed that the total rules obtained at supp = 0.1 for the classes unstable and stable are 47 and 25, respectively. At supp = 0.2, the total rules obtained for the classes unstable and stable are 29 and 1, respectively. At supp = 0.3, the total rules obtained for the classes unstable and stable are 1 and 1, respectively. At supp = 0.4, the total rules obtained for the classes unstable and stable are 1 and 0, respectively. At supp = 0.5, the total rules obtained for the classes unstable and stable are 1 and 0, respectively. At supp = 0.6, the total rules obtained for the classes unstable and stable are 1 and 0, respectively. At supp = 0.7, the total rules obtained for the classes unstable and stable are 0. At supp = 0.8, the total rules obtained for the classes unstable and stable are 0. At supp = 0.9, the total rules obtained for the classes unstable and stable are 0. At supp = 1, the total rules obtained for the classes unstable and stable are 0. The summary of the rules obtained at conf = 0.1 is given in Table 3.12. From this table, it is observed that all rules are Invalid.

In Figure 3.4(b), the rules are obtained at conf = 0.2 and varying supp value. From this figure, it is observed that the total rules obtained at supp = 0.1 for the classes unstable and stable are 47 and 25, respectively. At supp = 0.2, the total rules obtained for the classes unstable and stable are 29 and 1, respectively. At supp = 0.3, the total rules obtained for the classes unstable and stable are 1 and 1, respectively. At supp = 0.4, the total rules obtained for the classes unstable and stable are 1 and 0, respectively. At supp = 0.5, the total rules obtained for the classes unstable and stable are 1 and 0, respectively. At supp = 0.6, the total rules obtained for the classes unstable and stable are 1 and 0, respectively. At supp =

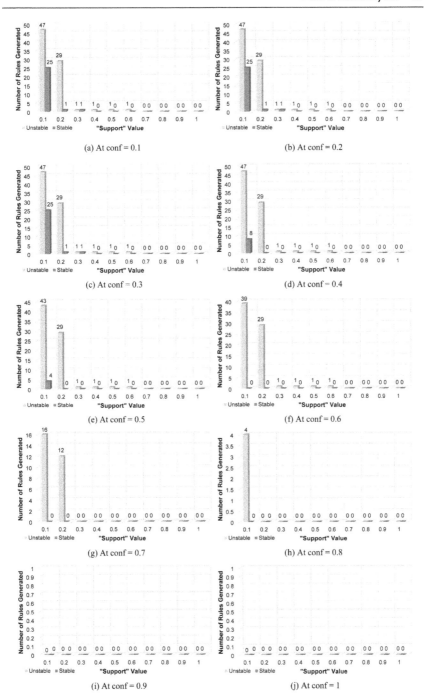

Figure 3.4 Total rules obtained for varying support values: (a) at conf = 0.1; (b) at conf = 0.2; (c) at conf = 0.3; (d) at conf = 0.4; (e) at conf = 0.5; (f) at conf = 0.6; (g) at conf = 0.7; (h) at conf = 0.8; (i) at conf = 0.9; and (j) at conf = 1

Table 3.13 Summary of rules obtained at conf = 0.2

Supp	Unstable		Stable	
0.1	47	Invalid	25	Invalid
0.2	29	Invalid	1	Invalid
0.3	1	Invalid	1	Invalid
0.4	1	Invalid	0	Invalid
0.5	1	Invalid	0	Invalid
0.6	1	Invalid	0	Invalid
0.7	0	Invalid	0	Invalid
0.8	0	Invalid	0	Invalid
0.9	0	Invalid	0	Invalid
1	0	Invalid	0	Invalid

0.7, the total rules obtained for the classes unstable and stable are 0. At supp = 0.8, the total rules obtained for the classes unstable and stable are 0. At supp = 0.9, the total rules obtained for the classes unstable and stable are 0. At supp = 1, the total rules obtained for the classes unstable and stable are 0. The summary of the rules obtained at conf = 0.2 is given in Table 3.13. From this table, it is observed that all rules are Invalid.

In Figure 3.4(c), the rules are obtained at conf = 0.3 and varying supp value. From this figure, it is observed that the total rules obtained at supp = 0.1 for the classes unstable and stable are 47 and 25, respectively. At supp = 0.2, the total rules obtained for the classes unstable and stable are 29 and 1, respectively. At supp = 0.3, the total rules obtained for the classes unstable and stable are 1 and 1, respectively. At supp = 0.4, the total rules obtained for the classes unstable and stable are 1 and 0, respectively. At supp = 0.5, the total rules obtained for the classes unstable and stable are 1 and 0, respectively. At supp = 0.6, the total rules obtained for the classes unstable and stable are 1 and 0, respectively. At supp = 0.7, the total rules obtained for the classes unstable and stable are 0. At supp = 0.8, the total rules obtained for the classes unstable and stable are 0. At supp = 0.9, the total rules obtained for the classes unstable and stable are 0. At supp = 1, the total rules obtained for the classes unstable and stable are 0. The summary of the rules obtained at conf = 0.3 is given in Table 3.15. From this table, it is observed that all rules are Invalid.

In Figure 3.4(d), the rules are obtained at conf = 0.4 and varying supp value. From this figure, it is observed that the total rules obtained at supp = 0.1 for the classes unstable and stable are 47 and 8, respectively. At supp = 0.2, the total rules obtained for the classes unstable and stable are 29 and 0, respectively. At supp = 0.3, the total rules obtained for the classes unstable and stable are 1 and 0, respectively. At supp = 0.4, the total rules obtained for the classes unstable and stable are 1 and 0, respectively. At supp = 0.5, the total rules obtained for the classes unstable and stable are

Table 3.14   Summary of rules obtained at conf = 0.4

Supp	Unstable		Stable	
0.1	47	Invalid	8	Valid
0.2	29	Invalid	0	Invalid
0.3	1	Invalid	0	Invalid
0.4	1	Invalid	0	Invalid
0.5	1	Invalid	0	Invalid
0.6	1	Invalid	0	Invalid
0.7	0	Invalid	0	Invalid
0.8	0	Invalid	0	Invalid
0.9	0	Invalid	0	Invalid
1	0	Invalid	0	Invalid

Table 3.15   Summary of rules obtained at conf = 0.3

Supp	Unstable		Stable	
0.1	47	Invalid	25	Invalid
0.2	29	Invalid	1	Invalid
0.3	1	Invalid	1	Invalid
0.4	1	Invalid	0	Invalid
0.5	1	Invalid	0	Invalid
0.6	1	Invalid	0	Invalid
0.7	0	Invalid	0	Invalid
0.8	0	Invalid	0	Invalid
0.9	0	Invalid	0	Invalid
1	0	Invalid	0	Invalid

1 and 0, respectively. At supp = 0.6, the total rules obtained for the classes unstable and stable are 1 and 0, respectively. At supp = 0.7, the total rules obtained for the classes unstable and stable are 0. At supp = 0.8, the total rules obtained for the classes unstable and stable are 0. At supp = 0.9, the total rules obtained for the classes unstable and stable are 0. At supp = 1, the total rules obtained for the classes unstable and stable are 0. The summary of the rules obtained at conf = 0.4 is given in Table 3.14. From the table, it is observed that the number of rule 8 at Stable with supp value 0.1 is Valid. All the remaining are Invalid.

In Figure 3.4(e), the rules are obtained at conf = 0.5 and varying supp value. From this figure, it is observed that the total rules obtained at supp = 0.1 for the classes unstable and stable are 43 and 4, respectively. At supp = 0.2, the total rules obtained for the classes unstable and stable are 29 and 0, respectively. At supp = 0.3, the total rules obtained for the classes unstable and stable are 1 and 0, respectively. At supp = 0.4, the total rules obtained for the classes unstable and stable are 1 and 0, respectively. At supp = 0.5, the total rules obtained for the classes unstable and stable are 1 and 0, respectively. At supp = 0.6, the total rules obtained for the classes unstable and stable are 1 and 0, respectively. At supp = 0.7, the total rules

Table 3.16 Summary of rules obtained at conf = 0.5

Supp	Unstable		Stable	
0.1	43	Invalid	4	Valid
0.2	29	Invalid	0	Invalid
0.3	1	Invalid	0	Invalid
0.4	1	Invalid	0	Invalid
0.5	1	Invalid	0	Invalid
0.6	1	Invalid	0	Invalid
0.7	0	Invalid	0	Invalid
0.8	0	Invalid	0	Invalid
0.9	0	Invalid	0	Invalid
1	0	Invalid	0	Invalid

obtained for the classes unstable and stable are 0. At supp = 0.8, the total rules obtained for the classes unstable and stable are 0. At supp = 0.9, the total rules obtained for the classes unstable and stable are 0. At supp = 1, the total rules obtained for the classes unstable and stable are 0. The summary of the rules obtained at conf = 0.5 is given in Table 3.16. From the table, it is observed that the number of rule 4 at Stable with supp value 0.1 is Valid. All the remaining are Invalid.

In Figure 3.4(f), the rules are obtained at conf = 0.6 and varying supp value. From this figure, it is observed that the total rules obtained at supp = 0.1 for the classes unstable and stable are 39 and 0, respectively. At supp = 0.2, the total rules obtained for the classes unstable and stable are 29 and 0, respectively. At supp = 0.3, the total rules obtained for the classes unstable and stable are 1 and 0, respectively. At supp = 0.4, the total rules obtained for the classes unstable and stable are 1 and 0, respectively. At supp = 0.5, the total rules obtained for the classes unstable and stable are 1 and 0, respectively. At supp = 0.6, the total rules obtained for the classes unstable and stable are 1 and 0, respectively. At supp = 0.7, the total rules obtained for the classes unstable and stable are 0. At supp = 0.8, the total rules obtained for the classes unstable and stable are 0. At supp = 0.9, the total rules obtained for the classes unstable and stable are 0. At supp = 1, the total rules obtained for the classes unstable and stable are 0. The summary of the rules obtained at conf = 0.6 is given in Table 3.17. From this table, it is observed that all rules are Invalid.

In Figure 3.4(g), the rules are obtained at conf = 0.7 and varying supp value. From this figure, it is observed that the total rules obtained at supp = 0.1 for the classes unstable and stable are 16 and 0, respectively. At supp = 0.2, the total rules obtained for the classes unstable and stable are 12 and 0, respectively. At supp = 0.3, the total rules obtained for the classes unstable and stable are 0. At supp = 0.4, the total rules obtained for the classes unstable and stable are 0. At supp = 0.5, the total rules obtained for the classes unstable and stable are 0. At supp = 0.6, the total rules obtained

Table 3.17 Summary of rules obtained at conf = 0.6

Supp	Unstable		Stable	
0.1	39	Invalid	0	Invalid
0.2	29	Invalid	0	Invalid
0.3	1	Invalid	0	Invalid
0.4	1	Invalid	0	Invalid
0.5	1	Invalid	0	Invalid
0.6	1	Invalid	0	Invalid
0.7	0	Invalid	0	Invalid
0.8	0	Invalid	0	Invalid
0.9	0	Invalid	0	Invalid
1	0	Invalid	0	Invalid

Table 3.18 Summary of rules obtained at conf = 0.7

Supp	Unstable		Stable	
0.1	16	Valid	0	Invalid
0.2	12	Valid	0	Invalid
0.3	0	Invalid	0	Invalid
0.4	0	Invalid	0	Invalid
0.5	0	Invalid	0	Invalid
0.6	0	Invalid	0	Invalid
0.7	0	Invalid	0	Invalid
0.8	0	Invalid	0	Invalid
0.9	0	Invalid	0	Invalid
1	0	Invalid	0	Invalid

for the classes unstable and stable are 0. At supp = 0.7, the total rules obtained for the classes unstable and stable are 0. At supp = 0.8, the total rules obtained for the classes unstable and stable are 0. At supp = 0.9, the total rules obtained for the classes unstable and stable are 0. At supp = 1, the total rules obtained for the classes unstable and stable are 0. The summary of the rules obtained at conf = 0.7 is given in Table 3.18. From the table, it is observed that the number of rules 16 and 12 at unstable with supp values 0.1 and 0.2, respectively, are Valid. All the remaining are Invalid.

In Figure 3.4(h), the rules are obtained at conf = 0.8 and varying supp value. From this figure, it is observed that the total rules obtained at supp = 0.1 for the classes unstable and stable are 4 and 0, respectively. At supp = 0.2, the total rules obtained for the classes unstable and stable are 0. At supp = 0.3, the total rules obtained for the classes unstable and stable are 0. At supp = 0.4, the total rules obtained for the classes unstable and stable are 0. At supp = 0.5, the total rules obtained for the classes unstable and stable are 0. At supp = 0.6, the total rules obtained for the classes unstable and stable are 0. At supp = 0.7, the total rules obtained for the classes unstable and stable are 0. At supp = 0.8, the total rules obtained for the classes unstable and stable are 0. At supp = 0.9, the total rules obtained for the classes unstable

Table 3.19 Summary of rules obtained at conf = 0.8

Supp	Unstable		Stable	
0.1	4	Valid	0	Invalid
0.2	0	Invalid	0	Invalid
0.3	0	Invalid	0	Invalid
0.4	0	Invalid	0	Invalid
0.5	0	Invalid	0	Invalid
0.6	0	Invalid	0	Invalid
0.7	0	Invalid	0	Invalid
0.8	0	Invalid	0	Invalid
0.9	0	Invalid	0	Invalid
1	0	Invalid	0	Invalid

Table 3.20 Summary of rules obtained at conf = 0.9

Supp	Unstable		Stable	
0.1	0	Invalid	0	Invalid
0.2	0	Invalid	0	Invalid
0.3	0	Invalid	0	Invalid
0.4	0	Invalid	0	Invalid
0.5	0	Invalid	0	Invalid
0.6	0	Invalid	0	Invalid
0.7	0	Invalid	0	Invalid
0.8	0	Invalid	0	Invalid
0.9	0	Invalid	0	Invalid
1	0	Invalid	0	Invalid

and stable are 0. At supp = 1, the total rules obtained for the classes unstable and stable are 0. The summary of the rules obtained at conf = 0.8 is given in Table 3.19. From the table, it is observed that the number of rule 4 at Unstable with supp value 0.1 is Valid. All the remaining are Invalid.

In Figure 3.4(i), the rules are obtained at conf = 0.9 and varying supp value. From this figure, it is observed that the total rules obtained at supp = 0.1 for the classes unstable and stable are 0. At supp = 0.2, the total rules obtained for the classes unstable and stable is 0. At supp = 0.3, the total rules obtained for the classes unstable and stable is 0. At supp = 0.4, the total rules obtained for the classes unstable and stable are 0. At supp = 0.5, the total rules obtained for the classes unstable and stable are 0. At supp = 0.6, the total rules obtained for the classes unstable and stable are 0. At supp = 0.7, the total rules obtained for the classes unstable and stable are 0. At supp = 0.8, the total rules obtained for the classes unstable and stable are 0. At supp = 0.9, the total rules obtained for the classes unstable and stable are 0. At supp = 1, the total rules obtained for the classes unstable and stable are 0. The summary of the rules obtained at conf = 0.9 is given in Table 3.20. From this table, it is observed that all rules are Invalid.

Table 3.21   Summary of rules obtained at conf = 1

Supp	Unstable		Stable	
0.1	0	Invalid	0	Invalid
0.2	0	Invalid	0	Invalid
0.3	0	Invalid	0	Invalid
0.4	0	Invalid	0	Invalid
0.5	0	Invalid	0	Invalid
0.6	0	Invalid	0	Invalid
0.7	0	Invalid	0	Invalid
0.8	0	Invalid	0	Invalid
0.9	0	Invalid	0	Invalid
1	0	Invalid	0	Invalid

In Figure 3.4(j), the rules are obtained at conf = 1 and varying supp value. From this figure, it is observed that the total rules obtained at supp = 0.1 for the classes unstable and stable are 0. At supp = 0.2, the total rules obtained for the classes unstable and stable are 0. At supp = 0.3, the total rules obtained for the classes unstable and stable are 0. At supp = 0.4, the total rules obtained for the classes unstable and stable are 0. At supp = 0.5, the total rules obtained for the classes unstable and stable are 0. At supp = 0.6, the total rules obtained for the classes unstable and stable are 0. At supp = 0.7, the total rules obtained for the classes unstable and stable are 0. At supp = 0.8, the total rules obtained for the classes unstable and stable are 0. At supp = 0.9, the total rules obtained for the classes unstable and stable are 0. At supp = 1, the total rules obtained for the classes unstable and stable are 0. The summary of the rules obtained at conf = 1 is given in Table 3.21. From this table, it is observed that all rules are Invalid.

3.5 CORRELATION ANALYSIS BETWEEN THE PARAMETERS USING ASSOCIATION RULES

The correlation between the parameters for the class unstable is shown in a network graph using the graph-based method. This network graph contains vertices and edges, where the vertices denote the set of items and the edges denote the relationship in rules. In this graph, the node size is based on the "supp" value, and the colour of the node is based on the lift value. The higher the supp value the higher the node size, and the higher the lift value the darker the node colour. The correlation between the parameters for the class unstable at supp = 0.1 and conf = 0.7 is shown in Figure 3.5 using 16 association rules. The summary of the correlation between the parameters with 16 rules for the class unstable is given in Table 3.22. In this table, the rules {13}–{16} have the highest lift value when compared to other rules, which represents that the parameters in these rules are more highly correlated with

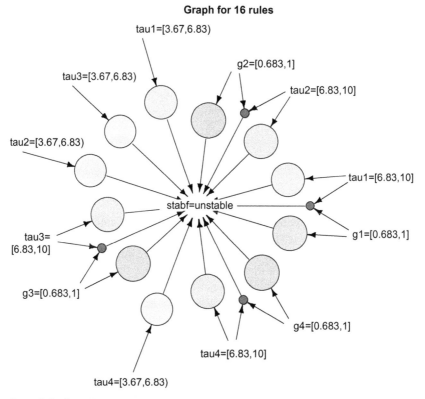

Figure 3.5 Correlation between the parameters with 16 rules for the class unstable.

each other than in other rules. Further, from rules 1 to 12, it is observed that the parameters tau1 through tau4 are unstable when the values are $3.67 \leq$ tau1, tau2, tau3, tau4 < 6.83 and also when the value is 6.83 or 10. Similarly, the parameters g1 through g4 are unstable when the value is 0.683 or 1.

The correlation between the parameters for the class unstable at supp = 0.1 and conf = 0.8 is shown in Figure 3.6 using four association rules. The summary of the correlation between the parameters with four rules for the class unstable is given in Table 3.23. In this table, the rules {1}–{4} have the highest lift value, which represents that the parameters in these rules are highly correlated with each other. Further, it is observed that the combination of the parameters tau1 and g1 is unstable when the tau1 value is 6.83 or 10 and the g1 value is 0.683 or 1. The combination of the parameters tau2 and g2 is unstable when the tau2 value is 6.83 or 10 and the g2 value is 0.683 or 1. The combination of the parameters tau3 and g3 is unstable when the tau3 value is 6.83 or 10 and the g3 value is 0.683 or 1. The combination of the parameters tau4 and g4 is unstable when the tau4 value is 6.83 or 10 and the g4 value is 0.683 or 1.

Table 3.22 Summary of correlation between the parameters with 16 rules for the class
unstable

Rule No.	LHS	RHS	Coverage	Confidence	Support	Lift	Count
[1]	{tau1=[3.67,6.83)} =>	{stabf= unstable}	0.3333000	0.7227723	0.2409000	1.132872	14454
[2]	{tau2=[6.83,10]} =>	{stabf= unstable}	0.3333333	0.7364000	0.2454667	1.154232	14728
[3]	{tau3=[3.67,6.83)} =>	{stabf= unstable}	0.3333333	0.7090000	0.2363333	1.111285	14180
[4]	{tau4=[3.67,6.83)} =>	{stabf= unstable}	0.3333333	0.7090000	0.2363333	1.111285	14180
[5]	{tau3=[6.83,10]} =>	{stabf= unstable}	0.3333333	0.7364000	0.2454667	1.154232	14728
[6]	{tau4=[6.83,10]} =>	{stabf= unstable}	0.3333333	0.7364000	0.2454667	1.154232	14728
[7]	{g2=[0.683,1]} =>	{stabf= unstable}	0.3333333	0.7575000	0.2525000	1.187304	15150
[8]	{g3=[0.683,1]} =>	{stabf= unstable}	0.3333333	0.7575000	0.2525000	1.187304	15150
[9]	{g4=[0.683,1]} =>	{stabf= unstable}	0.3333333	0.7575000	0.2525000	1.187304	15150
[10]	{tau2=[3.67,6.83)} =>	{stabf= unstable}	0.3333333	0.7090000	0.2363333	1.111285	14180
[11]	{g1=[0.683,1]} =>	{stabf= unstable}	0.3334000	0.7483503	0.2495000	1.172963	14970
[12]	{tau1=[6.83,10]} =>	{stabf= unstable}	0.3334000	0.7243551	0.2415000	1.135353	14490
[13]	{tau2=[6.83,10], g2=[0.683,1]} =>	{stabf= unstable}	0.1144333	0.8866880	0.1014667	1.389793	6088
[14]	{tau3=[6.83,10], g3=[0.683,1]} =>	{stabf= unstable}	0.1144333	0.8866880	0.1014667	1.389793	6088
[15]	{tau4=[6.83,10], g4=[0.683,1]} =>	{stabf= unstable}	0.1144333	0.8866880	0.1014667	1.389793	6088
[16]	{tau1=[6.83,10], g1=[0.683,1]} =>	{stabf= unstable}	0.1139000	0.8832309	0.1006000	1.384374	6036

Table 3.23 Summary of correlation between the parameters with four rules for the class
unstable

Rule No.	LHS	RHS	Coverage	Confidence	Support	Lift	Count
[1]	{tau2=[6.83,10], g2=[0.683,1]} =>	{stabf= unstable}	0.1144333	0.8866880	0.1014667	1.389793	6088
[2]	{tau3=[6.83,10], g3=[0.683,1]} =>	{stabf= unstable}	0.1144333	0.8866880	0.1014667	1.389793	6088
[3]	{tau4=[6.83,10], g4=[0.683,1]} =>	{stabf= unstable}	0.1144333	0.8866880	0.1014667	1.389793	6088
[4]	{tau1=[6.83,10], g1=[0.683,1]} =>	{stabf= unstable}	0.1139000	0.8832309	0.1006000	1.384374	6036

Table 3.24 Summary of correlation between the parameters with 12 rules for the class unstable

Rule No.	LHS	RHS	Coverage	Confidence	Support	Lift	Count
[1]	{tau1=[3.67,6.83)} =>	{stabf= unstable}	0.3333000	0.7227723	0.2409000	1.132872	14454
[2]	{tau2=[6.83,10]} =>	{stabf= unstable}	0.3333333	0.7364000	0.2454667	1.154232	14728
[3]	{tau3=[3.67,6.83)} =>	{stabf= unstable}	0.3333333	0.7090000	0.2363333	1.111285	14180
[4]	{tau4=[3.67,6.83)} =>	{stabf= unstable}	0.3333333	0.7090000	0.2363333	1.111285	14180
[5]	{tau3=[6.83,10]} =>	{stabf= unstable}	0.3333333	0.7364000	0.2454667	1.154232	14728
[6]	{tau4=[6.83,10]} =>	{stabf= unstable}	0.3333333	0.7364000	0.2454667	1.154232	14728
[7]	{g2=[0.683,1]} =>	{stabf= unstable}	0.3333333	0.7575000	0.2525000	1.187304	15150
[8]	{g3=[0.683,1]} =>	{stabf= unstable}	0.3333333	0.7575000	0.2525000	1.187304	15150
[9]	{g4=[0.683,1]} =>	{stabf= unstable}	0.3333333	0.7575000	0.2525000	1.187304	15150
[10]	{tau2=[3.67,6.83)} =>	{stabf= unstable}	0.3333333	0.7090000	0.2363333	1.111285	14180
[11]	{g1=[0.683,1]} =>	{stabf= unstable}	0.3334000	0.7483503	0.2495000	1.172963	14970
[12]	{tau1=[6.83,10]} =>	{stabf= unstable}	0.3334000	0.7243551	0.2415000	1.135353	14490

The correlation between the parameters for the class unstable at supp = 0.2 and conf = 0.7 is shown in Figure 3.7 using 12 association rules. The summary of the correlation between the parameters with 12 rules for the class unstable is given in Table 3.24. Further, from rules 1 to 12, it is observed that the parameters tau1 through tau4 are unstable when the values are 3.67 ≤ tau1, tau2, tau3, tau4 < 6.83 and also when the value is 6.83 or 10. Similarly, the parameters g1 through g4 are unstable when the value is 0.683 or 1. The correlation between the parameters for the class stable at supp = 0.1 and conf = 0.4 is shown in Figure 3.8 using eight association rules. The summary of the correlation between the parameters with eight rules for the class stable is given in Table 3.25. In this table, the rules {1} and {6}–{8} have the highest lift value, which represents that the parameters in these rules are more highly correlated with each other than in other rules. Further, it is observed that the parameters tau1 through tau4 lead to stability when the values are 0.501 ≤ tau1 < 3.67, and 0.5 ≤ tau2, tau3, tau4 < 3.67. Similarly, the parameters g1 through g4 lead to stability when the values are 0.05 ≤ g1, g2, g3, g4 < 0.367.

Graph for 4 rules

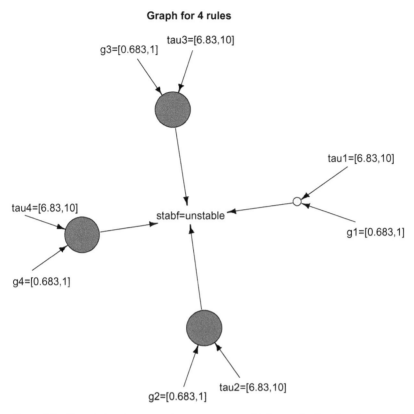

Figure 3.6 Correlation between the parameters with four rules for the class unstable.

Table 3.25 Summary of correlation between the parameters with eight rules for the class stable

Rule No.	LHS	RHS	Coverage	Confidence	Support	Lift	Count
[1]	{tau1=[0.501,3.67)} =>	{stabf= stable}	0.3333000	0.5331533	0.1777000	1.472799	10662
[2]	{g1=[0.05,0.367)} =>	{stabf= stable}	0.3333000	0.4740474	0.1580000	1.309523	9480
[3]	{g3=[0.05,0.367)} =>	{stabf= stable}	0.3333333	0.4861000	0.1620333	1.342818	9722
[4]	{g4=[0.05,0.367)} =>	{stabf= stable}	0.3333333	0.4861000	0.1620333	1.342818	9722
[5]	{g2=[0.05,0.367)} =>	{stabf= stable}	0.3333333	0.4861000	0.1620333	1.342818	9722
[6]	{tau2=[0.5,3.67)} =>	{stabf= stable}	0.3333333	0.5314000	0.1771333	1.467956	10628
[7]	{tau3=[0.5,3.67)} =>	{stabf= stable}	0.3333333	0.5314000	0.1771333	1.467956	10628
[8]	{tau4=[0.5,3.67)} =>	{stabf= stable}	0.3333333	0.5314000	0.1771333	1.467956	10628

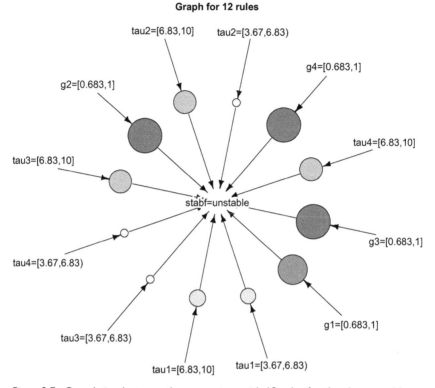

Figure 3.7 Correlation between the parameters with 12 rules for the class unstable.

Table 3.26 Summary of correlation between the parameters with four rules for the class stable

Rule No.	LHS	RHS	Coverage	Confidence	Support	Lift	Count
[1]	{tau1=[0.501,3.67)} =>	{stabf= stable}	0.3333000	0.5331533	0.1777000	1.472799	10662
[2]	{tau2=[0.5,3.67)} =>	{stabf= stable}	0.3333333	0.5314000	0.1771333	1.467956	10628
[3]	{tau3=[0.5,3.67)} =>	{stabf= stable}	0.3333333	0.5314000	0.1771333	1.467956	10628
[4]	{tau4=[0.5,3.67)} =>	{stabf= stable}	0.3333333	0.5314000	0.1771333	1.467956	10628

The correlation between the parameters for the class stable at supp = 0.1 and conf = 0.5 is shown in Figure 3.9 using four association rules. The summary of the correlation between the parameters with four rules for the class stable is given in Table 3.26. From this table, it is seen that the parameters tau1 through tau4 are stable when the values are $0.501 \leq tau1 < 3.67$ and $0.5 \leq tau2, tau3, tau4 < 3.67$.

Graph for 8 rules

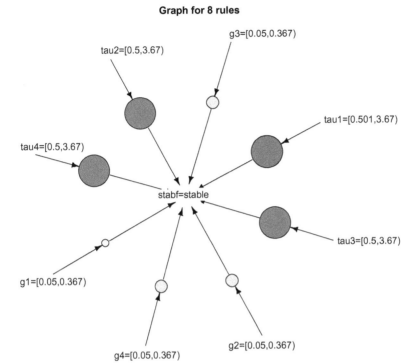

Figure 3.8 Correlation between the parameters with eight rules for the class stable.

3.6 CONCLUSIONS

This chapter discusses the correlation analysis between the parameters that impact the stability of the power system. To find the correlation among the parameters, an association rule mining that uses Apriori algorithm is applied to the considered smart grid stability dataset. The association rule mining has successfully identified the correlation between the parameters and their respective impact on the power system. From this correlation analysis, it was observed that the parameters tau1 through tau4 and g1 through g4 have a substantial influence on the power system's stability. Besides, the parameters p1–p4 have no noteworthy impression on the power system's stability. The constraints identified for the system's stability and instability are summarized as follows.

3.6.1 Constraints identified for the system stability

- The parameters tau1 through tau4 lead to a stable system when the values are $0.501 \leq tau1 < 3.67$, and $0.5 \leq tau2, tau3, tau4 < 3.67$.

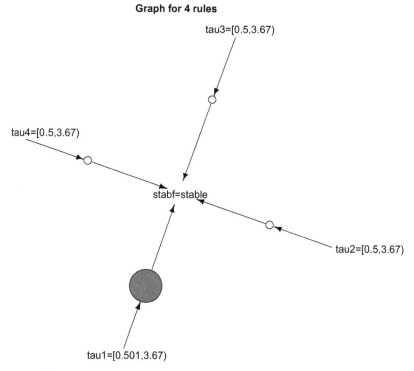

Figure 3.9   Correlation between the parameters with four rules for the class stable.

- Similarly, the parameters g1 through g4 lead to a stable system when the values are $0.05 \leq g1, g2, g3, g4 < 0.367$.

3.6.2 Constraints identified for the system instability

- The parameters tau1 through tau4 lead to an unstable system when the values are $3.67 \leq tau1, tau2, tau3, tau4 < 6.83$ and also when the value is 6.83 or 10.
- The parameters g1 through g4 lead an unstable system when the value is 0.683 or 1.
- Further, the combination of the parameters shows the effects as follows.
- A combination of tau1 and g1 leads to an unstable system when the tau1 value is 6.83 or 10 and the g1 value is 0.683 or 1.
- A combination of the parameters tau2 and g2 leads to an unstable system when the tau2 value is 6.83 or 10 and the g2 value is 0.683 or 1.
- A combination of the parameters tau3 and g3 leads to an unstable system when the tau3 value is 6.83 or 10 and the g3 value is 0.683 or 1.
- A combination of the parameters tau4 and g4 leads to an unstable system when the tau4 value is 6.83 or 10 and the g4 value is 0.683 or 1.

Thus, this work is useful to identify critical parameters and their combinations that are affecting the stability of the power system. This helps for better management and establishes absolute stability for the power system.

REFERENCES

1. S. Afzal, H. Mokhlis, H. A. Illias, N. N. Mansor, and H. Shareef, "State-of-the-art review on power system resilience and assessment techniques," *IET Generation Transmission and Distribution*, vol. 14, no. 25, pp. 6107–6121, Dec. 2020, https://doi.org/10.1049/iet-gtd.2020.0531.
2. O. A. Alimi, K. Ouahada, and A. M. Abu-Mahfouz, "A review of machine learning approaches to power system security and stability," *IEEE Access*, vol. 8, pp. 113512–113531, 2020, https://doi.org/10.1109/ACCESS.2020.3003568.
3. K. P. Prakash and Y. V. Pavan Kumar, "A systematic approach for exploration, behavior analysis, and visualization of redundant data anomalies in smart home energy consumption dataset," *International Journal of Renewable Energy Research (IJRER)*, vol. 12, no. 1, pp. 109–123, 2022, https://doi.org/10.20508/ijrer.v12i1.12613.g8381.
4. K. P. Prakash and Y. V. Pavan Kumar, "Simple and effective descriptive analysis of missing data anomalies in smart home energy consumption readings," *Journal of Energy Systems*, vol. 5, no. 3, pp. 199–220, Jan. 2023, https://doi.org/10.30521/jes.878318.
5. Z. Zou, M. Liserre, Z. Wang, and M. Cheng, "Modeling and stability analysis of a smart transformer-fed grid," *IEEE Access*, vol. 8, pp. 91876–91885, 2020, https://doi.org/10.1109/ACCESS.2020.2993558.
6. M. G. Taul, X. Wang, P. Davari, and F. Blaabjerg, "An overview of assessment methods for synchronization stability of grid-connected converters under severe symmetrical grid faults," *IEEE Transactions on Power Electron*, vol. 34, no. 10, pp. 9655–9670, Oct. 2019, https://doi.org/10.1109/TPEL.2019.2892142.
7. J. Chen, M. Liu, T. O'Donnell, and F. Milano, "Impact of current transients on the synchronization stability assessment of grid-feeding converters," *IEEE Transactions on Power Systems*, vol. 35, no. 5, pp. 4131–4134, Sep. 2020, https://doi.org/10.1109/TPWRS.2020.3009858.
8. L. Zhu, C. Lu, I. Kamwa, and H. Zeng, "Spatial-temporal feature learning in smart grids: A case study on short-term voltage stability assessment," *IEEE Transactions on Industrial Informatics*, vol. 16, no. 3, pp. 1470–1482, Mar. 2020, https://doi.org/10.1109/TII.2018.2873605.
9. V. Arzamasov, K. Bohm, and P. Jochem, "Towards concise models of grid stability," in 2018 IEEE International Conference on Communications, Control, and Computing Technologies for Smart Grids (SmartGridComm), Aalborg: IEEE, pp. 1–6, Oct. 2018, https://doi.org/10.1109/SmartGridComm.2018.8587498.
10. B. Schäfer, C. Grabow, S. Auer, J. Kurths, D. Witthaut, and M. Timme, "Taming instabilities in power grid networks by decentralized control," *European Physical Journal Special Topics*, vol. 225, no. 3, pp. 569–582, May 2016, https://doi.org/10.1140/epjst/e2015-50136-y.

11. Y. Zhou and P. Zhang, "Noise-resilient quantum machine learning for stability assessment of power systems," *IEEE Transactions on Power Systems*, vol. 38, no. 1, pp. 475–487, Jan. 2023, https://doi.org/10.1109/TPWRS.2022.3160384.

12. T. Meridji, G. Joós, and J. Restrepo, "A power system stability assessment framework using machine-learning," *Electric Power Systems Research*, vol. 216, p. 108981, Mar. 2023, https://doi.org/10.1016/j.epsr.2022.108981.

13. W. Jin, B. Zhou, S. A. Althubiti, T. R. Alsenani, and M. E. Ghoneim, "Transient stability assessment of power systems using support vector regressor and convolution neural network," *Sustainable Computing: Informatics and Systems*, vol. 37, p. 100826, Jan. 2023, https://doi.org/10.1016/j.suscom.2022.100826.

14. C. Ren, X. Du, Y. Xu, Q. Song, Y. Liu, and R. Tan, "Vulnerability analysis, robustness verification, and mitigation strategy for machine learning-based power system stability assessment model under adversarial examples," *IEEE Transactions on Smart Grid*, vol. 13, no. 2, pp. 1622–1632, Mar. 2022, https://doi.org/10.1109/TSG.2021.3133604.

15. X. Li, C. Liu, P. Guo, S. Liu, and J. Ning, "Deep learning-based transient stability assessment framework for large-scale modern power system," *International Journal of Electrical Power & Energy Systems*, vol. 139, p. 108010, Jul. 2022, https://doi.org/10.1016/j.ijepes.2022.108010.

16. J. Huang, L. Guan, Y. Chen, S. Zhu, L. Chen, and J. Yu, "A deep learning scheme for transient stability assessment in power system with a hierarchical dynamic graph pooling method," *International Journal of Electrical Power & Energy Systems*, vol. 141, p. 108044, Oct. 2022, https://doi.org/10.1016/j.ijepes.2022.108044.

17. D. R. Shrivastava, S. A. Siddiqui, and K. Verma, "New data driven scheme for real-time power system transient stability assessment," *Journal of Electrical Engineering & Technology*, Dec. 2022, https://doi.org/10.1007/s42835-022-01326-6.

18. Y. Zhang, Q. Zhao, B. Tan, and J. Yang, "A power system transient stability assessment method based on active learning," *The Journal of Engineering*, vol. 2021, no. 11, pp. 715–723, Nov. 2021, https://doi.org/10.1049/tje2.12068.

19. C. B. Saner, Y. Yaslan, and I. Genc, "An ensemble model for wide-area measurement-based transient stability assessment in power systems," *Electrical Engineering*, vol. 103, no. 6, pp. 2855–2869, Dec. 2021, https://doi.org/10.1007/s00202-021-01281-x.

20. H. K. Chappa et al., "Real time voltage instability detection in DFIG based wind integrated grid with dynamic components," *International Journal of Computing and Digital Systems (IJCDS)*, vol. 10, no. 1, pp. 795–804, Nov. 2021, https://doi.org/10.12785/ijcds/100173.

21. F. Darbandi, A. Jafari, H. Karimipour, A. Dehghantanha, F. Derakhshan, and K. Raymond Choo, "Real-time stability assessment in smart cyber-physical grids: A deep learning approach," *IET Smart Grid*, vol. 3, no. 4, pp. 454–461, Aug. 2020, https://doi.org/10.1049/iet-stg.2019.0191.

22. B. Tan, J. Yang, Y. Tang, S. Jiang, P. Xie, and W. Yuan, "A deep imbalanced learning framework for transient stability assessment of power system," *IEEE Access*, vol. 7, pp. 81759–81769, 2019, https://doi.org/10.1109/ACCESS.2019.2923799.

23. S. Wu, L. Zheng, W. Hu, R. Yu, and B. Liu, "Improved deep belief network and model interpretation method for power system transient stability assessment," *Journal of Modern Power Systems and Clean Energy*, vol. 8, no. 1, pp. 27–37, 2020, https://doi.org/10.35833/MPCE.2019.000058.
24. J. Huang, L. Guan, Y. Su, H. Yao, M. Guo, and Z. Zhong, "Recurrent graph convolutional network-based multi-task transient stability assessment framework in power system," *IEEE Access*, vol. 8, pp. 93283–93296, 2020, https://doi.org/10.1109/ACCESS.2020.2991263.
25. B. Tan et al., "Spatial-temporal adaptive transient stability assessment for power system under missing data," *International Journal of Electrical Power & Energy Systems*, vol. 123, p. 106237, Dec. 2020, https://doi.org/10.1016/j.ijepes.2020.106237.
26. W. Hu et al., "Real-time transient stability assessment in power system based on improved SVM," *Journal of Modern Power Systems and Clean Energy*, vol. 7, no. 1, pp. 26–37, Jan. 2019, https://doi.org/10.1007/s40565-018-0453-x.
27. X. Li et al., "A stratified method for large-scale power system transient stability assessment based on maximum relevance minimum redundancy arithmetic," *IEEE Access*, vol. 7, pp. 61414–61432, 2019, https://doi.org/10.1109/ACCESS.2019.2915965.
28. Y. Zhang, Y. Xu, Z. Y. Dong, and R. Zhang, "A hierarchical self-adaptive data-analytics method for real-time power system short-term voltage stability assessment," *IEEE Transactions on Industrial Informatics*, vol. 15, no. 1, pp. 74–84, Jan. 2019, https://doi.org/10.1109/TII.2018.2829818.
29. Y. Zhang, Y. Xu, and Z. Y. Dong, "Robust ensemble data analytics for incomplete PMU measurements-based power system stability assessment," *IEEE Transactions on Power Systems*, vol. 33, no. 1, pp. 1124–1126, Jan. 2018, https://doi.org/10.1109/TPWRS.2017.2698239.
30. https://www.kaggle.com/datasets/pcbreviglieri/smart-grid-stability.

Chapter 4

Data-driven machine learning models for load power forecasting in photovoltaic systems

Prem Prakash Vuppuluri, K. Pritam Satsangi, Pihu Agarwal, and Tania Arora

4.1 INTRODUCTION

Electrical load is an ever-changing parameter in any electrical system with different sources and loads. Knowing the load prior could give an edge in managing sources and serving loads properly. Load forecasting has been a keen research area for the past few decades in the field of energy management, particularly when sources are more in number and also when energy storage is part of the system. According to time periods, forecasting can be defined in four categories.

- Very short-term (minutes to hours ahead)
- Short-term (day to weeks ahead)
- Medium-term (months to 1 year ahead)
- Long-term (years ahead)

Forecasting plays a crucial role in the integration of renewable energy sources into the electricity grid. Renewable energy sources, such as solar and wind, are highly dependent on weather conditions and other environmental factors, making their power output inherently variable and uncertain. With electrical systems becoming more complex in recent times, accurate forecasting of load can lead to better operation of electrical systems in three perspectives, namely cost, optimization, and reliability. By accurately forecasting the power output of renewable energy sources, grid operators can plan and manage the balance between energy supply and demand, thereby avoiding potential shortages or overproduction. Additionally, forecasting can help grid operators optimize the use of conventional power plants and energy storage systems to meet the grid's electricity demand. Forecasting also provides renewable energy project developers with insights on the expected power output of their projects, which in turn would lead to well-planned maintenance and help in the effective optimization of design and operation of facilities. Thus, accurate forecasting of renewable energy sources is very

DOI: 10.1201/9781003470274-4

essential to ensure grid stability, reduce energy costs, and promote the integration of clean energy into the electricity grid. Solar load forecasting is typically done using historical solar irradiance data and other relevant weather variables, such as temperature, humidity, and wind speed, which can have a significant impact on electric load demand.

Load forecasting typically relies on historical data, with (possibly) non-linear dependence on a wide variety of environmental factors and other parameters. Time series analysis can capture different types of patterns and trends in historical data, such as seasonality (e.g., daily, weekly, or yearly patterns) and long-term trends, and generally handles data that are collected over a period of time very effectively. Regression analysis allows us to model the relationship between load and various influencing factors, such as temperature, day of the week, holidays, and economic indicators, thereby helping us quantify the impact of these factors on load, allowing for more accurate forecasts. Furthermore, regression analysis can accommodate both linear and non-linear relationships between the dependent (load) and independent (factors affecting load) variables; this flexibility makes it suitable for capturing complex relationships that may not be apparent from simple inspection. Hence, statistical approaches such as time series and regression analyses have been used widely for load forecasting.

In recent times, machine learning (ML) and deep learning (DL) approaches, which learn from data and make predictions or decisions without having to be explicitly programmed, have gained popularity in recent years for load forecasting and have been shown to be more effective than traditional statistical methods in certain situations, especially when dealing with large and diverse datasets. ML models have generally adapted better to the non-stationary behaviour exhibited by load data (wherein statistical properties change over time) and still provide reasonably accurate forecasts. Deep learning models automatically learn relevant features or representations from the data and capture highly complex and non-linear relationships in data. These have proven to be particularly useful when dealing with high-dimensional data and in scenarios where load forecasting depends on intricate interactions between various factors. These data-driven models have also gained popularity on account of their being more reliable with non-linear and noisy data. On the other hand, ML models typically require large amounts of training data for them to perform well. The type and size of the training dataset also play a significant role in these models. This may prove to be a limiting factor in certain load forecasting applications, in particular those with low or sparse data availability.

Broadly speaking, machine learning models may be categorized into three main types based on how they learn from data: supervised-, unsupervised-, and reinforcement learning models. In supervised machine learning, the model learns from (is "trained" on) labelled data, where each data point provides both the input parameters and the correct output or label. The model's goal is to learn the relationship between the inputs and outputs so that it can make predictions on new data. Models that are used for predicting categorical labels or classes are known as classification models; these include algorithms such as logistic regression, decision trees, support vector machines, and neural networks for image classification. Models that predict continuous numerical values are known as regression models: linear, polynomial, and support vector regression algorithms are some well-known regression models.

In unsupervised machine learning, the model learns from unlabelled data, so there are no correct answers provided at the training stage. Instead, it tries to find patterns or structures in the data on its own. Examples include clustering models such as K-means clustering and hierarchical clustering, which group similar data points together based on patterns or similarities in the data, dimensionality reduction models such as principal component analysis (PCA) and t-distributed stochastic neighbour embedding (t-SNE), which reduce the number of features or dimensions in the data while preserving important information, and generative models that learn to generate new data points similar to the training data seen by the model. Variational autoencoders (VAEs) and generative adversarial networks (GANs) are some popular generative models.

Lastly, reinforcement learning (RL) is used for sequential decision-making tasks in situations where agents interact with their environment and learn to make decisions aimed at maximizing a (problem-specific) reward. Examples of RL include Q-learning, deep Q-networks (DQNs), and policy gradient methods. The interested reader is referred to [1] and [2] for a more detailed review of machine learning approaches.

4.2 REVIEW OF LITERATURE

A prediction study by Abdallah et al. depicts various models like linear regression, support vector machines, ensemble models, decision tree models, and neural networks [3]. Multimillion datasets from different demographies have been used to train the models where ensemble models, particularly random forest, performed better than others with minimum root mean square error and mean absolute error values. A systematic comparative study of models has been presented by Liu where time series ARIMA, some classical regression models, and two deep learning models were assessed for performance, and also the extraction of the best feature set from the data is shown [4]. Linear models with linear kernels performed better in this study, and it is also shown that layer-wise trained deep learning methods can improve forecasting accuracy. A hybrid model by Dong et al. presents a mixed approach for forecasting residential load in single-family houses in the United States [5]. Five different techniques such as artificial neural network (ANN), Gaussian process regression (GPR), Gaussian mixture model (GMM), support vector regression (SVR), and least-squares support vector machine (LS-SVM) have been applied to residential datasets and were compared with a hybrid model. Results show that the hybrid model is better for hour-ahead forecasting only and for day-ahead forecasting all the techniques fare similarly. A city-scale building energy prediction is presented by Kontokosta and Tull [6]. Historical data from more than 20,000 buildings have been used as input to train linear regression, random forest, and support vector regression models. Consumption patterns in different types of buildings like offices, schools, malls, etc., have been studied. A primitive comparative review of data-driven approaches such as regression-based, ANN, SVM, and clustering-based models has been presented by Tardioli [7]. A detailed review of hybrid models for time series forecasting is presented by Deb et al. [8]. The advantages and disadvantages of individual models are explained, and then different combinations of models (hybrid models) are also presented including ANN, ARIMA, SVM, Fuzzy, random forest, evolutionary algorithms (EAs). A specific review on building energy forecasting methods using AI techniques such as SVM and ANN has been presented by Ahmad et al. [9]. In addition to this, the potentials of some hybrid methods like least-squares support vector machine (LSSVM) and group method of data handling (GMDH) have also been introduced. A novel recurrent neural network (RNN) model has been proposed by Rahman et al. which performed better than a three-layered perceptron model [10]. A brief review of building energy load forecasting methods is presented by Mat Daut et al. [11]. Conventional methods and AI techniques have been referred to apply in such applications; however, hybrid methods have been found to be performing better than a single technique. An exhaustive empirical evaluation of machine learning algorithms is presented by Akhtar et al. for load estimation [12]. In more than 20 such algorithms, the Bagged Tree algorithm was found to be more effective. A detailed review of demand prediction techniques in smart building integrated PV is presented by Liu et al. [13]. Techniques like nature-inspired intelligence, ANN, machine learning, and multiagent systems have been reviewed at length. These are found to be helpful under various challenging conditions. A critical review of the status of data-driven machine learning models for urban energy modelling is presented by Manandhar et al., Deb, and Amasyali and El-Gohary [14–16]. Electricity consumption prediction in a smart metering environment has been presented by Kim et al. [17]. Demand forecasting using time series clustering methods has been detailed using ARIMA, ARIMAX, double-seasonal Holt-Winters forecasting (DSHW), neural network autoregressive model (NNAR), and so on. A new dimension of user behaviour is considered as a variable in predicting household electricity consumption [18]. The authors have proposed some predictors and intervention strategies using a hybrid model comprising SVR, which applies Guassian function, and then optimized by genetic algorithm (GA). Three machine learning models were tuned with energy-related data from public agencies in Brazil [19]. Random forest, gradient boosting, and SVMs were trained and optimized

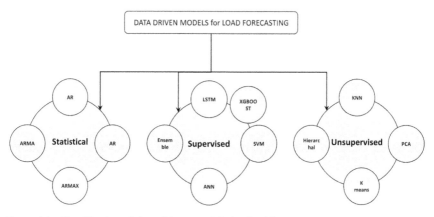

Figure 4.1   Classification of data-driven models for load forecasting.

to get accurate daily/monthly forecasts. Future electricity demand forecast of Brazil for 2021–2025 was presented by Velasquez et al. using time series approximation [20]. Regression with seasonality was found to be the best approach and the hybrid method combining different time series methods reduced the error. Stochastic optimization with load forecasting and deep neural networks based load forecasting model has been detailed by Prusty et al. and Selvaraj et al. [21, 22]. Both the papers have discussed about forecasting in smart buildings and smart grid networks.

Based on the above review, data-driven models for load forecasting can be depicted as shown in Figure 4.1.

The aim of this chapter is to develop and compare data-driven models that can make accurate day-ahead load forecasts. To forecast the necessary load for the following day, the model will make use of past load data. The objective is to judiciously select the right source to cater loads, to reduce reliance on non-renewable energy sources, and to promote sustainable energy practices. The approach taken in this article aims at providing new researchers in this field with an introduction to the application of statistical and machine learning models for forecasting and prediction. To this end, the datasets used in this work would also be made available upon request.

4.3 SOURCE OF DATA

A 40-kWp solar photovoltaic (PV) microgrid is being considered in this work, which is installed on one of the rooftops of Dayalbagh Educational Institute, Agra. The depiction of this grid-interactive microgrid is shown in Figure 4.2. As shown in Table 4.1, the system comprises PV arrays formed by 24 strings of 10 modules each, strings connected in parallel. The PV system is designed for a DC system voltage of 240 V. The output of PV is fed to

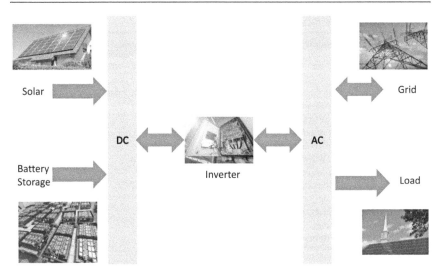

Figure 4.2   Structure of grid-interactive PV system with battery storage.

both the inverter (GSC) and the battery bank forming a DC bus. The battery bank is designed for a 4-h backup of the connected load. Lead acid batteries are chosen for energy storage due to their cost-effectiveness and well-known industrial use. 2 V and 700 Ah low maintenance lead acid (LMLA) OPzS batteries with SAN (styrene acrylonitrile resin) containers are connected in series to form a 240 V system. Hence, 120 batteries forming a string are installed such that the required system voltage is achieved. Although the battery bank is sized to cater 4 hours of total connected load, due to practical load conditions it can cater for more than the designated period. As it is necessary to ensure that the battery bank is in a charged state, the grid charging option is also available in the system, for situations when solar is not available.

A grid support conditioner (GSC) inverter comprises a converter and an integrated maximum power point tracking (MPPT) charge controller. Power conditioning unit (PCU) is the central core of the system. It acts as a mediator between DC and AC buses. The three-phase, digital signal processor (DSP)-based GSC is designed to operate as a multifunction power conditioning unit combining the functionality of a grid interface solar inverter with a true online single-conversion uninterruptible power supply (UPS). The GSC system allows the option of combining renewable energy sources on priority with the functionality of an industrial UPS system. Based on the solar power available, connected load, and battery state of charge, the unit configures itself as a charger or an inverter. In charging mode, the system maintains the battery voltage at a user-specified value and charges the battery in accordance with the manufacturer's procedures, thus maximizing the life of the battery bank. The DSP-based GSC provides output voltage conditioning

Table 4.1 PV array specifications

S. No.	Module parameters	Rating/value
1	Model – type	L24170 – monocrystalline silicon
2	Make	Bharat Heavy Electricals Ltd. (BHEL), India
3	Open-circuit voltage (V_{OC})	42 V
4	Short-circuit current (I_{SC})	5.2 A
5	Voltage at maximum power (V_{mp})	35 V
6	Current at maximum power (I_{mp})	4.86 A
7	Maximum power (P_{max})	170 Wp
8	Maximum system voltage	1000 V
9	Normal operating cell temperature (NOCT)	45°C–2°C
10	Modules in each string	10
11	No. of strings	24
12	Nominal string voltage	240 V

Table 4.2 Inverter specifications

S. No.	Inverter parameters	Rating
1	Type	Three phase
2	Output voltage	415V AC, 50 Hz
3	Input voltage	240 V–360 V DC
4	Power rating	40 kVA
5	Efficiency	94% (at rated load)
6	Total harmonic distortion (THD)	<4%

Table 4.3 Battery storage specifications

S. No.	Battery parameters	Value
1	Type	Lead acid
2	Make	EXIDE India
3	Ah capacity	400 Ah
4	Voltage per cell, V_{pc}	2 V
5	Charging rate	C 10
6	No. of batteries	120 (series)
7	DC system voltage	240
8	Depth of discharge	50% DoD

when operating in a grid-interactive mode, and it can export excess solar power to the grid. Detailed specifications of solar PV micro grid (SPVMG) under study are provided in Tables 4.1–4.4.

Table 4.5 specifies the details of different distributed microgrids installed at various locations in the institute. With such a huge setup, continuous data logging and monitoring are possible. The availability of live and field data motivates further research in this direction.

Table 4.4 Geographical specifications

1	Address of site	Dayalbagh Educational Institute, Dayalbagh, Agra 282005, Uttar Pradesh, India
2	Access Railhead Road	Agra Agra
3	Location	Agra city
4	Land ownership	Dayalbagh Educational Institute
5	Soil type	Not applicable. Roof projected system
6	Solar insolation level	5.33 kWh/m^2/day annual average
7	Latitude	27.50 North
8	Longitude	78.00 East
9	Ambient temperature	51°C max., 1°C min
10	Elevation	168 m approx. above mean sea level
11	Angle of tilt	27° – fixed

Table 4.5 Details of microgrids in Dayalbagh Educational Institute

S. No.	Location/faculty	Plant size (rated PV in kWp)	Inverter size (kVA)	Battery size (V, Ah, number)	year of installation
1	Arts	40	40	2 V, 400 Ah, 120	2010
2	Education	40	40	2 V, 700 Ah, 120	2010
3	Social science	40	40	2 V, 700 Ah, 120	2010
4	Science	147.5	150	2 V, 700 Ah, 180	2011
5	Music	100	100	2 V, 700 Ah, 120	2012
6	Engineering	147.5	150	2 V, 700 Ah, 180	2012
7	Boys hostel	5	5	2 V, 400 Ah, 60	2012
8	Girls hostel	20	20	2 V, 700 Ah, 60	2014
9	International seminar hall	20	20	2 V, 700 Ah, 60	2015
10	Dairy complex	50	50	2 V, 700 Ah, 120	2017
11	Tannery complex	50	50	2 V, 700 Ah, 120	2017

4.4 DATASET

A 40-kWp PV system installed in the Faculty of Arts, Dayalbagh Educational Institute, provided the data for this study. The primary motivation of the work is triggered with access to a continuous database of datalogs recorded by the monitoring system associated with the GSC inverter. The PV system is provided by such monitoring through the "OPS-Comms" interface supplied by the vendor. Self-explanatory pictures of this interface are given in Figures 4.3 and 4.4 and a screenshot of the datalog file recorded is shown in Figure 4.5.

Table 4.6 gives a list of parameters measured, as per IEC 61724, using sensors and devices. Irradiance is measured using a pyranometer in the plane of arrays measuring diffused radiation in W/m^2. Wind speed is another parameter. Due to occasional winds in the region, it is not included in the above parameters. Electrical parameters like voltage and current are measured for three different phases and the total value is also measured.

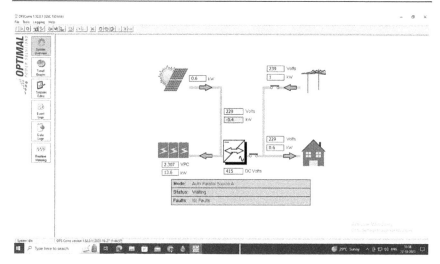

Figure 4.3 Monitoring interface depicting real-time status of the PV system.

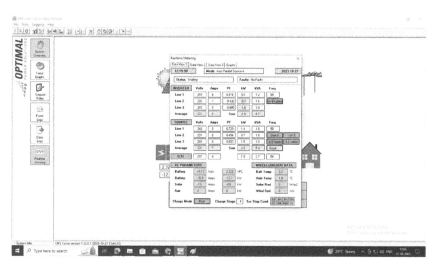

Figure 4.4 Monitoring interface with real-time parameter values.

Even though 231 parameters are measured and estimated by the measuring and datalogging system, only those useful in this study are presented here.

The dataset included historical solar panel and load data as well as meteorological conditions for a certain time period, which was 10 minutes for the dataset provided. Load data comprised 10-min load measurements at the DEI Arts Faculty, whereas meteorological data included ambient temperature and solar radiation. The load data and other data from the solar panels were obtained using an integrated monitoring device installed in the GSC inverter, which recorded the load readings at regular intervals (10 min).

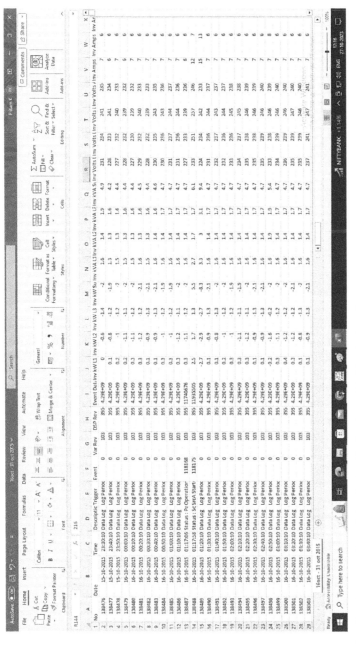

Figure 4.5 Sample screenshot of the datalog file (.csv) provided by the interface.

Table 4.6 Measured parameters

Parameter	Unit
Plane of array irradiance	W/m^2
Output voltage	V
Output current	A
Output power	kW
Ambient temperature	°C
Cell voltage	V
Battery voltage	V
Battery current	A
Battery power	kW
Load voltage	V
Load current	A
Load power	kW
Grid voltage	V
Grid current	A
Grid power	kW
Inverter	
Output voltage	V
Output current	A
Output power	kW

4.5 PREPROCESSING OF DATA

The datasets utilized in this study were provided by Dayalbagh Educational Institute. The data includes historical load data as well as meteorological conditions. Three months in 2015 were included in the dataset (October, November, and December). For analysis, the data were divided into six subgroups, which were then concatenated to create a new dataset. Before analysing the data, it was preprocessed. This included checking the data for missing values or outliers and, if necessary, removing them. Preprocessing is an important step in preparing data for analysis since it ensures the accuracy and dependability of the data. The original dataset had 10,778 rows and consisted of load measurements at 10-min intervals. This level of information in the data could be valuable for examining the load patterns of solar panels over short time periods, but analysing huge datasets with such high temporal resolution could be difficult. The data were resampled into a daily format using the resample function to ease the study. The 10-min load readings were aggregated into daily averages. The resampled dataset included 73 rows, which made the data easier to visualize and analyse. A plot of load (kW) versus days is shown in Figure 4.6.

4.6 SPLITTING OF DATASET

An important step in constructing a machine learning model is dividing the data into training and testing sets. The data in this study was divided

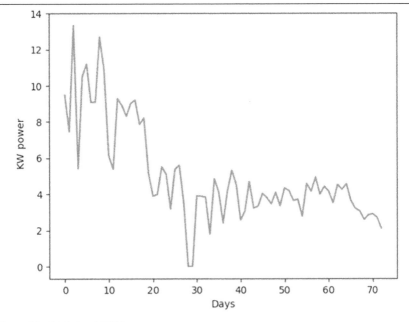

Figure 4.6 Daily load (kW).

into two groups: training and testing. The machine learning model was trained using the training set, and its performance was evaluated using the testing set. The split was done at random, but with the goal of ensuring that the proportion of data in each set was indicative of the full dataset. A popular split ratio for this step is 80/20 or 70/30, where 80% or 70% of the data is utilized for training and the remaining 20% or 30% is used for testing. A split ratio of 80/20 was used in this investigation. After partitioning the dataset, the training set had 54 rows and the testing set contained 19 rows.

4.7 BRIEF DESCRIPTION OF ALGORITHMS APPLIED

Five different algorithmic approaches were applied to the data, and a systematic comparison of their performance was made. Each of the algorithms used is described briefly as follows.

4.7.1 Autoregressive integrated moving average

ARIMA (autoregressive integrated moving average) is a time series forecasting model that is widely used in data analysis and statistical modelling. It combines three models: autoregression (AR), integrated (I), and moving average (MA).

The autoregressive (AR) model focuses on the past values of the time series data. It assumes that future values are influenced by previous values. ARIMA looks at how past observations, or lagged values, are related to the current value. The "auto" in autoregressive means that it uses the relationship within the series itself. Notionally, an AR(1) component means that the current value depends on just one previous value, AR(2) considers the current value's dependence on the two most recent values, and so on.

The "I" (integrated) component of ARIMA deals with differencing the data to make it stationary. Stationarity means that the statistical properties of the data, like its mean and variance, remain constant over time. Many time series data are not stationary by nature. By differencing the data (i.e., subtracting each value from the previous one), ARIMA aims to remove trends and seasonality, making the data stationary.

The moving average (MA) model considers past forecast errors. Specifically, it looks at how past errors in prediction impact future values. This helps capture the random noise in the data and correct it. Notionally, an MA(1) component implies that the current error depends only on the error from the previous time step, MA(2) considers the current error's dependence on the two previous errors, and so on.

ARIMA models are frequently used for projecting future values based on historical data in industries such as finance, economics, and engineering. ARIMA can also be used for solar load prediction, which can benefit utilities and grid operators by improving energy demand management and grid stability. This requires using historical data to identify patterns and trends, fitting an ARIMA model to the data, and generating forecasts of future solar load values. However, the accuracy of the prediction depends on factors such as the quality of the input data, the suitability of the ARIMA model, and the forecast horizon. The order parameter controls the order of the ARIMA model, which consists of three parameters: p, d, and q. "p" is the order of the autoregressive term. This parameter represents the number of previous observations used to forecast the current value. "d" is the degree of distinction. The number of times the data is different to make it stationary is represented by this parameter. Lastly, "q" is the moving average term's order. This parameter represents the number of previous prediction errors used to forecast the current value. In this investigation, the parameters p, d, and q were set to $start\_p=0$, $start\_q=0$, $max\_p=10$, and $max\_q=10$. The root mean squared error (RMSE) obtained by the best model was 2.574136. A plot of actual versus predicted load is shown in Figure 4.7.

4.7.2 K-nearest neighbour

The K-nearest neighbour (KNN) regressor is a machine learning algorithm that predicts the output of the query point based on the average of the output values of the nearest neighbours. It works by locating the K training

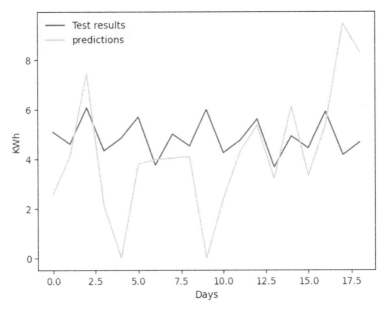

Figure 4.7 Actual versus predicted load using ARIMA.

examples (neighbours) in the feature space that are closest to a given query point. It is a non-parametric approach that is frequently used for small datasets and regression assignments because it can capture intricate non-linear interactions between the input and output variables. In order to predict the output of a given query point, the KNN algorithm locates the K training instances (neighbours) that are closest to the query point in the feature space and averages their output values. Solar radiation, temperature, and other weather factors, as well as the time of day and the day of the year, are frequently used as input elements for predicting solar load. Although KNN regressor is easy to use and does not require any training, the choice of distance measure and K value can have an impact on performance. KNN's capability to capture non-linear correlations between the input and output variables is one of its benefits for solar load prediction. Although the relationship between the meteorological factors and the solar load can be complicated and non-linear, this is significant in the forecast of solar load. Based on the similarities between the input features and the training data, KNN can recognize these patterns and provide precise predictions. Three relevant hyperparameters, "n_neighbors," "p," and "leaf_size," are explained as follows. The "n _neighbors" hyperparameter sets the number of nearest neighbours to take into account when producing a forecast. Just the nearest neighbour will be utilized to generate predictions in this work, as n_neighbors=1. The "p" hyperparameter determines the distance metric to be used for calculating the distance between feature space points. In this situation, $p=1$ indicates that the Manhattan distance metric, commonly known as the L1 distance, would be utilized. "leaf_size" represents the number of points to include in a leaf node while creating the KD-tree, which is utilized for the efficient closest neighbour search. In this scenario, leaf size=2 indicates that each leaf node shall have no more than two points.

4.7.3 Support vector machine regressor

Support vector machine (SVM) regressors are a widely used machine learning approach for classification and regression tasks. The method finds a hyperplane that separates the data into different groups while maximizing the margin between them. The margin is a region around the hyperplane where we want as few data points as possible. This margin is defined by two parallel lines. Data points that are closest to the margin lines are known as support vectors. These data points are important because they influence how we determine the position and orientation of the margin. The SVM regressor aims to minimize the error while keeping as many data points as possible outside the margin. The goal is to find a margin that is as wide as possible while satisfying this condition. The error in this context is the difference between the predicted value (position on or near the line/hyperplane) and the actual target value. In some cases, the data may not be linearly separable, meaning that a simple straight line or hyperplane would not fit the data well. SVM regressors can use kernel functions such as polynomial and radial basis function (RBF) kernels in such cases to map the data into a higher-dimensional space where it becomes linearly separable.

SVMs have been effectively applied in a variety of fields, including image classification, text classification, and bioinformatics. SVMs, on the other hand, require precise parameter tweaking and may be sensitive to the kernel function and kernel parameters used. Despite these challenges, SVMs remain a powerful tool for dealing with challenging classification and regression problems. SVM is a strong machine learning technique that can be used to forecast solar load. It entails preprocessing the data, dividing it into training and testing sets, training the SVM model, and generating forecasts of future solar load levels. The accuracy of SVM is determined by a variety of criteria, including thorough examination and analysis of the input data and model parameters.

4.7.4 Long short-term memory

Long short-term memory (LSTM) is a type of recurrent neural network (RNN) architecture, which is designed to handle and learn from sequences of data. It is known to be particularly well-suited for time series prediction, natural language processing, and sequence generation tasks. LSTMs are used for sequential data, such as sentences in text and time series data. In these sequences, each element (like a word or a data point) has some dependency on the ones that came before it. LSTMs have a unique component called a "memory cell." This cell can store and retrieve information over long sequences, making LSTMs capable of handling long-term dependencies in data. An LSTM network includes gates, which allow it to selectively remember or forget information, update the cell state with new information, and control what information is passed to the output. This gating mechanism helps LSTMs effectively capture and model long-range dependencies in sequential data, making them well-suited for tasks like natural language processing, speech recognition, and time series prediction.

LSTMs have three types of gates: Forget Gate, Input Gate, and Output Gate. The Forget Gate decides what information from the previous time step should be thrown away or kept in the memory cell. It takes as input the previous cell state and the current input and produces a value between 0 and 1 for each memory cell element, where 0 means "completely forget" and 1 means "completely remember." The Input Gate decides what new information should be stored in the memory cell. It takes the current input and the previous cell state as input and produces a candidate cell state. It combines this new information with the previous cell state to update the cell's content. The Output Gate decides what information should be read from the current memory cell to produce the output of the LSTM. It takes the current input and the updated cell state as input and produces the output. LSTMs update their memory cell states at each time step based on the information from the gates. This allows them to capture and remember important information from the past and adapt to the current input. LSTMs are trained using a process called backpropagation through time (BPTT). During training, the model makes predictions, and then the error between these predictions and the actual target values is calculated. The error is then propagated backward through time to adjust the LSTM's internal parameters (weights and biases) using gradient descent. This process is repeated iteratively until the model's predictions become more accurate. LSTM overcomes traditional RNN limitations in capturing long-term dependencies in sequential data. Because the hidden state in traditional RNNs can only hold information from the previous time step, the model may struggle to retain information over long sequences. LSTM networks address this problem by incorporating additional memory cells and gating mechanisms that enable the network to selectively remember or forget information from previous time steps. The training procedure for an LSTM network may be managed using the parameters: epochs, batch size, and verbose. Each of these parameters has the following meanings: Epochs: During the training phase, this option indicates how many times the complete training dataset should be iterated through. The training procedure will iterate over the full dataset 100 times when epochs=100. During the training phase, the batch size sets how many samples the network will handle in a single forward and backward pass. For instance, when batch size is 1, the network will train by processing one sample at a time. The "verbose" parameter regulates how much data is shown to the user during the training process. When the value is 0, no information is shown, when it is 1, progress bars are shown for each epoch, and when it is 2, progress bars are shown for each batch. The LSTM network was trained for 100 epochs, processing one sample at a time during each epoch when epochs=100, batch size=1, and verbose=2.

4.7.5 XGBoost

XGBoost is an abbreviation for Extreme Gradient Boosting. XGBoost is a gradient-boosted decision tree solution optimized for speed and performance. It is a fast gradient-boosting solution that can be used for regression predictive modelling. XGBoost's weak learners are decision trees, and it is well known for its capacity to handle complex non-linear correlations between input features and target variables. This includes a number of sophisticated features, such as early halting, regularization, and parallel processing, which can assist in reducing overfitting and increasing model efficiency. In this case, XGBoost is utilized for solar load prediction to develop a time series model that takes into consideration the solar panels' historical performance over time. This is accomplished by training the XGBoost model using previous data on solar panel performance. The parameters used in the XGBoost are as follows: objective='reg:squared error' argument defines the loss function to be optimized during training. The loss function in this example is a mean squared error, which is widely employed for regression situations. The model's purpose is to reduce the mean squared error between predicted and actual values. The option n estimators=1000 in XGBoost indicates the number of trees to be produced in the ensemble. 1000 trees will be planted in this situation. Raising the number of trees can enhance model accuracy while simultaneously increasing calculation time. These parameters indicate that the XGBoost model will be used to address a regression challenge with mean squared error as the loss function. An ensemble of 1000 decision trees will be used to construct a model, with each tree trained on a random subsample of the data. The model's objective is to predict continuous numerical values representing the solar load. Gradient boosting will be used to train the model, which entails repeatedly adding decision trees to the ensemble while minimizing the loss function.

4.8 CASE STUDY AND RESULTS

Using the dataset from Dayalbagh Educational Institute, training and results of five different forecasting techniques are presented as case study here. We use root mean squared error (RMSE) as the metric for evaluating the accuracy of the load forecast predictions. RMSE is the square root of the

Table 4.7   Root mean squared error obtained by
ARIMA, KNN, SVM, LSTM, and XGBoost

S. No.	Data-driven model	RMSE
1	ARIMA	2.574136
2	KNN	1.772
3	SVM	0.89413
4	LSTM	1.093071
5	XGBoost	1.7718

average of the squared differences between the predicted values and the actual values. The reason for using RMSE is that it is easy to interpret and provides a single numerical summary of the forecast accuracy, making it useful for comparing the performance of different forecasting models used in this study. Furthermore, RMSE gives more weight to larger errors, enabling to model to factor them appropriately. By taking the square root of the average of squared errors, RMSE emphasizes the importance of outliers, which can be particularly useful in identifying where a forecasting model needs improvement. The RMSE values obtained for the different models are provided in Table 4.7.

The results clearly show the superior performance obtained by the machine learning approaches over the statistical ARIMA technique. Furthermore, the best performance is obtained by the SVM model, as seen by the lowest RMSE value obtained for this approach.

4.9 CONCLUSIONS

Solar power generation is more variable and less predictable than traditional power sources, like coal or natural gas, due to its dependence on several other parameters. A large amount of fluctuation in solar power output can cause the dependent grid to become unstable and lead to power outages. Hence, the ability to accurately predict solar load can help grid operators maintain stable grid output. Furthermore, operators would be able to store excess energy during periods of high generation and use it during periods of low generation, thereby reducing the need for expensive backup power. In the long run, effective forecasting would also support easier integration of solar power into energy markets. This chapter presents a comparative study of five data-driven models for solar load forecasting. For this purpose, the required data is acquired from an actual 40 kWp solar photovoltaic microgrid installed on one of the rooftops of Dayalbagh Educational Institute, Agra. A well-known statistical model that has been used widely for time series prediction, the autoregressive integrated moving average (ARIMA) model, is implemented and used as the baseline model for comparisons. Several machine learning models such as K-nearest neighbour algorithm, support vector machine (SVM), long short-term memory (LSTM), and gradient boosting (XGBoost) are implemented, and their performance is compared on the dataset. The results show the effectiveness of the SVM approach for this dataset. The key steps followed in the implementation phase are systematically described to provide readers, especially new researchers with a practical introduction to the application of data-driven statistical and machine learning models for load forecasting purposes.

REFERENCES

1. Huaizhi Wang, Zhenxing Lei, Xian Zhang, Bin Zhou, Jianchun Peng, A review of deep learning for renewable energy forecasting, *Energy Conversion and Management*, Volume 198, 2019, 111799, ISSN 0196-8904, https://doi.org/10.1016/j.enconman.2019.111799.
2. S. Ray, A quick review of machine learning algorithms, *2019 International Conference on Machine Learning, Big Data, Cloud and Parallel Computing (COMITCon)*, Faridabad, India, 2019, Pages 35–39, https://doi.org/10.1109/COMITCon.2019.8862451.
3. Mohamed Abdallah, Manar Abu Talib, Mariam Hosny, Omnia Abu Waraga, Qassim Nasir, Muhammad Arbab Arshad, Forecasting highly fluctuating electricity load using machine learning models based on multimillion observations, *Advanced Engineering Informatics*, Volume 53, 2022, 101707, ISSN 1474-0346, https://doi.org/10.1016/j.aei.2022.101707.
4. Xin Liu, Zijun Zhang, Zhe Song, A comparative study of the data-driven day-ahead hourly provincial load forecasting methods: From classical data mining to deep learning, *Renewable and Sustainable Energy Reviews*, Volume 119, 2020, 109632, ISSN 1364-0321, https://doi.org/10.1016/j.rser.2019.109632.
5. Bing Dong, Zhaoxuan Li, S.M. Mahbobur Rahman, Rolando Vega, A hybrid model approach for forecasting future residential electricity consumption, *Energy and Buildings*, Volume 117, 2016, Pages 341–351, ISSN 0378-7788, https://doi.org/10.1016/j.enbuild.2015.09.033.
6. Constantine E. Kontokosta, Christopher Tull, A data-driven predictive model of city-scale energy use in buildings, *Applied Energy*, Volume 197, 2017, Pages 303–317, ISSN 0306-2619, https://doi.org/10.1016/j.apenergy.2017.04.005.
7. Giovanni Tardioli, Ruth Kerrigan, Mike Oates, James O'Donnell, Donal Finn, Data driven approaches for prediction of building energy consumption at urban level, *Energy Procedia*, Volume 78, 2015, Pages 3378–3383, ISSN 1876-6102, https://doi.org/10.1016/j.egypro.2015.11.754.
8. Chirag Deb, Fan Zhang, Junjing Yang, Siew Eang Lee, Kwok Wei Shah, A review on time series forecasting techniques for building energy consumption, *Renewable and Sustainable Energy Reviews*, Volume 74, 2017, Pages 902–924, ISSN 1364-0321, https://doi.org/10.1016/j.rser.2017.02.085.
9. A.S. Ahmad, M.Y. Hassan, M.P. Abdullah, H.A. Rahman, F. Hussin, H. Abdullah, R. Saidur, A review on applications of ANN and SVM for building electrical energy consumption forecasting, *Renewable and Sustainable Energy Reviews*, Volume 33, 2014, Pages 102–109, ISSN 1364-0321, https://doi.org/10.1016/j.rser.2014.01.069.

10. Aowabin Rahman, Vivek Srikumar, Amanda D. Smith, Predicting electricity consumption for commercial and residential buildings using deep recurrent neural networks, *Applied Energy*, Volume 212, 2018, Pages 372–385, ISSN 0306-2619, https://doi.org/10.1016/j.apenergy.2017.12.051.

11. Mohammad Azhar Mat Daut, Mohammad Yusri Hassan, Hayati Abdullah, Hasimah Abdul Rahman, Md Pauzi Abdullah, Faridah Hussin, Building electrical energy consumption forecasting analysis using conventional and artificial intelligence methods: A review, *Renewable and Sustainable Energy Reviews*, Volume 70, 2017, Pages 1108–1118, ISSN 1364-0321, https://doi.org/10.1016/j.rser.2016.12.015.

12. Shamim Akhtar, Muhamad Zahim Bin Sujod, Syed Sajjad Hussain Rizvi. 2022. An intelligent data-driven approach for electrical energy load management using machine learning algorithms, *Energies*, 15, no. 15: 5742, https://doi.org/10.3390/en15155742.

13. Zhengguang Liu, Zhiling Guo, Qi Chen, Chenchen Song, Wenlong Shang, Meng Yuan, Haoran Zhang, A review of data-driven smart building-integrated photovoltaic systems: Challenges and objectives, *Energy*, Volume 263, Part E, 2023, 126082, ISSN 0360-5442, https://doi.org/10.1016/j.energy.2022.126082.

14. Prajowal Manandhar, Hasan Rafiq, Edwin Rodriguez-Ubinas, Current status, challenges, and prospects of data-driven urban energy modeling: A review of machine learning methods, *Energy Reports*, Volume 9, 2023, Pages 2757–2776, ISSN 2352-4847, https://doi.org/10.1016/j.egyr.2023.01.094.

15. Deb, Chirag, *Data-Driven Urban Energy Modeling: Global Trends and India*, 2022. 10.1007/978-981-19-0412-7_9.

16. Kadir Amasyali, Nora M. El-Gohary, A review of data-driven building energy consumption prediction studies, *Renewable and Sustainable Energy Reviews*, Volume 81, Part 1, 2018, Pages 1192–1205, ISSN 1364-0321, https://doi.org/10.1016/j.rser.2017.04.095.

17. Hyojeoung Kim, Sujin Park, Sahm Kim, Time-series clustering and forecasting household electricity demand using smart meter data, *Energy Reports*, Volume 9, 2023, Pages 4111–4121, ISSN 2352-4847, https://doi.org/10.1016/j.egyr.2023.03.042.

18. Meng Shen, Yujie Lu, Kua Harn Wei, Qingbin Cui, Prediction of household electricity consumption and effectiveness of concerted intervention strategies based on occupant behaviour and personality traits, *Renewable and Sustainable Energy Reviews*, Volume 127, 2020, 109839, ISSN 1364-0321, https://doi.org/10.1016/j.rser.2020.109839.

19. João Vitor Leme, Wallace Casaca, Marilaine Colnago, Maurício Araújo Dias, Towards assessing the electricity demand in Brazil: Data-driven analysis and ensemble learning models, *Energies*, Volume 13, No. 6, 2020, Page 1407, https://doi.org/10.3390/en13061407.

20. Carlos E. Velasquez, Matheus Zocatelli, Fidellis B.G.L. Estanislau, Victor F. Castro, Analysis of time series models for Brazilian electricity demand forecasting, *Energy*, Volume 247, 2022, Page 123483, ISSN 0360-5442, https://doi.org/10.1016/j.energy.2022.123483.

21. B.R. Prusty, S.L. Arun, P. De Falco, Demand response in smart buildings. In A. Tomar, P.H. Nguyen, S. Mishra (eds.), *Control of Smart Buildings*. Studies in infrastructure and control, Springer, Singapore, 2022, https://doi.org/10.1007/978-981-19-0375-5_5.

22. K.R. Selvaraj, J. Chaudhary, R. Mantri, K. Bingi, B.R. Prusty, Stability prediction model for smart grid network that handles missing input variables, *2022 International Conference on Intelligent Controller and Computing for Smart Power (ICICCSP)*, Hyderabad, India, 2022, Pages 1–6, https://doi.org/10.1109/ICICCSP53532.2022.9862431.

Chapter 5

Forecasting of renewable energy using fractional-order neural networks

Bhukya Ramadevi, Venkata Ramana Kasi, Kishore Bingi, B Rajanarayan Prusty, and Madiah Omar

5.1 INTRODUCTION

Renewable energy resources have gained significant attention in government policies, academic research, and the power industry, with wind energy emerging as an up-and-coming option. It is recognized as a key renewable energy source due to its potential to contribute to sustainable power generation and mitigate carbon emissions [1]. Therefore, wind power forecasting is essential for integrating wind energy into the power grid. Accurate forecasts help grid operators and energy market players decide on energy scheduling, grid stability, and economic optimization. In recent years, neural network-based models have emerged as promising approaches for improving the accuracy of wind power forecasting [2, 3]. For instance, a novel approach for short-term wind power forecasting has been introduced [4]. The method involved making a hybrid model using multi-kernel regularized pseudo-inverse neural network techniques and variational mode decomposition. This hybrid approach aimed to enhance the accuracy of wind power prediction by incorporating both data decomposition and machine learning techniques. Further, the researchers in reference [5] have focused on feature extraction of numerical weather prediction data using 3D convolutional neural networks (CNNs) to improve wind power forecasting accuracy by capturing spatial and temporal information. Similarly, the work in reference [6] has evaluated the performance of attention-based recurrent neural networks (RNNs) for wind power forecasting. The attention mechanism allows the model to selectively focus on relevant temporal dependencies in the input sequence, enhancing forecasting accuracy compared to traditional RNN architectures. A novel forecasting model for wind power using an enhanced long short-term memory (LSTM) neural network has been proposed [7], demonstrating its effectiveness in accurately forecasting wind energy generation and outperforming conventional methods.

In addition, an LSTM-RNN and variable selection techniques to predict short-term wind power have been proposed [8]. In references [9] and [10], the investigators have implemented a deep learning-based predictive analytics framework and a mixed-input feature-based cascade-connected artificial

DOI: 10.1201/9781003470274-5

93

neural network (CF-CANN) for short-term wind power forecasting. The CF-CANN model incorporates multiple input features, including meteorological variables, historical wind power, and time-related information, to improve the accuracy of short-term wind power predictions. A novel approach using deep neural networks has been developed to generate multi-objective prediction intervals for wind power forecasting [11]. This offers a valuable tool for assessing uncertainty and improving decision-making in renewable energy integration and grid management. Moreover, Peiris et al. presented a case study from Sri Lanka, developed an ANN-based approach for wind power generation forecasting, and showed its effectiveness in accurately predicting wind power output [12]. Lin et al. investigated the use of deep learning networks for time-series forecasting in wind power prediction and highlighted their potential to enhance accuracy and reliability in renewable energy forecasting [13].

A comprehensive scientometrics analysis of recent advancements in wind energy forecasting has been conducted by Zhao et al. [14]. The work emphasized the significance of artificial intelligence and extensive data methodologies, providing valuable insights into emerging trends, methods, and future directions for enhancing the accuracy and efficiency of wind energy prediction. Sunder et al. have proposed a novel approach for forecasting the generated power of wind turbines by utilizing a combination of LSTM and non-linear autoregressive neural network models [15]. This combination of models has been specifically designed to tackle the issue of missing input data, a common challenge in wind power forecasting. Furthermore, by leveraging the strengths of both LSTM and non-linear autoregressive models, the authors aimed to improve the accuracy and reliability of their power generation predictions. Tian et al. presented a study on enhancing wind power forecasting accuracy using a backpropagation neural network combined with machine learning methods and improving the efficiency and reliability of wind power generation by leveraging advanced prediction techniques [16]. Alkesaiberi et al. have provided the effectiveness of various machine learning techniques for efficient wind power prediction, offering a comparative analysis to determine the most accurate and reliable approach for enhancing wind energy forecasting [17]. A novel method combining feature engineering and the informer model for accurate ultra-short-term wind power prediction has been proposed, offering promising advancements in renewable energy forecasting and grid stability management [18]. An optimized deep autoregressive (AR)-RNNs model for probabilistic wind power forecasting has been developed [19]. By incorporating historical weather and wind power data, the AR-RNN model captures complex temporal dependencies and generates probabilistic forecasts, enabling the estimation of forecast uncertainties. Miele et al. have proposed a multi-modal spatio-temporal neural network approach for multi-horizon wind power forecasting, combining multiple data sources to enhance prediction performance [20]. Finally, using a direct method, the authors have implemented a deep learning-based model for multistep ahead wind speed and power generation prediction [21]. The model combines LSTM networks and CNNs to capture short-term dependencies and spatial correlations in wind speed and power data.

Motivated by the literature mentioned above, this chapter proposes a model of the fractional-order single-layer feed-forward neural network to enhance prediction accuracy. Using fractional-order derivatives allows for improved tracking capability during training and testing. To achieve this, existing activation functions such as Rectified Linear Unit (ReLU) and Purelin are converted into fractional-order functions rather than creating hybrid functions using fractional calculus, which will be detailed below. These fractional-order activation functions have been integrated into the single-layer neural network model, forming a fractional-order single-layer neural network model. Furthermore, a simulation study has been conducted on a Texas wind turbine to forecast the generated power, comparing the performance of the fractional-order single-layer neural network model with that of the classical model. This evaluation aims to assess the effectiveness of the different activation functions.

5.2 FRACTIONAL CALCULUS

Fractional calculus is a mathematical tool used to define and study derivatives of arbitrary orders. Unlike traditional calculus, which deals with integer-order derivatives, fractional calculus extends this concept by allowing derivatives of fractional orders. This fractional-order derivative can describe non-integer-order dynamics in various systems. Fractional-order derivatives have been shown to have applications in many fields, including neural networks. In this context, fractional-order derivatives can be used to fractionally order various activation functions to enable better modelling of complex neural network dynamics. The following section summarizes the concept of a fractional-order derivative using fractional calculus. Then, this fractional-order derivative will be used for the fractional ordering of various neural network activation functions.

The integer-order derivative of a function $f(x)$ is generally defined over natural values. For instance, the first, second, and third-order derivatives of $f(x)$ are expressed as

$$f'(x) = \frac{d}{dx}f(x),$$

$$f''(x) = \frac{d^2}{dx^2}f(x),$$

$$f'''(x) = \frac{d^3}{dx^3}f(x). \tag{5.1}$$

For a power function $f(x) = x^n$, the natural k-derivatives can be computed as

$$\frac{d}{dx}f(x) = nx^{n-1},$$

$$\frac{d^2}{dx^2}f(x) = n(n-1)x^{n-2},$$

$$\frac{d^3}{dx^3}f(x) = n(n-1)(n-2)x^{n-3}, \ldots,$$

$$\frac{d^k}{dx^k}f(x) = n(n-1)(n-2)\ldots(n-k)x^{n-k}. \tag{5.2}$$

Using the factorial function, Eq. (5.2) can be rewritten as follows:

$$\frac{d}{dx}f(x) = nx^{n-1},$$

$$\frac{d^2}{dx^2}f(x) = \frac{n!}{(n-2)!}x^{n-2},$$

$$\frac{d^3}{dx^3}f(x) = \frac{n!}{(n-3)!}x^{n-3},$$

$$\vdots$$

$$\frac{d^k}{dx^k}f(x) = \frac{n!}{(n-k)!}x^{n-k}, \tag{5.3}$$

where $k < n$ and both are real integer numbers.

Fractional calculus can be used to extend the notion of integer-order derivatives to non-integer numbers in the same way it can be applied to integer-order derivatives [22]. Thus, the integer number k in Equation (5.3) can be extended to a fractional value α as

$$\frac{d^\alpha}{dx^\alpha}f(x) = \frac{n!}{(n-\alpha)!}x^{n-\alpha}. \tag{5.4}$$

However, in the above case, it is well known that the factorial operator can only be defined for non-negative integer numbers. Thus, for the fractional values, the factorial operator can be replaced by the Gamma function (Γ) which is defined as in reference [23],

$$\Gamma(n) = (n-1)!. \tag{5.5}$$

By shifting the above equation by 1, one can obtain an expression for $n!$ as follows:

$$\Gamma(n+1) = (n)!. \tag{5.6}$$

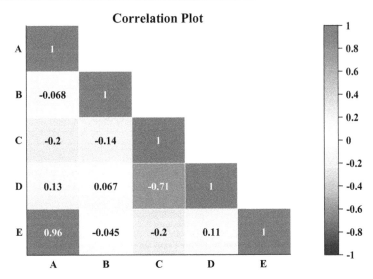

Figure 5.1   Correlation plot for (A) wind speed (m/s), (B) wind direction (deg), (C) pressure (atm), (D) air temperature (°C), and (E) generated power (kW)

Therefore, Equation (5.4) can be rewritten using the above Gamma function as

$$\frac{d^\alpha}{dx^\alpha} f(x) = \frac{\Gamma(n+1)}{\Gamma(n-\alpha+1)} x^{n-\alpha}. \qquad (5.7)$$

The above definition represents the fractional-order derivative of a function $f(x) = x^n$ valid for $n, \alpha, x \geq 0$.

5.3 SYSTEM DESCRIPTION

The Texas wind turbine dataset contains time-series data on energy produced by single wind turbines with a rated output of 3600 kW in Texas, USA. The wind turbine's rotor diameter and hub height are 111 and 80 m, respectively. The Electric Reliability Council of Texas administers Texas's electrical system and collects the data. Researchers and data analysts utilize the dataset to examine wind turbine performance, weather conditions, and other factors affecting electricity generation [24]. The dataset includes the date, time, total power generated (kW), wind speed (m/s), wind direction (deg), pressure (atm), and air temperature (°C).

Figure 5.1 presents a correlation plot displaying the Pearson correlation coefficient values among several parameters: wind speed, wind direction, pressure, air temperature, and generated power (kW). In this plot, positive correlation coefficients are represented in red, while negative coefficients are highlighted in blue. The colour scale ranges from −1 to 1, where −1 signifies a perfect negative linear relationship between the parameters, 1 represents a

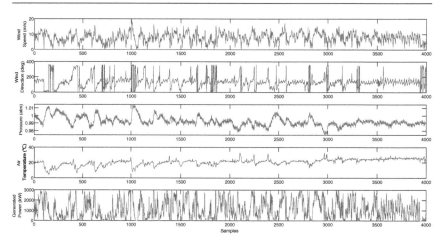

Figure 5.2   Input and output parameters of the Texas wind turbine system

perfect positive linear relationship, and 0 indicates no relationship between the parameters.

This simulation study examines the hourly wind turbine dataset with four input parameters: wind speed (m/s), wind direction (deg), pressure (atm), and air temperature (°C). Generated power (kW) is the output parameter. As shown in Figure 5.2, each dataset parameter comprises 4000 samples. The graphic illustrates that the dataset is comprehensive and noise-free. Additionally, the data is chaotic and non-linear. All parameters exhibit aperiodic behaviour.

5.4 PROPOSED METHODOLOGY

The proposed methodology for this work follows the steps presented in Figure 5.3. The initial step involves data collection from the Texas wind turbine, including various input parameters such as wind speed, wind direction, pressure, and air temperature, and the corresponding output parameter is wind-generated power. The correlation between these input and output parameters is calculated in the subsequent step. Additionally, data preprocessing is essential in utilizing data for a fractional-order neural network within the range of [0, 1]. Data normalization is a widely used technique to preprocess data before feeding it into a neural network model. Normalization aims to rescale the numerical values in the dataset to a standardized scale while preserving the relative differences in the value ranges and avoiding information loss. The normalization formula is provided below:

$$x_n = \frac{x - x_{\min}}{x_{\max} - x_{\min}} \tag{5.8}$$

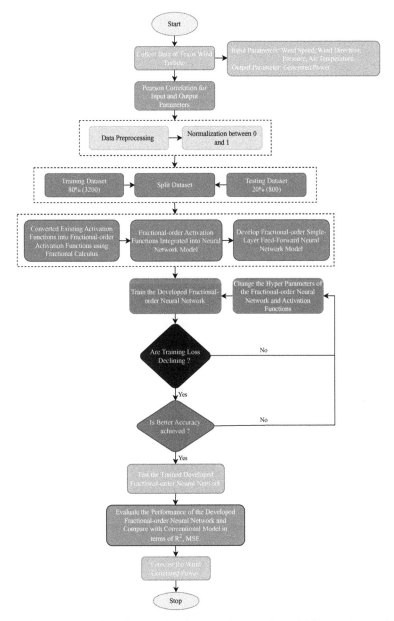

Figure 5.3 Flowchart of the fractional-order neural network model for training, testing, and forecasting.

where x_n represents the normalized data, x collected dataset (wind speed, wind direction, pressure, air temperature, generated power), while $x_{\max}$ and $x_{\min}$, respectively, denote the maximum and minimum values present in the dataset.

The next step involves dividing the dataset into training and testing sets. It is the best practice to allocate 80% of the dataset for training and 20% for testing. However, this distribution can be adjusted based on the dataset's characteristics and the specific requirements of the application domain. Following the other step, the commonly used activation functions are converted into fractional-order activation functions using fractional calculus and integrated into the neural network model. This transformation leads to developing of a single-layer fractional-order feed-forward neural network model. In the fifth step, train the fractional-order neural network model. The fractional-order neural network model learns from training datasets. During the learning process, if the training loss does not decrease, it indicates the need for improvement in both the datasets and the network structure. This can be achieved by cleaning the datasets to ensure data quality and modifying the hyperparameters of the fractional-order neural network model and activation functions. By refining the datasets and adjusting the model's parameters, it is possible to enhance the learning process and improve the performance of the neural network model. The network is still in continuous learning mode if the training loss declines. The learning process continues until better accuracy is achieved. At this point, the fractional-order neural network model has completed its learning process successfully. However, accuracy has yet to be achieved. In that case, it is necessary to continue training the network model up to a specified maximum number of iterations to improve its performance further. Further, in the sixth and final step of the flowchart, test the fractional-order neural network model: testing datasets are used to test the performance of the fractional-order neural network model after learning. This evaluation is crucial to determine the accuracy of the model's predictions, and it involves the use of MSE and R^2 metrics as indicators of prediction accuracy. These metrics allow for a thorough assessment of the fractional-order neural network model's performance.

5.5 FRACTIONAL-ORDER NEURAL NETWORK

This simulation study employed a single-layer feed-forward neural network to forecast system-generated power (kW) using four input variables, including wind speed (m/s), wind direction (deg), pressure (atm), and air temperature (°C) as shown in Figure 5.4. The neural network architecture consisted of an input layer with four nodes, a hidden layer with ten nodes, and an output layer with one node. The bias values at the hidden and output layers are denoted as b [13, 21]. In addition, the activation function used at the input layer is "ReLU," and at the output is "Purelin" to evaluate the neural network's performance.

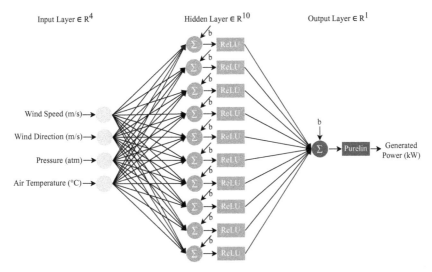

Figure 5.4 Architecture of single-layer feed-forward neural network.

5.5.1 Fractional ordering of activation functions

This section computes the fractional ordering of the activation functions for Purelin and ReLU using concepts of fractional calculus which is mentioned in the previous section to enhance the neural network's tracking capabilities significantly.

5.5.1.1 Fractional-order ReLU activation function

The ReLU activation function is widely used in neural networks, especially deep learning architectures. Its more precise element-wise operation requirements make it more computationally efficient than other activation functions, allowing more information to pass through the network. This helps to avoid the vanishing gradient problem and accelerate convergence during neural network training. The function is a simple non-linear function that returns the maximum of 0 and the input value. The ReLU activation function is described as in references [25, 26]:

$$f(x) = \max(0, x). \tag{5.9}$$

In the above equation, x is the input and $\max(0, x)$ is the maximum of input value, which can also be rewritten as follows:

$$f(x) = \begin{cases} x & \text{if } x \geq 0, \\ 0 & \text{if } x < 0. \end{cases} \tag{5.10}$$

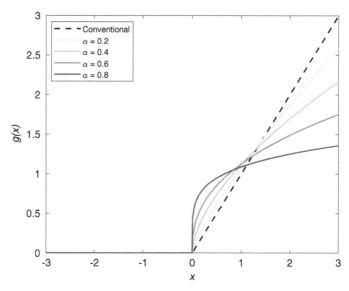

Figure 5.5 Response for fractional-order derivative of ReLU activation function for various α even orders.

However, the ReLU activation function is not differentiable at $x = 0$, which can cause problems for gradient-based optimization techniques. During training, it can lead "dead neurons" to stop responding to any input. Additionally, it's not suitable for negative input values, as it outputs 0 for negative input values. Therefore, the fractional ordering of the ReLU function can help achieve a smoother response than the conventional function. This smoother response will help avoid dead neurons, and the fractional ordering is differentiable at $x = 0$, addressing the non-differentiability problem. Finally, the fractional ordering of the ReLU function handles negative input values better, which can be crucial in specific tasks.

Therefore, the fractional ordering of ReLU function for an order $\alpha \in (0, 0.8)$ can be computed using Equation (5.7) as follows:

$$D^\alpha f(x) = g(x) = D^\alpha \begin{cases} x & \text{if } x \geq 0 \\ 0 & \text{if } x < 0 \end{cases},$$

$$g(x) = \begin{cases} \frac{1}{\Gamma(2-a)} x^{1-a} & \text{if } x \geq 0 \\ 0 & \text{if } x < 0 \end{cases}. \tag{5.11}$$

The response of the fractional-order derivative of the ReLU activation function for various α orders in the $(0, 0.9)$ compared with the conventional is shown in Figures 5.5 and 5.6. The traditional ReLU response indicates that the function's output is 0 for negative input values; thus, it is unsuitable for all negative input values. On the other hand, the fractional-order derivative

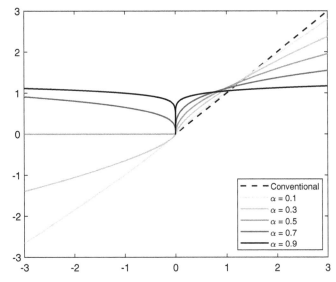

Figure 5.6   Response for fractional-order derivative of ReLU activation function for various α odd orders.

of ReLU in the figure shows a smoother response than the traditional function, which will help prevent the issue of dead neurons.

5.5.1.2 Fractional-order purelin function

The Purelin activation function is frequently used as a linear activation function in various machine learning and neural network applications. Its fundamental principle is to generate an output directly proportional to the input provided. Thus, the function returns kx in response to an input of x. For $k = 1$, the function acts as an identity function. The mathematical definition of the Purelin function can be written as follows [27]:

$$f(x) = kx, \tag{5.12}$$

where k is the hyperparameter.

This simple, efficient, and well-suited function handles regression issues when linearity captures the input–output relationship. However, it may not be suitable for more complex relationships where non-linear correlations between inputs and outputs are present, which limits the application of Purelin functions in many real-life situations. Therefore, fractional-order derivatives can add non-linearity to the function without affecting its linearity. As a result, this will allow the function to capture more complex and non-linear input–output relationships, thereby improving its suitability for broader applications.

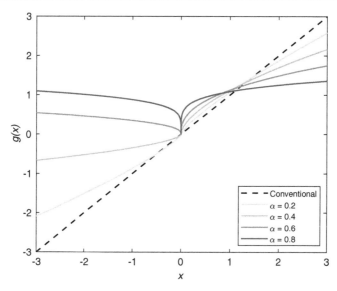

Figure 5.7 Response for fractional-order derivative of Purelin activation function for various α even orders.

The fractional ordering of Purelin function in Equation (5.12) for an order $\alpha \in (0, 0.9)$ can be computed using Equation (5.7) as follows:

$$D^{\alpha}f(x) = g(x) = kD^{\alpha}x, \tag{5.13}$$

$$g(x) = \frac{k}{\Gamma(2 - \alpha)}x^{1-\alpha}. \tag{5.14}$$

The response for the fractional-order derivative of the Purelin function for various α orders in the range $(0, 0.9)$ compared with the conventional was depicted in Figures 5.7 and 5.8. As shown in the figure, unlike the traditional model, the activation property will vary depending on the order α, where the output is linear and non-linear. For instance, the activation function will act linear when $\alpha = 0$ and non-linear when α is in the range $(0, 0.9)$.

Incorporating the abovementioned fractional-order activation functions, including fractional ReLU and fractional Purelin, into a neural network can create a fractional-order neural network. The architecture of the fractional-order single-layer feed-forward neural network is presented in Figure 5.9.

5.6 RESULTS AND DISCUSSION

This section presents the results and discussion of two models used for predicting the generated power of the Texas wind turbine. Firstly, an analysis

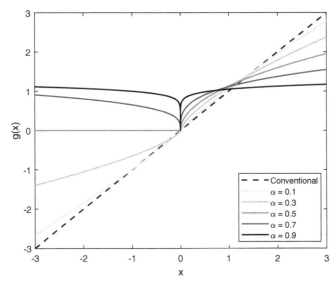

Figure 5.8 Response for fractional-order derivative of Purelin activation function for various α odd orders.

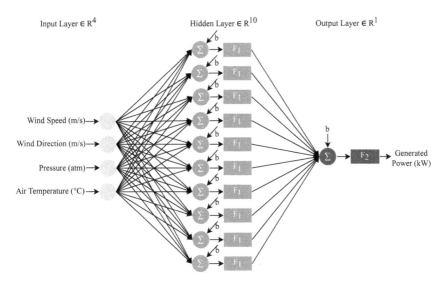

Figure 5.9 Architecture of fractional-order single-layer feed-forward neural network.

of the performance of the single-layer neural network model is provided. Next, the performance of the fractional-order single-layer neural network model is presented. Subsequently, a numerical comparison between the conventional and developed neural network models is shown in Table 7.2.

As mentioned in Section 7.2.1, this study utilizes 4000 samples. Of which, 80% (3200 samples) are used for training, while the remaining 20% (800 samples) are used for testing. For both models, the Levenberg–Marquardt algorithm is selected as the training algorithm. The activation functions employed in the hidden and output layers differ between the conventional and developed functions, and performance has been evaluated using both models, which will be discussed in detail below. The performance metrics used in this work are MSE and R^2, which have been calculated as follows:

$$\text{MSE} = \frac{1}{N} \sum_{i=1}^{N} (Y_i - \widehat{Y}_i)^2, \tag{5.15}$$

$$R^2 = 1 - \frac{\sum_{i=1}^{N} (Y_i - \widehat{Y}_i)^2}{\sum_{i=1}^{N} (Y_i - \overline{Y}_i)^2}, \tag{5.16}$$

where

- "N" is the number of samples,
- Y_i is the actual values,
- $\widehat{Y}_i$ is the predicted values,
- $\overline{Y}_i$ is the average value of $\widehat{Y}_i$.

The results in Table 7.2 present a performance comparison of neural network models such as single-layer neural networks and fractional-order single-layer neural networks for forecasting wind power using four input parameters: wind speed, wind direction, pressure, and air temperature. The models are evaluated with different activation functions at various α values, measuring their performance in terms of R^2 (coefficient of determination) and MSE (mean square error) metrics. The performance of the model varies with different combinations of activation functions, including ReLU, FReLU (fractional ReLU), Purelin, and FPurelin (fractional Purelin), and α values $(0.1, 0.2, 0.3, \ldots, 0.9)$ can lead to different levels of accuracy in wind-generated power forecasting. Table 7.2 provides the R^2 and MSE values obtained for each combination during the training and testing phases. The R^2 values indicate the proportion of the variance in the data that the function predicts, with values closer to 1 indicating a better fit. The MSE values represent the average squared difference between the predicted and actual values, with lower values indicating better accuracy. From the obtained results, the analysis of activation functions is given as follows: when α is 0, using ReLU in the hidden layer and Purelin in the output layer achieves relatively high R^2 values of 0.9593 and 0.9614 as well as low MSE values of 0.0304 and 0.0278 for both training and testing datasets, respectively. These results indicate that the model predicted the generated power depicted in Figure 5.10.

As α value increases, the FReLU activation function tends to outperform ReLU in terms of both R^2 and MSE values with Purelin, which are shown in Figures 5.11–5.19, illustrating the actual and predicted generated power for both the training and testing datasets. In addition, the FPurelin activation

Table 5.1 Performance comparison on both neural network models with various activation functions and α values

Derivative order α	Function		Training		Testing	
	Hidden layer	Output layer	R^2	MSE	R^2	MSE
$\alpha = 0$	ReLU	Purelin	0.9593	0.0304	0.9614	0.0278
$\alpha = 0.1$	FReLU	Purelin	0.9895	0.0077	0.9933	0.0049
	ReLU	FPurelin	0.7748	0.4486	0.8327	0.4398
	FReLU	FPurelin	0.8079	0.4949	0.8168	0.4833
$\alpha = 0.2$	FReLU	Purelin	0.9922	0.0057	0.9927	0.0053
	ReLU	FPurelin	0.6484	0.5215	0.7148	0.5104
	FReLU	FPurelin	0.8289	0.5555	0.8326	0.5554
$\alpha = 0.3$	FReLU	Purelin	0.9931	0.0051	0.9941	0.0046
	ReLU	FPurelin	0.6801	0.5857	0.7096	0.5543
	FReLU	FPurelin	0.7325	0.5845	0.7456	0.5792
$\alpha = 0.4$	FReLU	Purelin	0.9937	0.0047	0.9943	0.0042
	ReLU	FPurelin	0.7207	0.8534	0.7319	0.8389
	FReLU	FPurelin	0.7865	0.6989	0.8013	0.6321
$\alpha = 0.5$	FReLU	Purelin	0.9978	0.0017	0.9981	0.0015
	ReLU	FPurelin	0.6369	1.6717	0.6741	1.5987
	FReLU	FPurelin	0.8178	0.7749	0.8388	0.7687
$\alpha = 0.6$	FReLU	Purelin	0.9951	0.0036	0.9953	0.0034
	ReLU	FPurelin	0.6207	1.6717	0.6589	1.5987
	FReLU	FPurelin	0.7872	0.9223	0.8064	0.9212
$\alpha = 0.7$	FReLU	Purelin	0.9909	0.0067	0.9919	0.0057
	ReLU	FPurelin	0.9065	1.0095	0.9096	0.9914
	FReLU	FPurelin	0.8519	0.9056	0.8557	0.8715
$\alpha = 0.8$	FReLU	Purelin	0.9901	0.0072	0.9908	0.0071
	ReLU	FPurelin	0.7286	1.8205	0.7442	1.7363
	FReLU	FPurelin	0.5892	1.4095	0.5933	1.3661
$\alpha = 0.9$	FReLU	Purelin	0.9813	0.0136	0.9848	0.0115
	ReLU	FPurelin	0.7204	1.7402	0.7351	1.7104
	FReLU	FPurelin	0.4785	1.6157	0.5464	1.5437

function in the output layer generally performs better than Purelin, as it consistently achieves higher R^2 values and lower MSE values. Furthermore, using FReLU in the hidden layer and Purelin in the output layer with α value 0.5 achieves the highest R^2 values of 0.9978, 0.9981 and the lowest MSE values of 0.0017, 0.0015 for both the training and testing, respectively. Thus, it indicates that this activation function is highly suitable for predicting the generated power of the Texas wind turbine system. As α increases beyond a certain point, the model's performance declines for some functions, as indicated by decreasing R^2 values and increasing MSE values, as shown in Table 7.2. Therefore, the results suggest that using the FReLU activation function in the hidden layer and FPurelin in the output layer, with an

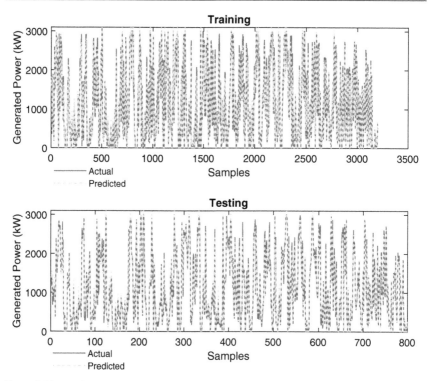

Figure 5.10 Performance of single-layer neural network with a combination of ReLU and Purelin at $\alpha = 0$ during training and testing.

appropriate α value, can yield better wind power forecasting performance than other functions.

Table 7.2 explores the performance of neural network models across a range of α values, including higher values such as 1.0, 1.1, 1.2, and so on up to 1.9. Each specific α value is associated with three sets of results, each corresponding to different activation functions that have been applied to the neural networks' hidden and output layers. These activation functions include FReLU, ReLU, Purelin, and FPurelin. The results have been observed that performance decreases as the α value increases. In addition, the FReLU activation function provides better performance predictions than ReLU in terms of R^2 and MSE during both the training and testing datasets. For a more visual representation of these results, Figures 5.20–5.29 are included in this study. These figures provide graphical insights into the actual and predicted generated power, showcasing the model's performance on the training and testing datasets. From both the results, Tables 7.2 and 5.2 provide a detailed evaluation of neural network models' performance in predicting wind-generated power, considering various activation functions and the impact of the derivative parameter α on model accuracy. Including training and testing metrics offers a comprehensive understanding of model

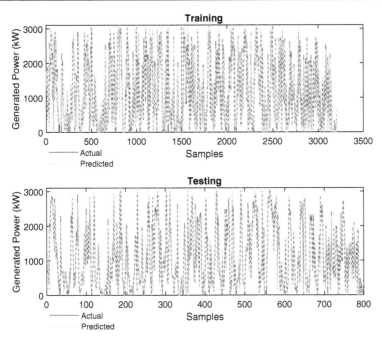

Figure 5.11 Performance of single-layer neural network with a combination of FReLU and Purelin at $\alpha = 0.1$ during training and testing.

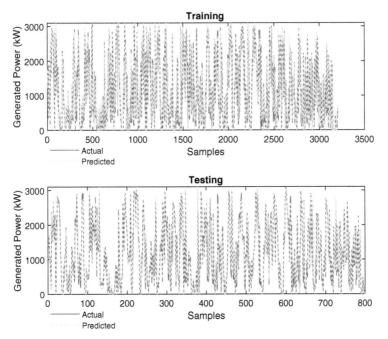

Figure 5.12 Performance of single-layer neural network with a combination of FReLU and Purelin at $\alpha = 0.2$ during training and testing.

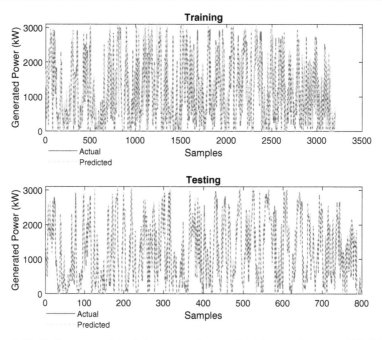

Figure 5.13 Performance of single-layer neural network with a combination of FReLU and Purelin at $\alpha = 0.3$ during training and testing.

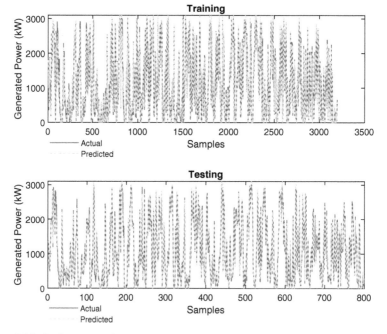

Figure 5.14 Performance of single-layer neural network with a combination of FReLU and Purelin at $\alpha = 0.4$ during training and testing.

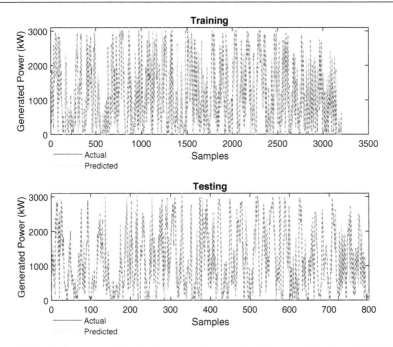

Figure 5.15 Performance of single-layer neural network with a combination of FReLU and Purelin at $\alpha = 0.5$ during training and testing.

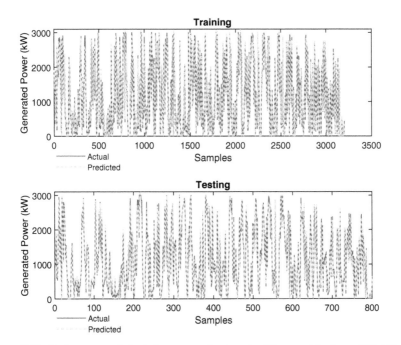

Figure 5.16 Performance of single-layer neural network with a combination of FReLU and Purelin at $\alpha = 0.6$ during training and testing.

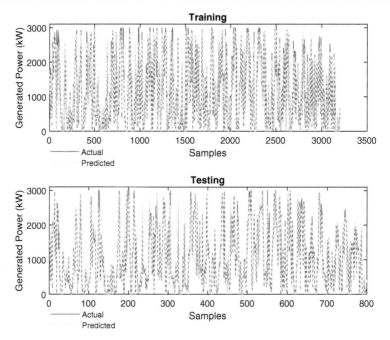

Figure 5.17 Performance of single-layer neural network with a combination of FReLU and Purelin at $\alpha = 0.7$ during training and testing.

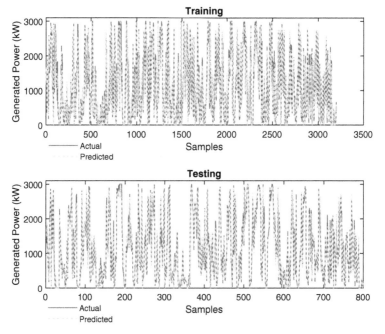

Figure 5.18 Performance of single-layer neural network with a combination of FReLU and Purelin at $\alpha = 0.8$ during training and testing.

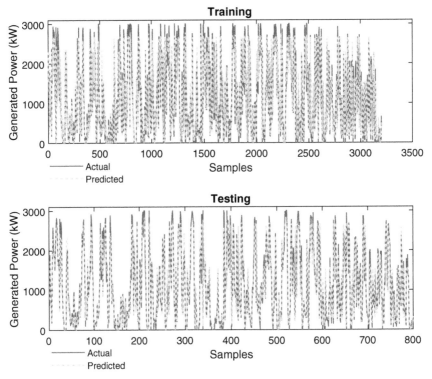

Figure 5.19 Performance of single-layer neural network with a combination of FReLU and Purelin at $\alpha = 0.9$ during training and testing.

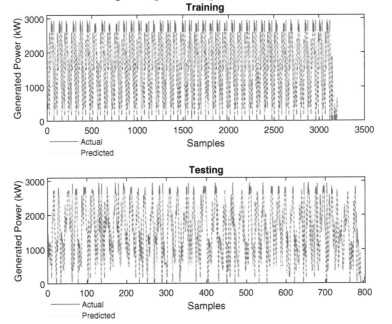

Figure 5.20 Performance of single-layer neural network with a combination of FReLU and Purelin at $\alpha = 1$ during training and testing.

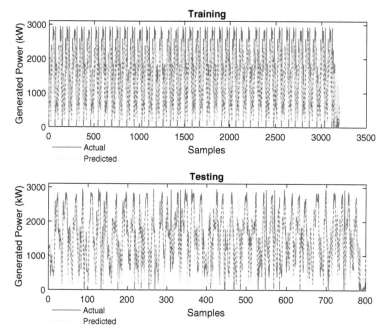

Figure 5.21 Performance of single-layer neural network with a combination of FReLU and Purelin at $\alpha = 1.1$ during training and testing.

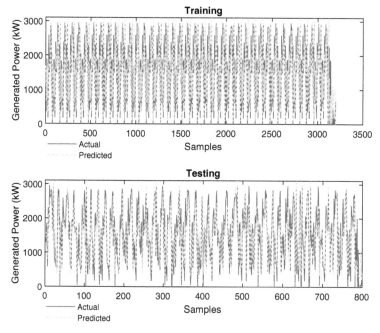

Figure 5.22 Performance of single-layer neural network with a combination of FReLU and Purelin at $\alpha = 1.2$ during training and testing.

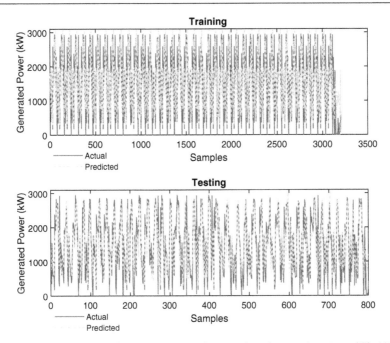

Figure 5.23 Performance of single-layer neural network with a combination of FReLU and Purelin at $\alpha = 1.3$ during training and testing.

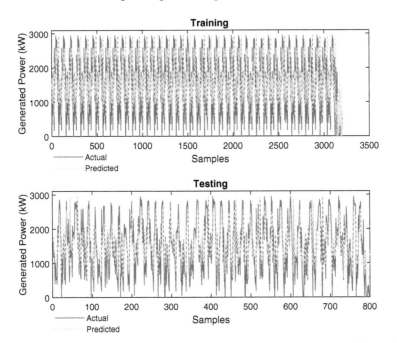

Figure 5.24 Performance of single-layer neural network with a combination of FReLU and Purelin at $\alpha = 1.4$ during training and testing.

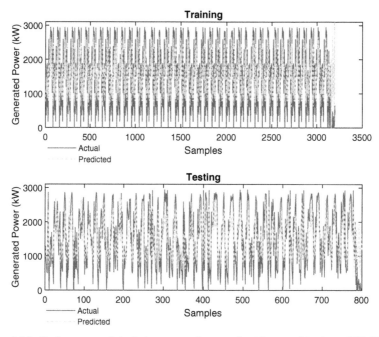

Figure 5.25 Performance of single-layer neural network with a combination of FReLU and Purelin at $\alpha = 1.5$ during training and testing.

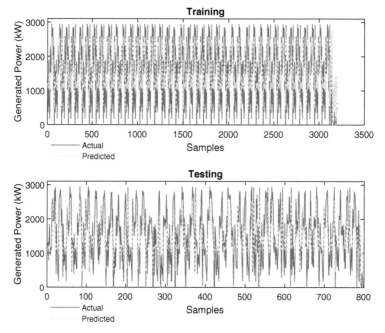

Figure 5.26 Performance of single-layer neural network with a combination of FReLU and Purelin at $\alpha = 1.6$ during training and testing.

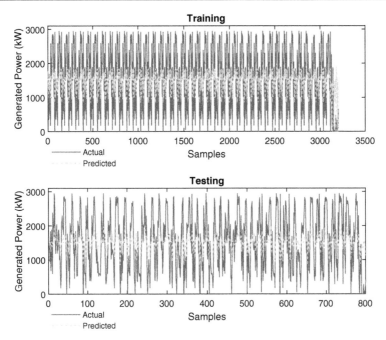

Figure 5.27 Performance of single-layer neural network with a combination of FReLU and Purelin at $\alpha = 1.7$ during training and testing.

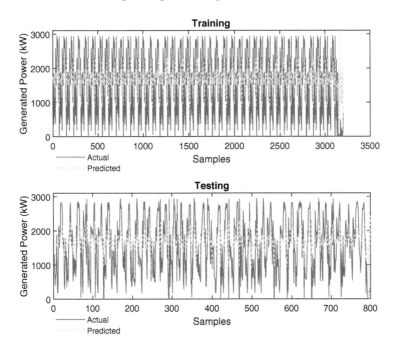

Figure 5.28 Performance of single-layer neural network with a combination of FReLU and Purelin at $\alpha = 1.8$ during training and testing.

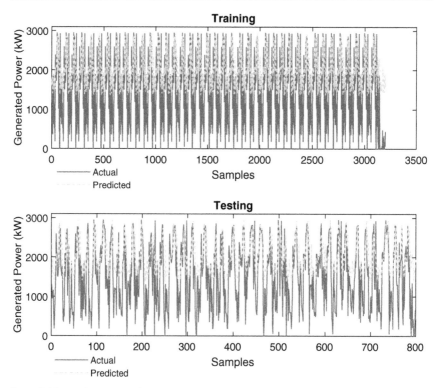

Figure 5.29 Performance of single-layer neural network with a combination of FReLU and Purelin at $\alpha = 1.9$ during training and testing.

performance across different configurations. This analysis is particularly valuable for those involved in renewable energy prediction, where accurate forecasts of wind-generated power are essential for efficient energy management.

Therefore, the results suggest that using the FReLU activation function in the hidden layer and Purelin in the output layer, with an appropriate α value, can yield better wind power forecasting performance than other functions. The analysis shows that using fractional-order derivatives in neural networks solves the problems with traditional activation functions, such as being unable to differentiate, the problem of vanishing gradients, and the fact that they are not always the same. These limitations often lead to issues when employing gradient-based techniques, including the activation function becoming inactive with negative inputs and a delayed network training process. However, it should be noted that the selection of the appropriate activation function may vary depending on the specific problem and the characteristics of the available data.

Table 5.2 Performance comparison on neural network model with various activation
functions and higher α values

Derivative	Function		Training		Testing	
order α	Hidden layer	Output layer	R^2	MSE	R^2	MSE
$\alpha = 1$	FReLU	Purelin	0.9667	0.0209	0.9671	0.0209
	ReLU	FPurelin	0	1.237	0	1.221
	FReLU	FPurelin	0	1.2381	0	1.2166
$\alpha = 1.1$	FReLU	Purelin	0.9197	0.0512	0.9204	0.0469
	ReLU	FPurelin	0.9072	1.0002	0.9108	0.9733
	FReLU	FPurelin	0.9006	1.0317	0.9091	1.0218
$\alpha = 1.2$	FReLU	Purelin	0.9123	0.0568	0.9141	0.0522
	ReLU	FPurelin	0.9267	0.8811	0.9006	0.8844
	FReLU	FPurelin	0.9909	0.7918	0.9826	0.7949
$\alpha = 1.3$	FReLU	Purelin	0.8926	0.0658	0.9055	0.0626
	ReLU	FPurelin	0.8758	0.5558	0.8946	0.5327
	FReLU	FPurelin	0.6419	0.8769	0.7004	0.8206
$\alpha = 1.4$	FReLU	Purelin	0.8648	0.1074	0.8701	0.0991
	ReLU	FPurelin	0.8494	0.5932	0.8552	0.5669
	FReLU	FPurelin	0.6592	0.7894	0.6644	0.7661
$\alpha = 1.5$	FReLU	Purelin	0.8121	0.1186	0.8254	0.1183
	ReLU	FPurelin	0.7737	0.2745	0.7702	0.2718
	FReLU	FPurelin	0.6832	0.4592	0.6952	0.4539
$\alpha = 1.6$	FReLU	Purelin	0.8401	0.1475	0.8387	0.1378
	ReLU	FPurelin	0.8111	0.2872	0.7893	0.2643
	FReLU	FPurelin	0.6117	0.4055	0.6207	0.3932
$\alpha = 1.7$	FReLU	Purelin	0.7985	0.2075	0.8416	0.2066
	ReLU	FPurelin	0.8253	0.3887	0.8347	0.3722
	FReLU	FPurelin	0.5515	0.4911	0.5644	0.4718
$\alpha = 1.8$	FReLU	Purelin	0.8366	0.2302	0.8438	0.2226
	ReLU	FPurelin	0.5653	0.3285	0.5781	0.3242
	FReLU	FPurelin	0.4597	0.2997	0.4753	0.2902
$\alpha = 1.9$	FReLU	Purelin	0.8318	0.2332	0.8355	0.2156
	ReLU	FPurelin	0.8023	0.2637	0.7881	0.2603
	FReLU	FPurelin	0.5769	0.2405	0.5962	0.2362

5.7 CONCLUSION

This chapter has focused on improving generated wind power (kW) forecasting by utilizing four input parameters: wind speed (m/s), wind direction
(deg), pressure (atm), and air temperature (°C), collected from a Texas
wind turbine. By incorporating neural network models and fractional-order
calculus, the proposed model aims to enhance the accuracy of wind energy
forecasts. Fractional-order calculus is employed to transform conventional
activation functions, such as Purelin and ReLU, into fractional-order activation functions, which are known to improve the precision of wind-generated

power forecasting. The performance of the enhanced model is compared with that of a traditional model using evaluation metrics such as MSE and R^2. From the results obtained, it has been observed that the combination of fractional-order ReLU and Purelin activation functions has shown more flexible behaviour with R^2 values of 0.9895, 0.9933 and lower MSE values of 0.0077, 0.0049 on both the training and testing datasets, respectively, when compared to conventional activation functions. These findings highlight the potential of employing fractional-order calculus in neural networks for wind power forecasting. The improved accuracy achieved through this approach holds promise for future research and applications in renewable energy.

REFERENCES

1. Bikash Kumar Sahu, Moonmoon Hiloidhari, and DC Baruah. Global trend in wind power with special focus on the top five wind power producing countries. *Renewable and Sustainable Energy Reviews*, 19:348–359, 2013.
2. Madiah Binti Omar, Rosdiazli Ibrahim, Rhea Mantri, Jhanavi Chaudhary, Kaushik Ram Selvaraj, and Kishore Bingi. Smart grid stability prediction model using neural networks to handle missing inputs. *Sensors*, 22(12):4342, 2022.
3. Bhukya Ramadevi and Kishore Bingi. Chaotic time series forecasting approaches using machine learning techniques: A review. *Symmetry*, 14(5):955, 2022.
4. Jyotirmayee Naik, Sujit Dash, PK Dash, and Ranjeeta Bisoi. Short term wind power forecasting using hybrid variational mode decomposition and multi-kernel regularized pseudo inverse neural network. *Renewable Energy*, 118:180–212, 2018.
5. Kazutoshi Higashiyama, Yu Fujimoto, and Yasuhiro Hayashi. Feature extraction of nwp data for wind power forecasting using 3d-convolutional neural networks. *Energy Procedia*, 155:350–358, 2018.
6. Umit Cali and Vinayak Sharma. Short-term wind power forecasting using long-short term memory based recurrent neural network model and variable selection. *International Journal of Smart Grid and Clean Energy*, 8(2):103–110, 2019.
7. Jianing Wang, Hongqiu Zhu, Yingjie Zhang, Fei Cheng, and Can Zhou. A novel prediction model for wind power based on improved long short-term memory neural network. *Energy*, 265:126283, 2023.
8. Bin Huang, Yuying Liang, and Xiaolin Qiu. Wind power forecasting using attention-based recurrent neural networks: A comparative study. *IEEE Access*, 9:40432–40444, 2021.
9. Noman Shabbir, Lauri Kütt, Muhammad Jawad, Oleksandr Husev, Ateeq Ur Rehman, Akber Abid Gardezi, Muhammad Shafiq, and Jin-Ghoo Choi. Short-term wind energy forecasting using deep learning-based predictive analytics. *Computers, Materials & Continua*, 72:1017–1033, 2022.

10. Qin Chen and Komla Agbenyo Folly. Short-term wind power forecasting using mixed input feature-based cascade-connected artificial neural networks. *Frontiers in Energy Research*, 411, 2021.

11. Min Zhou, Bo Wang, Shudong Guo, and Junzo Watada. Multi-objective prediction intervals for wind power forecast based on deep neural networks. *Information Sciences*, 550:207–220, 2021.

12. Amila T Peiris, Jeevani Jayasinghe, and Upaka Rathnayake. Forecasting wind power generation using artificial neural network: "pawan danawi—A case study from Sri Lanka. *Journal of Electrical and Computer Engineering*, 2021:1–10, 2021.

13. Wen-Hui Lin, Ping Wang, Kuo-Ming Chao, Hsiao-Chung Lin, Zong-Yu Yang, and Yu-Huang Lai. Wind power forecasting with deep learning networks: Time-series forecasting. *Applied Sciences*, 11(21):10335, 2021.

14. Erlong Zhao, Shaolong Sun, and Shouyang Wang. New developments in wind energy forecasting with artificial intelligence and big data: A scientometric insight. *Data Science and Management*, 5(2):84–95, 2022.

15. M Sunder, R Abishek, M Maiti, K Bingi, PAM Devan, and M Assaad. Forecasting of wind turbines generated power with missing input variables. In *2022 International Conference on Future Trends in Smart Communities (ICFTSC)*, pages 98–103. IEEE, 2022.

16. Weihua Tian, Yan Bao, and Wei Liu. Wind power forecasting by the bp neural network with the support of machine learning. *Mathematical Problems in Engineering*, 2022, 2022.

17. Abdulelah Alkesaiberi, Fouzi Harrou, and Ying Sun. Efficient wind power prediction using machine learning methods: A comparative study. *Energies*, 15(7):2327, 2022.

18. Hui Wei, Wen-Sheng Wang, and Xiao-Xuan Kao. A novel approach to ultra-short-term wind power prediction based on feature engineering and informer. *Energy Reports*, 9:1236–1250, 2023.

19. Parul Arora, Seyed Mohammad Jafar Jalali, Sajad Ahmadian, BK Panigrahi, PN Suganthan, and Abbas Khosravi. Probabilistic wind power forecasting using optimized deep auto-regressive recurrent neural networks. *IEEE Transactions on Industrial Informatics*, 19(3):2814–2825, 2022.

20. Eric Stefan Miele, Nicole Ludwig, and Alessandro Corsini. Multi-horizon wind power forecasting using multi-modal spatio-temporal neural networks. *Energies*, 16(8):3522, 2023.

21. Maryam Yaghoubirad, Narjes Azizi, Meisam Farajollahi, and Abolfazl Ahmadi. Deep learning-based multistep ahead wind speed and power generation forecasting using direct method. *Energy Conversion and Management*, 281:116760, 2023.

22. Manuel Duarte Ortigueira. *Fractional Calculus for Scientists and Engineers*, volume 84. Springer Science & Business Media, Cham, Switzerland, 2011.

23. Sverre Holm and Sven Peter Näsholm. A causal and fractional all-frequency wave equation for lossy media. *The Journal of the Acoustical Society of America*, 130(4):2195–2202, 2011.

24. Pravdomir Dobrev. Texas wind turbine dataset. https://www.kaggle.com/datasets/pravdomirdobrev/texas-wind-turbine-dataset-simulated.

25. Megha S Job, Priyanka H Bhateja, Muskan Gupta, Kishore Bingi, and B Raja-narayan Prusty. Fractional rectified linear unit activation function and its variants. *Mathematical Problems in Engineering*, 2022, 2022.
26. Chigozie Nwankpa, Winifred Ijomah, Anthony Gachagan, and Stephen Mar-shall. Activation functions: Comparison of trends in practice and research for deep learning. arXiv preprint arXiv:1811.03378, 2018.
27. Sagar Sharma, Simone Sharma, and Anidhya Athaiya. Activation functions in neural networks. *Towards Data Science*, 6(12):310–316, 2017.

Chapter 6

Data-driven photovoltaic system characteristic determination using non-linear system identification

Yellapragada Venkata Pavan Kumar, Challa Pradeep Reddy, Ramani Kannan, and Purna Prakash Kasaraneni

6.1 INTRODUCTION

The energy systems that use non-renewable energy sources such as coal, oil, and nuclear energy are rapidly shifting towards the usage of renewable energy sources such as solar, biomass, and wind. The very important reasons to use renewable energy sources are due to the nature of pollution-free, reliable, and noiseless operation. This integration of green energy with power systems reduces the adverse impact on human health as well as the environment. Among all the renewable energy sources, solar energy is abundantly available and easily accessible. Hence, the deployment of photovoltaic (PV) systems throughout the globe has been on the streak for the last decade [1–4]. The shift towards green energy is becoming one of the solutions for ever-increasing global warming [5, 6]. The maintenance of large deployments of PV systems is challenging. Experiencing the occurrence of abnormalities in the recorded data of these PV systems is a common phenomenon during daily operations [7]. An abnormality or a fault can be a deviation from the actual expectation of the operation. The kinds of abnormalities are anomalous readings, garbage readings, redundant readings, missing readings, and outlier readings [8–12]. To find the faults in the large-scale PV systems, the collaborative filtering techniques and model-based approach were discussed [13, 14]. Further, the literature works discussed various methods to find the abnormalities or faults in the PV systems and are given in Section 6.1.1.

6.1.1 State-of-the-art literature review

In the detection and diagnosis of faults, irradiation variance has significant importance [15]. A logistic regression method was implemented to diagnose the faults in the PV array [16]. To find the faults every hour, a hybrid method with unsupervised weather status pattern recognition and the blending fitting model was implemented [17]. An artificial neural network-based approach was discussed for finding the faults in isolated PV systems [18]. A

DOI: 10.1201/9781003470274-6

model was proposed to implement the algorithm online for finding the faults in the PV systems [19]. A vertices principal component analysis was realized to find the faults in the grid-connected PV system [20]. A statistical tool-based fault detection system was employed to find the faults in large-scale grid-connected solar PV plants [21]. An approach based on the residuals was implemented to find the faults in the solar PV systems [22]. An artificial neural network-based fault detection model was proposed to find the faults in PV systems [23]. An unsupervised one-class support vector machine-based monitoring technique was implemented to find anomalies in PV systems [24].

The abovesaid literature works discussed the methods for finding faults in PV systems. But up to the best of the authors' knowledge, all the discussed methods are complex, and no method has discussed the simple analytical models for finding the possible abnormalities such as missing readings, redundant readings, outlier readings, and garbage readings in PV systems' data. Hence, this chapter proposes various analytical models for finding the abovementioned abnormalities in PV systems. This is the major contribution of this chapter.

6.1.2 Description of the dataset

The dataset named "Photovoltaic Power and Weather Parameters" [25] is a publicly available PV power measurements dataset. This dataset can be freely used for research and scientific purposes. The PV power measurements were recorded at an interval of one minute at SolarTech Lab, Politecnico di Milano, Italy, during the production. The variables of this dataset are, namely, "Time" contains the timestamp with the format "dd-MM-yyyy hh:mm:ss" which is always stated in the Central European Time. In timestamp, dd represents a day, MM represents a month, yyyy represents a year, hh represents an hour, mm represents a minute, and ss represents a second. "PV_Power" contains the recordings of the power readings of the PV module with the module tilt (30°). "T_air" contains the details of the ambient temperature in (°C) which is measured by the weather station. The ambient temperature is the temperature measured in the surrounding area. "G_h" contains the recordings of global horizontal irradiance in W/m^2. "G_tilt" contains the recordings of global irradiance on the plane of the array (30°). "W_s" contains the recordings of wind speed in m/s. "W_d" contains the recordings of wind direction (°), supposing 0° east, positive south. All the variables of this dataset contain original measurements. This dataset contains 525,600 records that represent the measurements recorded at every minute in a year, i.e., from 01-Jan-2017 to 31-Dec-2017. The hours of the day in this dataset are from 0 through 23. Besides, the key point to be noted about this dataset is that the missing measurements in this dataset are represented with "not a number (NaN)," which is usually represented as "not available (NA)."

6.2 METHODOLOGY

The flow of implementation for the proposed methodology to detect the abnormalities in the PV system characteristics is shown in Figure 6.1. Initially, the process starts with the reading of the considered PV dataset. The proposed analytical model cannot be applied directly to this raw dataset as all the characteristics data are available in a single-column format. Hence, the preparation of the dataset is essential to apply the proposed analytical model. As a next step to the reading of the dataset, the dataset is split into multiple variables. Further, the variable that contains the timestamp is split into four variables, namely ST_Date, ST_Hour, ST_Minute, and ST_Second, where ST stands for SolarTech which is considered from the SolarTech Lab. Further, verify the data type of each variable and update the datatype with the respective datatype and save it into the same variable for effective implementation of the proposed methodology. Because the data type of all variables is available as a single column in the raw dataset, it is observed as a character type.

Once the dataset preparation is done, this newly prepared dataset is divided into sub-datasets that contain timestamps and measurement data. Consider each sub-dataset and search for missing readings. If the variable consists of an NA value or an empty cell, then the reading value is said to be missing. If the missing values exist, then identify the records with missing data and quantify them for further analysis.

Next, search for the redundant readings in each sub-dataset. When the two records are identical then those are said to be redundant. If redundancy exists, identify the records with redundant records and quantify them for further analysis. Continue the search process to identify the outlier readings. An outlier is a value that is out of the range. A reading value that falls out of the range is an outlier reading. Outliers are identified by using a boxplot analysis. Finally, search for the garbage readings in each sub-dataset. A garbage reading is a reading that consists of a value other than a numeric value. The detailed explanation for the proposed methodology is explained as follows. The algorithmic steps for dataset reading and preparation are given in Table 6.1. This helps to convert the raw data that is normally available in the dataset into the format that is required to implement the proposed analytical models.

The algorithmic steps for finding abnormalities, namely the missing readings, the redundant readings, the outlier readings, and the garbage readings, in a systematic way are provided in Tables 6.2–6.5, respectively. All these models are executed sequentially, thereby enumerating and visualizing the existence of all possible anomalies.

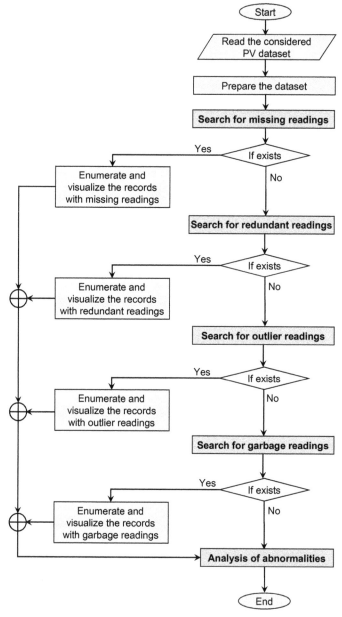

Figure 6.1   Flow of implementation for the proposed methodology to detect abnormalities.

Once all the possible abnormalities in the data are found, then calculate and visualize the count and proportions of the identified abnormalities to understand the impact of these abnormalities on the dataset.

Table 6.1   Algorithmic steps for dataset reading and preparation

Algorithm description

- Read the PV dataset considered.
- Prepare the dataset by splitting the single column into multiple columns in the raw dataset. Further, the variable "Time" is split into four new columns such as ST_Date, ST_Hour, ST_Minute, and ST_Second.
- Update the datatypes of each variable with the appropriate datatype.
- Divide the dataset into the sub-datasets that contain timestamp and measurement columns and save them separately as objects. The sub-datasets for each measurement are as follows.

  - ST_Date, ST_Hour, ST_Minute, ST_Second, and PV_Power
  - ST_Date, ST_Hour, ST_Minute, ST_Second, and T_air
  - ST_Date, ST_Hour, ST_Minute, ST_Second, and G_h
  - ST_Date, ST_Hour, ST_Minute, ST_Second, and G_tilt
  - ST_Date, ST_Hour, ST_Minute, ST_Second, and W_s
  - ST_Date, ST_Hour, ST_Minute, ST_Second, and W_d

Table 6.2   Algorithmic steps for the identification of the missing readings

Algorithm description

- If the recorded reading value in the measurement variable of the sub-dataset is "not available" or "an empty cell" or "not a number" then it is considered to be missing.
- The reading values are marked as missing when any of the abovementioned cases appear and the pseudo-code for the same is given as follows.
- Read the object.
- Check each element of the object to find missing values.
  for (p in 1:length(object)) {
- Check the object for NA, NaN, and empty cells.
  if (object[p] = = NA || object[p] = = NaN || object[p] = = " ") {
- Mark the missing values with the logical element TRUE if the above condition is TRUE or else mark with the logical element FALSE, which represents that there are no missing values.
  missing_values[p] ← TRUE
  else {
  missing_values[p] ← FALSE } } }
- Return the identified missing values.
- Retrieve the records with missing readings.

6.3 RESULTS AND DISCUSSION

The results of the implementation of the proposed methodology are presented in this section. The implementation of the proposed approach has provided the following results. The number of missing readings in the dataset is presented in Figure 6.2. The proportions of the missing readings are presented in Figure 6.3. The consolidated information on the proportions of the missing readings is presented in Figure 6.4. Hour-wise count and the

Table 6.3 Algorithmic steps for the identification of the redundant readings

Algorithm description

- Read the object.
- Check each element of the object from the second record in the object to find missing values.
  for (p in 2:length(object)) {
- If the present data element is equal to the previous data element, then mark the respective data element with the logical element TRUE, if the present data element is not equal to the previous data element move to the next data element and do the same process if there is no matching then mark the respective data element with the logical element FALSE.
  if (object[p] = = object[p-1]) {
  redundant[p] ← TRUE
  else{
  redundant[p] ← FALSE
  } } }
- Return the identified redundant reading values.
- Retrieve the records with the redundant readings.

Table 6.4 Algorithmic steps for the identification of the outlier readings

Algorithm description

- The outliers in readings are identified by using boxplot analysis. The outliers are visualized by using a box-and-whisker plot. To draw the boxplot, the five-number summary i.e., minimum value, first quartile (Q1), median value, third quartile (Q3), and maximum value is to be calculated.
- The five-number summary is represented as follows. (minimum, Q1, median, Q3, maximum)
- Read the object.
- Determine the lower bound (i.e., minimum) and upper bound (i.e., maximum) values by calculating the interquartile range (IQR).
- The IQR is obtained by calculating the difference between Q3 and Q1.
  IQR = Q3 − Q1
- The outliers in the data are determined as follows.
  The data elements that are below the (Q1 - 1.5 * IQR) or above the (Q3 + 1.5 * IQR) are treated as outliers.
- Retrieve the records with outlier readings.

distribution of missing readings are presented in Figure 6.5. The number and the proportions of outlier readings in the dataset are presented in Figures 6.6 and 6.7, respectively.

The subplots from Figure 6.2a through Figure 6.2f provide quantitative information on the missing readings in each variable. In each subplot, the variable name is available on the top, the count of missing readings in each variable on the bottom, the number of rows on the left, and the existence of missing readings encoded with the binary values 0 and 1, where 0 for non-existence and 1 for existence. From Figure 6.2a, it is observed that there

Table 6.5 Algorithmic steps for the identification of the garbage readings

Algorithm description

- The garbage readings mean the readings that are other than numerical values. Also, the cells that contain "NaN" in the dataset are garbage values.
- The garbage values can be identified based on the pattern or regular expression. The pattern that is identified other than the numerical value is a garbage value.
- The regular expression to find the garbage values is given below. The regular expression can match either an optional sign followed by zero or more digits, a dot, and one or more digits, representing a floating-point number with an optional integer part, or an optional sign followed by one or more digits, representing an integer.
  [-+]?([0-9]*\\.[0-9]+|[0-9]+
- Read the object.
- Apply the regular expression.
- Retrieve the records with garbage readings.

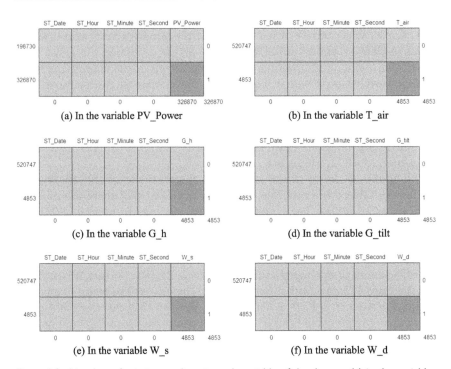

(a) In the variable PV_Power

(b) In the variable T_air

(c) In the variable G_h

(d) In the variable G_tilt

(e) In the variable W_s

(f) In the variable W_d

Figure 6.2 Number of missing readings in each variable of the dataset: (a) in the variable PV_Power; (b) in the variable T_air; (c) in the variable G_h; (d) in the variable G_tilt; (e) in the variable W_s; and (f) in the variable W_d.

are no missing values in the variables ST_Date, ST_Hour, ST_Minute, and ST_Second. Further, it is noticed that the number of missing readings in the PV_Power variable is 326,870. Hence, in this variable, it is identified that out of 525,600, there are 326,870 rows with the existence of missing values and 198,730 rows with the non-existence of missing values. From Figure 6.2b through Figure 6.2f, it is observed that there are no missing values in the variables ST_Date, ST_Hour, ST_Minute, and ST_Second. Further, it is noticed that the number of missing readings in the variables T_air, G_h, G_tilt, W_s, and W_d is 4853. Hence, in these variables, it is identified that out of 525,600, there are 4853 rows with the existence of missing values and 520,747 rows with the non-existence of missing values.

The subplots from Figure 6.3a through Figure 6.3f provide the proportions of the missing readings in each variable. In each subplot, the proportion and the pattern of the missing values are shown. The variable names are taken on the x-axis and the proportion of the missing values is taken on the y-axis. From Figure 6.3a, it is observed that the proportion of the missing readings in the PV_Power variable is 0.62 and the proportion of non-missing values in all the variables is 0.38. From Figure 6.3b through Figure 6.3f, it is observed that the proportion of the missing readings in the variables T_air, G_h, G_tilt, W_s, and W_d is 0.0092 and the proportion of non-missing values in all the variables is 0.9908.

The consolidated information on the proportions of the missing readings in each variable is shown in Figure 6.4. The names of the variables are taken on the x-axis and the proportion of the missing readings is taken on the y-axis. From this figure, it is evident that the variable PV_Power has the highest proportion (0.62) of missing readings than the other variables. The remaining variables T_air, G_h, G_tilt, W_s, and W_d have a very less proportion (0.0092) of missing readings.

The hour-wise count of the missing readings in the variable PV_Power is given in Table 6.6. From this table, it is observed that there are missing readings at all hours. The count of missing readings in hour 0 is 21840. Further, it is noticed that there are 364 days with missing readings in hour 0. The count of missing readings in hours 1, 2, and 3 is 21,900, respectively. Further, it is noticed that there are 365 days with missing readings in each hour. The count of missing readings in hour 4 is 21,581. Further, it is noticed that there are 365 days with missing readings in hour 4. The count of missing readings in hour 5 is 17,949. Further, it is noticed that there are 364 days with missing readings in hour 5. The count of missing readings in hour 6 is 13,507. Further, it is noticed that there are 299 days with missing readings in hour 6. The count of missing readings in hour 7 is 9914. Further, it is noticed that there are 238 days with missing readings in hour 7. The count of missing readings in hour 8 is 6518. Further, it is noticed that there are 221 days with missing readings in hour 8. The count of missing readings in hour 9 is 5194. Further, it is noticed that there are 170 days with missing readings in hour 9. The count of missing readings in hour 10 is 4820. Further, it is noticed that there are 141 days with missing readings in hour 10. The count of missing readings in hour 11 is 4693. Further, it is noticed that there are 132 days with missing readings in hour 11. The count of missing readings in hour 12

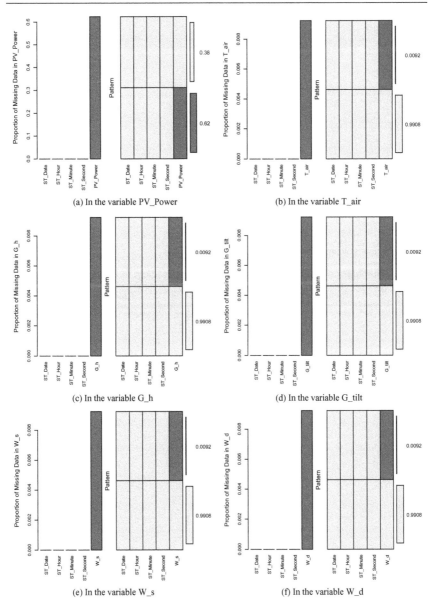

Figure 6.3 Proportions of missing readings in each variable of the dataset: (a) in the variable PV_Power; (b) in the variable T_air; (c) in the variable G_h; (d) in the variable G_tilt; (e) in the variable W_s; and (f) in the variable W_d.

is 4543. Further, it is noticed that there are 132 days with missing readings in hour 12. The count of missing readings in hour 13 is 4629. Further, it is noticed that there are 141 days with missing readings in hour 13. The count of missing readings in hour 14 is 4760. Further, it is noticed that there are 144

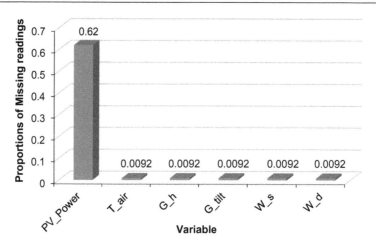

Figure 6.4 Consolidated proportions of missing readings.

Table 6.6 Summary of the hour-wise count of missing readings in PV_Power

Hour	No_of_Days_with_Missing_Readings	Count_of_Missing_Readings
0	364	21,840
1	365	21,900
2	365	21,900
3	365	21,900
4	365	21,581
5	364	17,949
6	299	13,507
7	238	9914
8	221	6518
9	170	5194
10	141	4820
11	132	4693
12	132	4543
13	141	4629
14	144	4760
15	158	5051
16	211	6416
17	247	10,348
18	295	14,185
19	364	18,276
20	365	21,785
21	364	21,810
22	362	21,711
23	363	21,640

days with missing readings in hour 14. The count of missing readings in hour 15 is 5051. Further, it is noticed that there are 158 days with missing readings in hour 15. The count of missing readings in hour 16 is 6416. Further, it is noticed that there are 211 days with missing readings in hour 16. The count of missing readings in hour 17 is 10,348. Further, it is noticed that there are 247 days with missing readings in hour 17. The count of missing readings in hour 18 is 14,185. Further, it is noticed that there are 295 days with missing readings in hour 18. The count of missing readings in hour 19 is 18,276. Further, it is noticed that there are 364 days with missing readings in hour 19. The count of missing readings in hour 20 is 21,785. Further, it is noticed that there are 365 days with missing readings in hour 20. The count of missing readings in hour 21 is 21,810. Further, it is noticed that there are 364 days with missing readings in hour 21. The count of missing readings in hour 22 is 21,711. Further, it is noticed that there are 362 days with missing readings in hour 22. The count of missing readings in hour 23 is 21,640. Further, it is noticed that there are 363 days with missing readings in hour 23. Besides, from this table, it is evident that hours 1, 2, and 3 consist of the highest count of missing readings 21,900.

Similarly, the hour-wise count of the missing readings in the variables T_air, G_h, G_tilt, W_s, and W_d is given in Table 6.7. From this table, it is observed that there are missing readings at all hours. The count of missing readings in hour 0 is 180. Further, it is noticed that there are 3 days with missing readings in hour 0. The count of missing readings in hour 1 is 181. Further, it is noticed that there are 4 days with the missing readings in hour 1.

The count of missing readings in hour 2 is 240. Further, it is noticed that there are 4 days with the missing readings in hour 2. The count of missing readings in hours 3, 4, 5, and 6 is 180, respectively. Further, it is noticed that there are 3 days with missing readings in each hour. The count of missing readings in hour 7 is 228. Further, it is noticed that there are 4 days with missing readings in hour 7. The count of missing readings in hour 8 is 277. Further, it is noticed that there are 5 days with the missing readings in hour 8. The count of missing readings in hour 9 is 214. Further, it is noticed that there are 7 days with the missing readings in hour 9. The count of missing readings in hour 10 is 159. Further, it is noticed that there are 7 days with the missing readings in hour 10. The count of missing readings in hour 11 is 179. Further, it is noticed that there are 4 days with missing readings in hour 11. The count of missing readings in hour 12 is 132. Further, it is noticed that there are 3 days with missing readings in hour 12. The count of missing readings in hour 13 is 158. Further, it is noticed that there are 4 days with missing readings in hour 13. The count of missing readings in hour 14 is 237. Further, it is noticed that there are 7 days with the missing readings in hour 14. The count of missing readings in hour 15 is 214. Further, it is noticed that there are 7 days with the missing readings in hour 15. The count of missing readings in hour 16 is 173. Further, it is noticed that there are 5 days with the missing readings in hour 16. The count of missing readings in hour 17 is 120. Further, it is noticed that there are 2 days with missing readings in hour 17. The count of missing readings in hour 18 is 129. Further, it is noticed that there are 3 days with missing readings in hour 18.

Table 6.7 Summary of hour-wise distribution of missing readings in T_air, G_h, G_tilt, W_s, and W_d

Hour	No_of_Days_with_Missing_Readings	Count_of_Missing_Readings
0	3	180
1	4	181
2	4	240
3	3	180
4	3	180
5	3	180
6	3	180
7	4	228
8	5	277
9	7	214
10	7	159
11	4	179
12	3	132
13	4	158
14	7	237
15	7	214
16	5	173
17	2	120
18	3	129
19	3	172
20	3	180
21	3	180
22	3	180
23	10	600

The count of missing readings in hour 19 is 172. Further, it is noticed that there are 3 days with missing readings in hour 19. The count of missing readings in hours 20, 21, and 22 is 180, respectively. Further, it is noticed that there are 3 days with missing readings in each hour. The count of missing readings in hour 23 is 600. Further, it is noticed that there are 363 days with missing readings in hour 10. Besides, from this table, it is evident that hour 23 consists of the highest count of missing readings 600.

The hour-wise count and distribution of missing readings for each variable in the dataset are shown in Figure 6.5. The hour information is taken on the *x*-axis and the count of missing readings is taken on the *y*-axis.

The number of outlier readings in each variable of the dataset is shown in Figure 6.6. From Figure 6.6a, it is observed that there are 26 outlier readings in the variable PV_Power. From Figure 6.6b, it is observed that there are 52 outlier readings in the variable T_air. From Figure 6.6c, it is observed that there are 45,368 outlier readings in the variable G_h. From Figure 6.6d, it is observed that there are 48,966 outlier readings in the variable G_tilt. From Figure 6.6e, it is observed that there are 15,887 outlier readings in the variable W_s. From Figure 6.6f, it is observed that there are 0 outlier readings in the variable W_d.

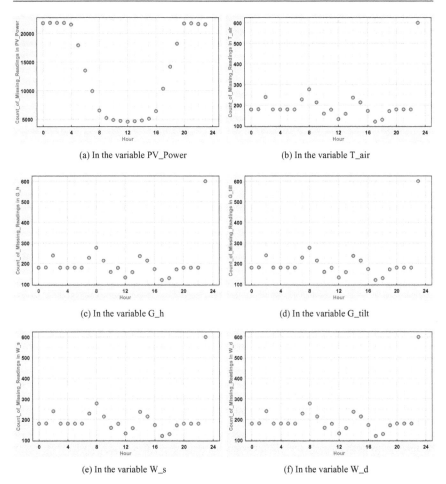

Figure 6.5 Hour-wise count and distribution of missing readings in the dataset: (a) in the variable PV_Power; (b) in the variable T_air; (c) in the variable G_h; (d) in the variable G_tilt; (e) in the variable W_s; and (f) in the variable W_d.

The proportions of outlier readings in each variable of the dataset are shown in Figure 6.7. From this figure, it is observed that the proportion of outlier readings in the variable PV_Power is 0.0049. The proportion of outlier readings in the variable T_air is 0.0098. The proportion of the outlier readings in the variable G_h is 8.6316. The proportion of the outlier readings in the variable G_tilt is 9.3162. The proportion of the outlier readings in the variable W_s is 3.0226. The proportion of the outlier readings in the variable W_d is 0. Overall, from Figures 6.6 and 6.7, it is noticed that the variable G_tilt has the highest number (48,966) and the proportion (9.3162) of outlier readings in the dataset.

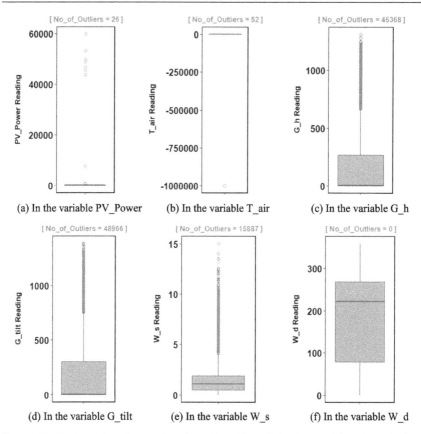

Figure 6.6 Number of outlier readings in each variable of the dataset: (a) in the variable PV_Power; (b) in the variable T_air; (c) in the variable G_h; (d) in the variable G_tilt; (e) in the variable W_s; and (f) In the variable W_d.

6.4 CONCLUSIONS

This chapter discusses the identification of abnormalities in the dataset of PV systems. The abnormalities, namely, missing readings, outlier readings, and garbage readings are identified. Interestingly, no redundant readings are identified. Besides, the garbage readings and the missing readings are the same as the missing readings are represented with "NaN."

The significant observations from the analysis are as follows.

- No abnormalities were found in the variables ST_Date, ST_Hour, ST_Minute, and ST_Second.
- The count and the proportion of missing readings in the variable PV_Power are 326,870 and 0.62, respectively.

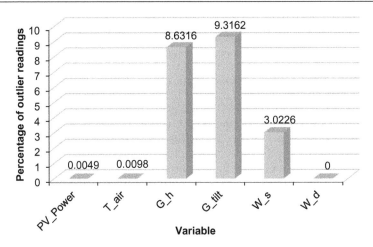

Figure 6.7 Proportions of outlier readings in each variable of the dataset.

- The count and proportion of missing readings in the variables T_air, G_h, G_tilt, W_s, and W_d are 4853 and 0.0092, respectively.
- The hour-wise count and distribution of missing readings in the variable PV_Power, the hours 1, 2, and 3, consist of the highest count (21,900) of missing readings.
- The hour-wise count and distribution of missing readings in the variables T_air, G_h, G_tilt, W_s, and W_d, hour 23, consist of the highest count of missing readings 600.
- The variable G_tilt has the highest number (48,966) and the proportion (9.3162) of outlier readings in the dataset.

Therefore, this work is advantageous to identify various abnormalities that impact the integrity of the PV systems' characteristics.

6.4.1 Future scope

The future scope of the proposed analytical models is to identify all possible abnormalities in the real-time data of PV systems by considering various characteristics. This helps novice researchers to interpret the trends of abnormalities between historical and real-time data.

REFERENCES

1. S. Leva, A. Nespoli, S. Pretto, M. Mussetta, and E. G. C. Ogliari, "PV plant power nowcasting: A real case comparative study with an open access dataset," *IEEE Access*, vol. 8, pp. 194428–194440, 2020, https://doi.org/10.1109/ACCESS.2020.3031439.

2. L. Chen and X. Wang, "Adaptive fault localization in photovoltaic systems," *IEEE Transactions on Smart Grid*, vol. 9, no. 6, pp. 6752–6763, Nov. 2018, https://doi.org/10.1109/TSG.2017.2722821.
3. E. Garoudja, F. Harrou, Y. Sun, K. Kara, A. Chouder, and S. Silvestre, "Statistical fault detection in photovoltaic systems," *Solar Energy*, vol. 150, pp. 485–499, Jul. 2017, http://doi.org/10.1016/j.solener.2017.04.043.
4. A. Mellit, G. M. Tina, and S. A. Kalogirou, "Fault detection and diagnosis methods for photovoltaic systems: A review," *Renewable and Sustainable Energy Reviews*, vol. 91, pp. 1–17, Aug. 2018, https://doi.org/10.1016/j.rser.2018.03.062.
5. S. Prakash, S. Purwar, and S. R. Mohanty, "Adaptive detection of islanding and power quality disturbances in a grid-integrated photovoltaic system," *Arabian Journal for Science and Engineering*, vol. 45, no. 8, pp. 6297–6310, Aug. 2020, https://doi.org/10.1007/s13369-020-04378-w.
6. D. S. Pillai and N. Rajasekar, "A comprehensive review on protection challenges and fault diagnosis in PV systems," *Renewable and Sustainable Energy Reviews*, vol. 91, pp. 18–40, Aug. 2018, https://doi.org/10.1016/j.rser.2018.03.082.
7. Y. Zhao, Q. Liu, D. Li, D. Kang, Q. Lv, and L. Shang, "Hierarchical anomaly detection and multimodal classification in large-scale photovoltaic systems," *IEEE Transactions on Sustainable Energy*, vol. 10, no. 3, pp. 1351–1361, Jul. 2019, https://doi.org/10.1109/TSTE.2018.2867009.
8. K. P. Prakash and Y. V. P. Kumar, "Simple and effective descriptive analysis of missing data anomalies in smart home energy consumption readings," *Journal of Energy Systems*, vol. 5, no. 3, pp. 199–220, Aug. 2021, https://doi.org/10.30521/jes.878318.
9. K. P. Prakash and Y. V. P. Kumar, "Analytical approach to exploring the missing data behavior in smart home energy consumption dataset," *Journal of Renewable Energy and Environment*, vol. 9, no. 2, pp. 37–48, May 2022, https://doi.org/10.30501/jree.2021.313536.1277.
10. K. P. Prakash and Y. V. P. Kumar, "Exploration of anomalous tracing of records in smart home energy consumption dataset," *ECS Transactions*, vol. 107, no. 1, pp. 18271–18280, Apr. 2022, https://iopscience.iop.org/article/10.1149/10701.18271ecst.
11. K. P. Prakash, Y. V. P. Kumar, G. L. K. Moganti, and A. Flah, "Analytical enumeration of redundant data anomalies in energy consumption readings of smart buildings with a case study of Darmstadt smart city in Germany," *Sustainability*, vol. 14, no. 17, p. 10842, Aug. 2022, https://doi.org/10.3390/su141710842.
12. K. P. Prakash and Y. V. P. Kumar, "A systematic approach for exploration, behavior analysis, and visualization of redundant data anomalies in smart home energy consumption dataset," *International Journal of Renewable Energy Research*, vol. 12, no. 1, pp. 109–123, 2022, https://doi.org/10.20508/ijrer.v12i1.12613.g8381.
13. Y. Zhao, D. Li, T. Lu, Q. Lv, N. Gu, and L. Shang, "Collaborative fault detection for large-scale photovoltaic systems," *IEEE Transactions on Sustainable Energy*, vol. 11, no. 4, pp. 2745–2754, Oct. 2020, https://doi.org/10.1109/TSTE.2020.2974404.

14. V. Carletti, A. Greco, A. Saggese, and M. Vento, "An intelligent flying system for automatic detection of faults in photovoltaic plants," *Journal of Ambient Intelligence and Humanized Computing*, vol. 11, no. 5, pp. 2027–2040, May 2020, https://doi.org/10.1007/s12652-019-01212-6.

15. M. Hajji, Z. Yahyaoui, M. Mansouri, H. Nounou, and M. Nounou, "Fault detection and diagnosis in grid-connected PV systems under irradiance variations," *Energy Reports*, vol. 9, pp. 4005–4017, Dec. 2023, https://doi.org/10.1016/j.egyr.2023.03.033.

16. M. Wang, X. Xu, and Z. Yan, "Online fault diagnosis of PV array considering label errors based on distributionally robust logistic regression," *Renewable Energy*, vol. 203, pp. 68–80, Feb. 2023, https://doi.org/10.1016/j.renene.2022.11.126.

17. J. Qu, Z. Qian, Y. Pei, L. Wei, H. Zareipour, and Q. Sun, "An unsupervised hourly weather status pattern recognition and blending fitting model for PV system fault detection," *Applied Energy*, vol. 319, p. 119271, Aug. 2022, https://doi.org/10.1016/j.apenergy.2022.119271.

18. A. Aallouche and H. Ouadi, "Online fault detection and identification for an isolated PV system using ANN," *IFAC-PapersOnLine*, vol. 55, no. 12, pp. 468–475, 2022, https://doi.org/10.1016/j.ifacol.2022.07.356.

19. R. Platon, J. Martel, N. Woodruff, and T. Y. Chau, "Online fault detection in PV systems," *IEEE Transactions on Sustainable Energy*, vol. 6, no. 4, pp. 1200–1207, Oct. 2015, https://doi.org/10.1109/TSTE.2015.2421447.

20. L. Rouani, M. F. Harkat, A. Kouadri, and S. Mekhilef, "Shading fault detection in a grid-connected PV system using vertices principal component analysis," *Renewable Energy*, vol. 164, pp. 1527–1539, Feb. 2021, https://doi.org/10.1016/j.renene.2020.10.059.

21. M. S. Iqbal, Y. A. K. Niazi, U. Amir Khan, and B.-W. Lee, "Real-time fault detection system for large scale grid integrated solar photovoltaic power plants," *International Journal of Electrical Power & Energy Systems*, vol. 130, p. 106902, Sep. 2021, https://doi.org/10.1016/j.ijepes.2021.106902.

22. A. Dhoke, R. Sharma, and T. K. Saha, "An approach for fault detection and location in solar PV systems," *Solar Energy*, vol. 194, pp. 197–208, Dec. 2019, https://doi.org/10.1016/j.solener.2019.10.052.

23. P. Jenitha and A. I. Selvakumar, "Fault detection in PV systems," *Applied Solar Energy*, vol. 53, no. 3, pp. 229–237, Jul. 2017, https://doi.org/10.3103/S0003701X17030069.

24. F. Harrou, A. Dairi, B. Taghezouit, and Y. Sun, "An unsupervised monitoring procedure for detecting anomalies in photovoltaic systems using a one-class support vector machine," *Solar Energy*, vol. 179, pp. 48–58, Feb. 2019, https://doi.org/10.1016/j.solener.2018.12.045.

25. Sonia Leva, Alfredo Nespoli, Silvia Pretto, Marco Mussetta, Emanuele Ogliari, September 23, 2020, "Photovoltaic power and weather parameters," *IEEE Dataport*, https://doi.org/10.21227/42v0-jz14.

Chapter 7

Fractional feed-forward neural network-based smart grid stability prediction model

*Bhukya Ramadevi, Venkata Ramana Kasi, Kishore Bingi,
Rosdiazli Ibrahim, and B Rajanarayan Prusty*

7.1 INTRODUCTION

The current power system, which relies on fossil fuels, faces several limitations such as privacy issues, cybersecurity threats, and power losses caused by one-way communication. As energy bills continue to rise and the demand for renewable energy increases, it is crucial to update the grid [1]. To overcome these challenges, it is necessary to implement a smart grid system that uses renewable energy sources and enables bidirectional communication. Bidirectional communication optimizes smart grid components, making them more sustainable and reliable [2]. Unlike the traditional grid, smart grids allow users to consume, produce, store, and exchange energy. With demand response and dynamic pricing based on supply and demand evaluation, customers have more control over their energy usage. Smart grids also optimize resource allocation, and predicting their stability is a primary requirement for these systems [3].

As renewable energy sources become more integrated into smart grids, predicting their stability through neural networks has become increasingly important. The complexity of grid data requires the ability to capture complex patterns and nonlinear relationships, which neural networks excel at. Recent studies have demonstrated the effectiveness of neural networks in predicting grid stability, including voltage stability, frequency stability, and power system oscillations. This information is valuable to grid operators, who can proactively maintain grid stability. For example, Gupta et al. proposed a neural network-based early warning system to detect and predict blackouts in smart grid power networks, which highlighted the importance of neural networks in blackout prediction. Additionally, researchers have explored the effectiveness of convolutional neural networks (CNNs) in short-term electrical load forecasting and improving load forecasting accuracy. Other models, such as the modified backpropagation neural network-based model combined with chaotically improved meta-heuristics, have been proposed to improve the accuracy of energy demand prediction

DOI: 10.1201/9781003470274-7

in smart grids. Finally, predictive models have been developed to address the challenges of integrating renewable energy sources and optimizing grid operations in smart grids.

Advanced dispatch strategies and price forecasting models have been developed by researchers through the use of deep learning techniques. In their study [4], the authors explored the application of a deep learning approach using an enhanced CNN for price forecasting in smart grid systems. They discussed the advantages of using CNNs for accurate price prediction and highlighted the potential of deep learning techniques in improving price forecasting in smart grid environments. The authors proposed enhanced CNN and support vector regression models, which demonstrated improved accuracy and performance when compared to traditional methods [5]. The significance of these advanced models for forecasting in smart grid applications was also highlighted. In another study [6], researchers proposed a deep neural network model for energy load forecasting in smart grids. The model utilized deep learning techniques to accurately predict energy load demand, enabling efficient energy management and grid stability. A deep learning method for predicting short-term residential load in smart grids was also implemented by the authors in reference [7]. The method utilized deep learning techniques to improve load forecasting accuracy, thereby contributing to the efficient management and optimization of smart grid systems. A novel hybrid method for short-term load forecasting in smart grids using multiple linear regression (MLR) and long short-term memory (LSTM) neural network was developed by the researchers as in reference [8], which showed promising results for load forecasting in smart grid systems. Lastly, a novel approach using a multidirectional LSTM model for smart grid stability prediction was introduced [9]. The model showed promising results in accurately forecasting grid stability and offered the potential for enhancing the stability management of smart grids.

A recent study by Xia et al. introduced a new approach that combines stacked gated recurrent unit neural networks with a recurrent neural network to forecast variables in smart grid operations [10]. This method showed promising results in accurately predicting renewable energy generation and electricity load, contributing to improved smart-grid operations and planning. Massaoudi et al. proposed integrated deep learning approaches, such as bidirectional gated units and simulated annealing, to predict smart grid stability using point and interval estimation techniques [11]. Their method leverages the power of deep learning algorithms to achieve precise predictions, emphasizing the importance of accurate stability forecasting for smart-grid operations. Breviglieri et al. developed optimized deep learning models for predicting smart grid stability, highlighting the importance of model optimization to achieve high-performance results [12]. Bingi et al. provided an overview of various neural network-based approaches for predicting smart grid stability, emphasizing the potential of neural networks in capturing complex patterns and relationships in grid data to enhance prediction accuracy and reliability [13]. Additionally, they highlighted the importance of optimizing neural network architectures and training processes to achieve accurate smart grid stability predictions. Mohsen et al. developed an efficient artificial neural network (ANN) with high testing accuracy and validated performance metrics for smart grid stability prediction [14].

This chapter proposes a novel approach for predicting the stability of a smart grid by designing a fractional feed-forward neural network model. The use of fractional-order derivatives enhances the tracking capability during training, testing, and validation. Instead of creating hybrid functions using fractional calculus, we developed activation functions such as Tansig, HardTansig, LiSHT, LeCunTanh, ArchTan, and Purelin using fractional-order derivatives. These functions were then incorporated into a single-layer neural network model, resulting in a fractional feed-forward neural network model. A simulation study was conducted on a smart grid to forecast stability, and the performance of the fractional feed-forward neural network was compared to that of the traditional model. The evaluation aimed to assess the effectiveness of the different activation functions by evaluating the prediction accuracy and stability assessment of the fractional-order model. This assessment demonstrated the advantages of our proposed approach.

7.2 SMART GRID DATA DESCRIPTION AND ANALYSIS

7.2.1 Dataset description

The simulation results of a 4-node network with star topology, as illustrated in Figure 7.1 and previously investigated by Schafer et al. [15], are analysed in this study. The dataset contains 12 independent variables and one dependent variable, publicly available from the University of California Irvine (UCI). The original sample size of 5000 has been expanded to 60,000 to account for the grid's symmetric nature.

The dataset includes several independent variables, namely τ_1 through τ_4. These variables represent each participant's reaction time in the network and have values ranging from 0.5 to 10. Specifically, τ_1 corresponds to the supplier node, while τ_2 through τ_4 correspond to the consumer nodes. Additionally, the dataset includes P_1 through P_4, which indicates the nominal power produced (when positive) or consumed (when negative) by each participant. For consumers (P_2 through P_4), the values range between -2.0 and -0.5. To calculate the total power consumed, one should take the negative sum of P_2, P_3, and P_4, while the supplier node's power is represented by P_1. Further, the γ_1 values to γ_4 indicate the price elasticity coefficient for each participant, ranging from 0.05 to 1.00. Specifically, γ_1 refers to the supplier node, while γ_2 to γ_4 refer to the consumer nodes. The dependent variable, "Stability," determines the maximum real part of the characteristic differential equation root, indicating linear stability if negative and linear instability if positive. The dataset is generated from simulations without missing values, so there is no need to preprocess non-numerical or missing values since all variables are numerical. The dataset consists of figures that display the independent variables (Figure 7.2a–c) and the dependent variable "Stability" (Figure 7.2d), with a focus on the first 400 samples in the zoomed-in region. It is important to note that the variable values represent the real parts of the roots in the dynamic equation of the decentral smart grid control (DSGC) system [16].

7.2.2 Correlation Analysis

This study involves a thorough analysis of the smart grid dataset, utilizing Pearson's correlation matrix to determine the linear relationship between the independent variables (τ_j, P_j, γ_j) and the dependent variable (stability). The correlation coefficient is crucial in establishing the strength and direction of this relationship. Our findings are presented in Figure 7.3 and Table 7.1 (based on reference [17]), which categorizes correlation coefficient values into various ranges with specific interpretations. It is important to note that a value close to -1 or 1 signifies a very strong correlation, while values between -0.7 and -0.95 (or between 0.7 and 0.95) indicate a strong correlation. A correlation coefficient between -0.5 and -0.7 (or between 0.5 and 0.7) implies a moderate correlation, whereas values between -0.3 and -0.5 (or between 0.3 and 0.5) represent a weak correlation. Correlation coefficients near 0 indicate negligible correlation [18].

In the correlation matrix shown in Figure 7.3, each value represents the correlation coefficient between two variables. This helps to observe

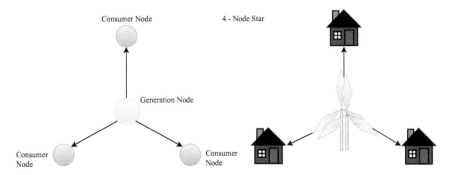

Figure 7.1   Architecture of 4-node star network.

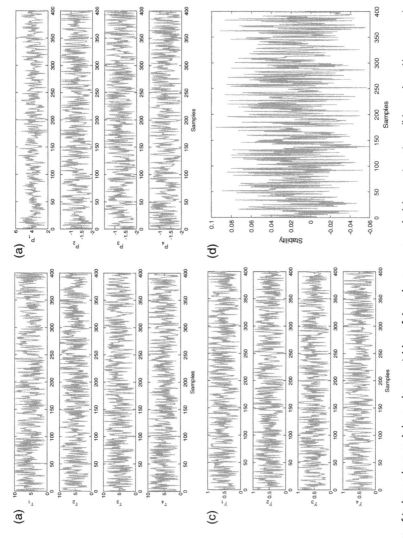

Figure 7.2 Dataset of independent and dependent variables of 4-node star network: (a) reaction time; (b) produced/consumed power; (c) price elasticity coefficient; and (d) stability.

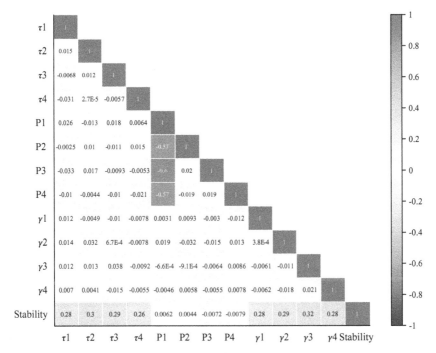

Figure 7.3 Correlation plot for dataset variables.

Table 7.1 Correlation coefficient values and their corresponding interpretations

Correlation coefficient	Strength of correlation
−1 to −0.95 or 0.95 to 1	Very strong correlation
−0.7 to −0.95 or 0.7 to 0.95	Strong correlation
−0.5 to −0.7 or 0.5 to 0.7	Moderate correlation
−0.3 to −0.5 or 0.3 to 0.5	Weak correlation
−0.3 to 0.3	Negligible correlation

the correlation levels between the variables. A positive value indicates a positive linear relationship, while a negative value represents a negative linear relationship. The magnitude of the correlation coefficient determines the strength of the relationship. Upon analysing the correlation matrix, it has been discovered a weak positive correlation between the variables (P_2 and γ_4), with a correlation coefficient of 0.015. Moreover, a slightly stronger positive correlation with a correlation coefficient of 0.018 between P_1 and γ_3 has been found. Conversely, a moderate negative correlation has been observed with a correlation coefficient of −0.57 between P_1 to P_2 and P_4. This analysis has provided valuable insights into the relationships between different variables in the smart grid simulated dataset.

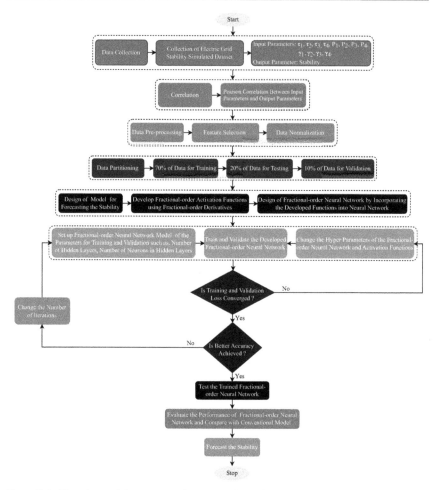

Figure 7.4 Flowchart of the proposed smart grid stability prediction model.

7.3 PROPOSED SMART GRID STABILITY PREDICTION MODEL

7.3.1 Methodology Flowchart

In this work, the proposed methodology for predicting the smart grid stability involves the steps shown in Figure 7.4. To begin the process, data collection is crucial. The UCI machine learning repository provided the necessary dataset in this specific instance. As depicted in the figure, this is the initial stage.

The Pearson correlation coefficients were computed for all parameters in the second step. Following that, data preprocessing plays a crucial role in enhancing both the data quality and the neural network's performance. Normalization is a frequently used technique for data preprocessing in neural network models. This work implements normalization to boost model performance by reducing bias towards higher-weighted values in the smart grid dataset. The normalization formula is employed to standardize data into a standardized range, which is represented as follows:

$$x_n = \frac{x - x_{\min}}{x_{\max} - x_{\min}} \tag{7.1}$$

In this context, x_n denotes the normalized data, while x represents the collected smart grid data set. Additionally, $x_{\min}$ and $x_{\max}$, respectively, indicate the minimum and maximum values present in the dataset. To make variables with different scales and units comparable and easier to analyse, the formula scales the data within the range of 0 and 1 by subtracting the minimum value and dividing by the range.

The data from the smart grid is preprocessed and divided into three subsets: 70% for training, 20% for testing, and 10% for validation. However, this partitioning can be adjusted depending on the specific needs of the dataset and the application domain. The next step involves designing a model for predicting smart grid stability. In this design, Tangential activation functions are developed using fractional-order derivatives, which are commonly used in this context. A fractional feed-forward neural network model is created using the developed activation functions. This model is trained and validated using the training and validation datasets, setting parameters such as the number of hidden layers and neurons in each layer. Suppose the loss for both the training and validation sets does not converge. In that case, the data quality and network structure can be improved by refining the datasets and modifying the model's hyperparameters and activation functions. This enhances the learning process and improves the neural network model's performance. Once the desired accuracy is achieved, the fractional-order neural network model has completed its learning process. However, if the desired accuracy is not reached, the network model must continue to be trained and validated up to a maximum number of iterations to improve its performance. Finally, the trained and validated fractional-order neural network model is tested using the testing dataset to evaluate its performance. Measures such as R^2 and MSE are used to assess the model's performance, and the results are compared with those of a conventional neural network model on the smart grid dataset. More details on the fractional feed-forward neural network model and the conventional network model used in this work are discussed below.

7.3.2 Fractional feed-forward neural network

This section computes the fractional ordering of the activation functions for Purelin and tangential functions using concepts of fractional calculus which is mentioned in reference [19] to enhance the feed forward neural network's tracking capabilities significantly.

7.3.2.1 Fractional-ordering tangential activation functions

The Tansig activation function, which is also referred to as the hyperbolic tangent Sigmoid function [20], is a widely used function in hidden layers for classification problems. It effectively transforms input values from the $(-\infty, +\infty)$ range to the $(-1, 1)$ range. The Tansig function is mathematically represented as follows:

$$f(x) = \frac{2}{1 + e^{-2x}} - 1. \tag{7.2}$$

When compared to the Sigmoid function, the Tansig function boasts a higher derivative, and its output values have an average of 0 as the input values approach 0. Consequently, utilizing the Tansig function during neural network training can greatly enhance the convergence rate and expedite the training process. Similar to the Sigmoid function, the Tansig function is also affected by the vanishing gradient issue, which can impede the training process. To tackle this problem, introducing non-linear components through the fractional ordering of the Tansig function can be helpful, as suggested in [21]. This can be achieved by rewriting the aforementioned equation using the MacLaurin series expansion.

$$f(x) = \sum_{n=0}^{\infty} \frac{4^n(4^n - 1)B_{2n}}{(2n)!} x^{2n-1}. \tag{7.3}$$

Then, the fractional ordering of the Tansig function for an order $\alpha \in (0, 1)$ can be computed as follows:

$$D^\alpha f(x) = g(x) = D^\alpha \sum_{n=0}^{\infty} \frac{4^n(4^n - 1)B_{2n}}{(2n)!} x^{2n-1},$$

$$g(x) = \sum_{n=0}^{\infty} \frac{4^n(4^n - 1)B_{2n}(2n - 1)!}{(2n)! \, \Gamma(2n - \alpha)} x^{2n-1-\alpha}. \tag{7.4}$$

Figure 7.5 shows the response of the Tansig activation function's fractional-order derivative for different values of α. The conventional function displays an S-shaped curve, similar to the Sigmoid function and its variations. However, the fractional-order derivative of the Tansig activation function exhibits an S-shaped curve only for lower values of α. For higher values of α, the function becomes non-linear due to the fractional ordering, which helps solve the vanishing gradient problem.

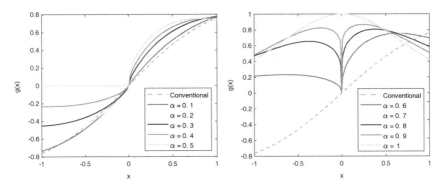

Figure 7.5 Response for a fractional-order derivative of the Tansig activation function for various orders of α.

The HardTansig function is a modified version of the commonly utilized Tansig function in deep learning applications. It provides computational benefits over the standard Tansig function while preserving its efficiency. Unlike the Tansig function, the HardTansig function has a value range of -1 to 1. Its definition is stated in references [20, 22].

$$f(x) = \begin{cases} -1 & \text{if } x < -1, \\ x & \text{if } -1 \leq x \leq 1, \\ 1 & \text{if } x > 1. \end{cases} \qquad (7.5)$$

The fractional-order derivative of the HardTansig function, for an order $\alpha \in (0, 1)$ can be computed as follows:

$$D^\alpha f(x) = g(x) = D^\alpha \begin{cases} -1 & \text{if } x < -1 \\ x & \text{if } -1 \leq x \leq 1 \,, \\ 1 & \text{if } x > 1 \end{cases}$$

$$g(x) = \begin{cases} \frac{-1}{\Gamma(1-\alpha)} x^{-\alpha} & \text{if } x < -1 \\ \frac{1}{\Gamma(2-\alpha)} x^{1-\alpha} & \text{if } -1 \leq x \leq 1 \,. \\ \frac{1}{\Gamma(1-\alpha)} x^{-\alpha} & \text{if } x > 1 \end{cases} \qquad (7.6)$$

The response of the fractional-order derivative of the HardTansig activation function for various values of (α) is shown in Figure 7.6, as compared to the conventional derivative. The plot reveals that the functions have non-zero gradients only during specific intervals, determined by (α), while maintaining zero gradients at other times. This characteristic of the function helps address the vanishing gradient problem, as long as most units operate within intervals where the gradient is equal to 1. Moreover, the responses indicate that the fractional-order derivative introduces non-linearity into

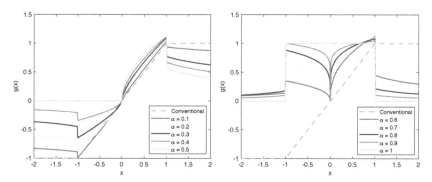

Figure 7.6 Response for a fractional-order derivative of the HardTansig activation function for various orders of α.

the function, which is beneficial for tackling the vanishing gradient problem.

The LiSHT function, a variation of the widely used Tansig function in deep learning, addresses the "dead ReLU" issue. This problem arises when the ReLU activation function becomes inactive for negative inputs, resulting in a zero gradient and preventing weight updates during backpropagation. The LiSHT function solves this problem by multiplying the input element-wise with the hyperbolic tangent. Unlike ReLU activation functions, the LiSHT function operates within the range of $[-1, 1]$, ensuring that negative gradients are not eliminated. This characteristic helps optimize learning and training stability in deep neural networks. Mathematically, the LiSHT function can be expressed as the product of the input and the Tansig function [22],

$$f(x) = x \cdot \delta(x), \tag{7.7}$$

where $\delta(x)$ represents the Tansig function which is defined in Equation (7.2) as follows:

$$\delta(x) = \frac{2}{1 + e^{-2x}} - 1. \tag{7.8}$$

Alternatively, the LiSHT function Equation (7.7) can be written using the MacLaurin series expansion as:

$$f(x) = \sum_{n=0}^{\infty} \frac{4^n(4^n - 1)B_{2n}}{(2n)!} x^{2n}. \tag{7.9}$$

To determine the fractional ordering of the LiSHT activation function, one can calculate α within the $(0, 1)$ range using Eq. (5) mentioned in the reference [19].

$$D^\alpha f(x) = g(x) = D^\alpha \sum_{n=0}^{\infty} \frac{4^n(4^n - 1)B_{2n}}{(2n)!} x^{2n},$$

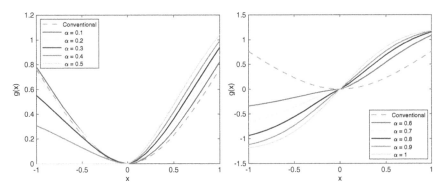

Figure 7.7 Response for a fractional-order derivative of the LiSHT activation function for various orders of α.

$$g(x) = \sum_{n=0}^{\infty} \frac{4^n(4^n - 1)B_{2n}\Gamma(2n + 1)}{(2n)!\,\Gamma(2n - \alpha + 1)}x^{2n-\alpha}. \qquad (7.10)$$

The response shown in Figure 7.7 illustrates the response of the LiSHT activation function's fractional-order derivative for different values of α, in comparison to the conventional response. It is evident that the conventional LiSHT produces a positive output response. The fractional ordering of LiSHT displays similar behaviour for lower α values, while for higher α values, the response indicates that fractional ordering introduces more non-linearity than other activation functions.

The LeCunTanh activation function, introduced by Yann LeCun, is a variant of the hyperbolic tangent function. It is mathematically defined as follows [18]:

$$f(x) = 1.7159 \cdot \tanh\left(\frac{2}{3}x\right), \qquad (7.11)$$

where tanh is the hyperbolic tangent function defined as,

$$\tanh(x) = \frac{(e^x - e^{-x})}{(e^x + e^{-x})}. \qquad (7.12)$$

Yann LeCun determined the constants for the LeCunTanh function through empirical observations and experimentation. The purpose of these constants is to maintain an output variance close to 1, since the gain of the Sigmoid function is nearly 1 over its acceptable range. The LeCunTanh function has a broader range than the traditional Tansig function, spanning from -1.7159 to 1.7159. This expanded range enables the activation function to represent a greater range of values, preventing output neuron saturation. However, it is important to note that the LeCunTanh function is not zero-centred, which can cause gradient descent to be biased towards certain directions in the weight space, especially when used with other non-zero-centred layers.

To address the issue and capture a wider range of patterns and dynamics in the data, the LeCunTanh function can be fractionally ordered for added flexibility. This can be achieved by rewriting the equation mentioned above using the MacLaurin series expansion to obtain the fractional-order LeCun-Tanh function.

$$f(x) = 1.7159 \sum_{n=0}^{\infty} \frac{4^n(4^n - 1)(\frac{2}{3})^{2n-1}B_{2n}}{(2n)!} x^{2n-1}, \qquad (7.13)$$

Based on the series representation provided above, one can determine the LeCunTanh activation function's fractional-order derivative for an order $\alpha \in (0, 1)$ by utilizing Eq. (5) in [19]. The equation is as follows:

$$D^{\alpha} f(x) = g(x) = D^{\alpha} \left(1.7159 \sum_{n=0}^{\infty} \frac{4^n(4^n - 1)(\frac{2}{3})^{2n-1}B_{2n}}{(2n)!} x^{2n-1} \right),$$

$$g(x) = 1.7159 \sum_{n=0}^{\infty} \frac{4^n(4^n - 1)(\frac{2}{3})^{2n-1}B_{2n}\Gamma(2n)}{(2n)! \, \Gamma(2n - \alpha)} x^{2n-1-\alpha}. \qquad (7.14)$$

Figure 7.8 highlights the difference between the response of the fractional-order derivative of the LeCunTanh function and its conventional version. While the conventional version has a symmetric S-shaped curve suitable for modelling positive and negative inputs, the fractional-order derivative's response resolves the non-zero-centeredness issue for higher orders of α. Additionally, the function's responses are more flexible for different orders of α, enabling it to capture a wider range of patterns and dynamics in data. For lower orders of α, the response of the fractional-order derivative is similar to the conventional one.

The ArcTan function is a powerful activation function that effectively solves the vanishing gradient problem associated with the Tansig function. Although both functions are non-linear and map inputs to outputs in the $-\pi/2$ range to $\pi/2$, the ArcTan function maintains a more consistent gradient throughout its input range. This allows for enhanced stability and reliability in network performance. As a differentiable function, it can be effectively used in gradient-based optimization algorithms for training neural networks. Ultimately, the ArcTan function combines the benefits of the Tansig function, including non-linearity and a wide range of output values, while avoiding the vanishing gradient issue. This makes it an incredibly valuable activation function for deep learning applications. Mathematically, the ArcTan function is expressed as in [23].

$$f(x) = \tan^{-1}(x). \qquad (7.15)$$

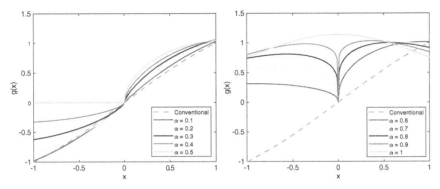

Figure 7.8 Response for a fractional-order derivative of the LeCunTanh activation function for various orders of α.

The above equation can be rewritten using MacLaurin series expansion as:

$$f(x) = \sum_{n=0}^{\infty} \frac{(-1)^n}{2n+1} x^{2n+1}. \tag{7.16}$$

Although the ArcTan activation function has its benefits, it can be difficult to optimize through gradient-based methods due to its non-monotonic behaviour with several turning points. However, this issue can be resolved by implementing fractional ordering within the ArcTan function. The fractional-order derivative considers the function's entire history, effectively smoothing out the non-monotonic behaviour. Moreover, this method enables the ArcTan function to display smoother derivatives, making it easier to optimize using gradient-based methods.

The fractional-order derivative of the ArcTan activation function for an order $\alpha \in (0, 1)$ can be computed as follows:

$$D^{\alpha} f(x) = g(x) = D^{\alpha} \sum_{n=0}^{\infty} \frac{(-1)^n}{2n+1} x^{2n+1},$$

$$g(x) = \sum_{n=0}^{\infty} \frac{(-1)^n \Gamma(2n+3)}{(2n+1)\Gamma(2n+2-\alpha)} x^{2n+1-\alpha}. \tag{7.17}$$

The response in Figure 7.9 illustrates how the fractional-order derivative of the ArcTan activation function performs in comparison to the traditional derivative across different α orders. It is clear from the results that the fractional-order derivative of ArcTan yields smoother derivatives, which makes it easier for gradient-based optimization techniques to work effectively. As a result, this approach is a promising solution to the non-monotonicity issue that is common with the ArcTan function.

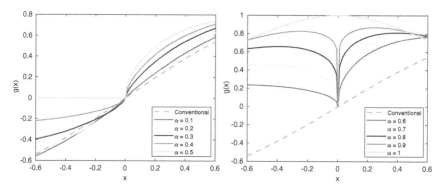

Figure 7.9 Response for a fractional-order derivative of the ArchTan activation function for various orders of α.

7.3.2.2 Fractional-ordering of purelin function

The Purelin function is a linear activation function that generates an output directly proportional to the input. It gives a value of Px when presented with an input of x, with P being a hyperparameter. The function acts as an identity function when P equals 1. According to [24], the Purelin function can be mathematically defined as follows:

$$f(x) = Px \qquad (7.18)$$

The Purelin function is a straightforward and effective method for regression problems requiring a linear relationship between input and output variables. However, its linearity can hinder when trying to capture complex correlations and non-linear connections between inputs and outputs. In most real-world scenarios, the relationship between inputs and outputs tends to be non-linear, making the Purelin function less applicable. To solve this issue, fractional-order derivatives can be used to introduce a non-linear component to the Purelin function, without compromising its linearity. This addition allows for a more comprehensive and intricate analysis of the non-linear interactions between input and output variables, making it more versatile for a broader range of applications.

The fractional ordering of the Purelin function for an order $\alpha \in (0, 1)$ can be computed as follows:

$$D^\alpha f(x) = g(x) = PD^\alpha x$$

$$g(x) = \frac{P}{\Gamma(2 - \alpha)} x^{1-\alpha} \qquad (7.19)$$

Figure 7.10 displays the response of the Purelin activation function's fractional-order derivative for different orders of α within the range of $(0, 1)$, alongside the standard response. The figure highlights how the function's

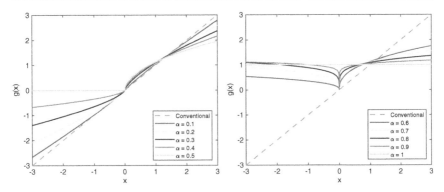

Figure 7.10 Response for a fractional-order derivative of the Purelin activation function for various orders of α.

activation property changes with varying α values. When $\alpha = 0$, the output remains linear, but for α values between $(0, 1)$, the function displays both linear and non-linear behaviour. This suggests that by utilizing fractional-order derivatives, the Purelin function can effectively capture both linear and non-linear relationships, making it a more versatile and suitable option for a broader range of applications.

A neural network model with fractional-order activation functions has been developed. These functions include FTansig, FHardTansig, FLiSHT, FLeCunTanh, FArchTan, and FPurelin. A fractional-order model can be created by incorporating them into a neural network. Figure 7.11 shows the architecture of the single-layer feed-forward neural network model with fractional-order functions. The "F" indicates the activation functions have been varied between conventional and fractional-order functions, while the Purelin function remains constant at the output layer.

To predict stability, a simulated study utilizes a fractional feed-forward neural network model that considers 12 input variables, including τ_j, P_j, and γ_j with j ranging from 1 to 4, as shown in Figure 7.11. The neural network includes an input layer with four nodes, a hidden layer with ten nodes, and an output layer with one node. The bias values for the hidden and output layers are noted as b [19].

The neural network model utilizes input variables to perform computations with fractional-order activation functions in the hidden layer and generate an output in the output layer. These activation functions, including FTansig, FHardTansig, FLiSHT, FLeCunTanh, FArchTan, and FPurelin, introduce non-linear components that enable the network to capture intricate relationships and non-linear interactions between the input and output variables. By incorporating fractional-order activation functions, the model can handle complex and non-linear datasets, thus improving its performance in stability forecasting tasks. This work employs the mean square error (MSE) and coefficient of determination (R^2) as performance measures,

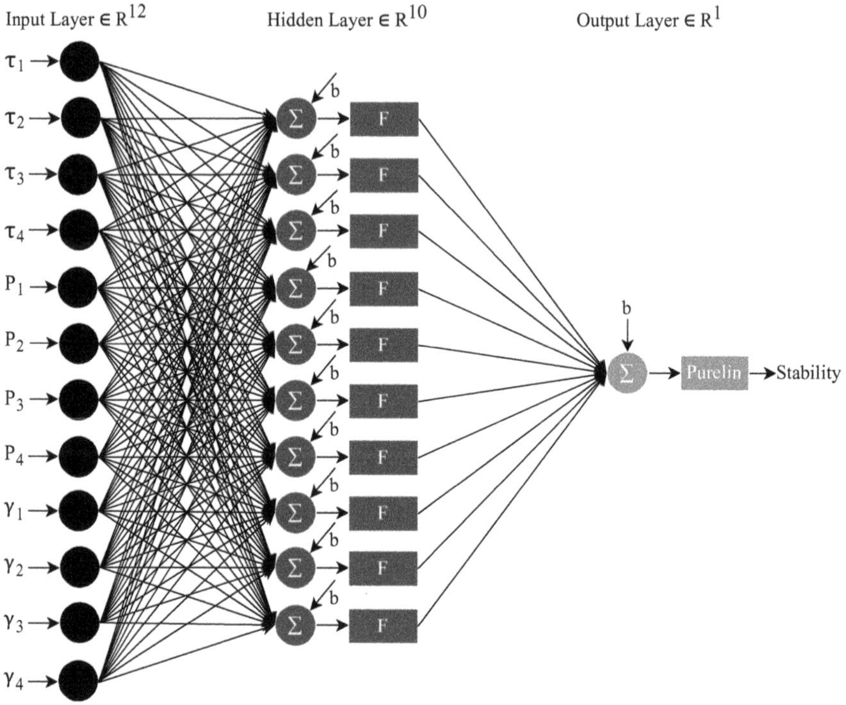

Input Layer $\in R^{12}$ Hidden Layer $\in R^{10}$ Output Layer $\in R^{1}$

Figure 7.11   Architecture of fractional feed-forward neural network model.

which have been calculated accordingly.

$$\text{MSE} = \frac{1}{N}\sum_{i=1}^{N}(Y_i - \widehat{Y_i})^2,$$

$$R^2 = 1 - \frac{\sum_{i=1}^{N}(Y_i - \widehat{Y_i})^2}{\sum_{i=1}^{N}(Y_i - \overline{Y_i})^2}, \tag{7.20}$$

In this equation, "N" represents the total number of samples. Y_i refers to the actual values, while the predicted values are denoted by $\widehat{Y_i}$. Lastly, $\overline{Y_i}$ represents the average value of predicted values.

7.4 RESULTS AND DISCUSSION

In this section, the findings and analyses of the neural network model for predicting stability using conventional and fractional-order tangential activation functions at the hidden layer and Purelin activation function at the output layer across different derivative order (α) values are presented.

Table 7.2 illustrates the comparison of the performance of the conventional and fractional tangential activation functions in terms of training, testing, and validation metrics for stability prediction. The measured performance metrics are R^2 and MSE for the training, testing, and validation datasets.

For the derivative order of 0, "HardTansig" emerges as the most effective function, consistently displaying high R^2 values and low MSE across training, testing, and validation. On the contrary, "Tansig" generally underperforms, yielding the lowest R^2 and higher MSE values compared to the other functions. The Tansig function displays an R^2 value of 0.6008 during training, 0.6169 during testing, and 0.6209 during validation, with corresponding MSE values. However, the HardTansig function, depicted in Figures 7.12–7.14, outperforms the Tansig function with R^2 values of 0.9065, 0.9075, and 0.9097, respectively. The LiSHT and LeCunTanh functions also demonstrate good performance, but the ArchTan function surpasses them with R^2 values of 0.9168, 0.9218, and 0.9226, as shown in Figures 7.15–7.17.

As the derivative order increases to 0.1, "LeCunTanh" and "ArcTan" also prove to be competitive, delivering high R^2 values and low MSE. "Tansig" still lags behind with the least favourable R^2 and higher MSE. At higher derivative orders (0.2, 0.3, 0.4, 0.5, 0.6, 0.7, 0.8, and 0.9), "HardTansig" consistently performs exceptionally well, showcasing the highest R^2 and lowest MSE among the functions. Conversely, "Tansig" consistently exhibits the poorest performance, displaying the lowest R^2 and higher MSE. However, at $\alpha = 0.5$ the HardTansig function, depicted in Figures 7.18–7.20, outperforms the Tansig function with R^2 values of 0.9769, 0.9782, and 0.9723, during training, testing, and validation, respectively. Furthermore, at $\alpha = 0.8$, HardTansig performs good with R^2 values of 0.9602, 0.9632, and 0.9605 during training, testing, and validation, respectively, are shown in Figures 7.21–7.23. In addition, at $\alpha = 0.2$, the LeCunTanh function also demonstrate better performance, with R^2 values of 0.9589, 0.9621, and 0.9661 during training, testing and validation, as shown in Figures 7.24–7.26.

According to the study, using fractional-order tangential activation functions in the hidden layer, while keeping the Purelin activation function constant in the output layer with various α values, can enhance the performance in terms of R^2 and MSE. This indicates that the fractional-order activation functions are more effective in the designed model than conventional tangential functions. The study also shows that incorporating fractional-order derivatives in neural networks can overcome the limitations of traditional activation functions, such as the inability to differentiate and the vanishing gradient problem. These limitations often make it difficult to use gradient-based techniques, leading to inactive activation functions with negative inputs and slow network training. However, it is important to note that the choice of the most appropriate activation function may differ

Table 7.2 Performance comparison of tangential activation functions with developed
functions in the neural network model at various α values

Derivative order α	Function Hidden layer	Training R^2	Training MSE	Testing R^2	Testing MSE	Validation R^2	Validation MSE
0	Tansig	0.6008	0.0976	0.6169	0.0941	0.6209	0.0831
	HardTansig	0.9065	0.0268	0.9075	0.0263	0.9097	0.0253
	LiSHT	0.5661	0.1027	0.5987	0.0961	0.5865	0.0968
	LeCunTanh	0.9082	0.0262	0.9094	0.0261	0.9114	0.0255
	ArcTan	0.9168	0.0239	0.9218	0.0231	0.9226	0.0214
0.1	Tansig	0.6333	0.0891	0.6498	0.0878	0.6751	0.0844
	HardTansig	0.8949	0.0298	0.9007	0.0291	0.9052	0.0285
	LiSHT	0.5013	0.1144	0.5231	0.1082	0.5082	0.1119
	LeCunTanh	0.9291	0.0205	0.9313	0.0204	0.9399	0.0177
	ArcTan	0.9321	0.0196	0.9345	0.0192	0.9368	0.0184
0.2	Tansig	0.9103	0.0337	0.9132	0.0325	0.9145	0.0318
	HardTansig	0.9292	0.0271	0.9315	0.0253	0.9301	0.0257
	LiSHT	0.6325	0.1189	0.6489	0.1099	0.6672	0.1068
	LeCunTanh	0.9589	0.0156	0.9621	0.0151	0.9661	0.0128
	ArcTan	0.9367	0.0238	0.9398	0.0228	0.9374	0.0246
0.3	Tansig	0.9275	0.0272	0.9331	0.0259	0.9318	0.0256
	HardTansig	0.9388	0.0234	0.9407	0.0223	0.9478	0.0195
	LiSHT	0.6450	0.1152	0.6548	0.1107	0.6903	0.1077
	LeCunTanh	0.9436	0.0211	0.9525	0.0186	0.9555	0.0182
	ArcTan	0.8813	0.0442	0.8873	0.0414	0.8864	0.0404
0.4	Tansig	0.8809	0.0442	0.8826	0.0432	0.8618	0.0478
	HardTansig	0.9423	0.0222	0.9448	0.0205	0.9433	0.0209
	LiSHT	0.6503	0.1131	0.6574	0.1124	0.6643	0.1058
	LeCunTanh	0.9544	0.0173	0.9556	0.0171	0.9507	0.0193
	ArcTan	0.6954	0.1026	0.7369	0.0899	0.7075	0.0861
0.5	Tansig	0.8484	0.0553	0.8614	0.0506	0.8409	0.0547
	HardTansig	0.9769	0.0086	0.9782	0.0089	0.9723	0.0099
	LiSHT	0.5462	0.1395	0.5991	0.1242	0.6014	0.1338
	LeCunTanh	0.9575	0.0165	0.9579	0.0159	0.9425	0.0204
	ArcTan	0.6554	0.1119	0.6773	0.1044	0.7315	0.0967
0.6	Tansig	0.8612	0.0515	0.8695	0.0493	0.8597	0.0445
	HardTansig	0.9323	0.0232	0.9454	0.0209	0.9452	0.0205
	LiSHT	0.7475	0.0861	0.7573	0.0838	0.7368	0.0911
	LeCunTanh	0.9102	0.0313	0.9162	0.0344	0.8957	0.0361
	ArcTan	0.6199	0.1234	0.6316	0.1165	0.5954	0.1213
0.7	Tansig	0.8797	0.0441	0.8838	0.0439	0.8727	0.0464
	HardTansig	0.9497	0.0193	0.9543	0.0177	0.9587	0.0151
	LiSHT	0.7488	0.0851	0.7737	0.0819	0.7589	0.0819
	LeCunTanh	0.6094	0.1248	0.6269	0.1187	0.5597	0.1198
	ArcTan	0.5599	0.1353	0.5628	0.1333	0.5997	0.1222
0.8	Tansig	0.8973	0.0376	0.9091	0.0355	0.9059	0.0362
	HardTansig	0.9602	0.0154	0.9632	0.0138	0.9605	0.0148
	LiSHT	0.7471	0.0883	0.7442	0.0825	0.7137	0.0919
	LeCunTanh	0.7402	0.0884	0.7473	0.0844	0.7558	0.0882
	ArcTan	0.6396	0.1172	0.6441	0.1161	0.6122	0.1662

Continued

Table 7.2 Continued

Derivative order α	Function Hidden layer	Training		Testing		Validation	
		R^2	MSE	R^2	MSE	R^2	MSE
	ArcTan	0.5599	0.1353	0.5628	0.1333	0.5997	0.1222
	Tansig	0.9402	0.0231	0.9385	0.0228	0.9408	0.0218
	HardTansig	0.9478	0.0201	0.9521	0.0189	0.9397	0.0233
0.9	LiSHT	0.7418	0.0899	0.7512	0.0832	0.7679	0.0779
	LeCunTanh	0.7406	0.0904	0.7431	0.0831	0.7535	0.0791
	ArcTan	0.6892	0.1024	0.7109	0.0996	0.6619	0.1126

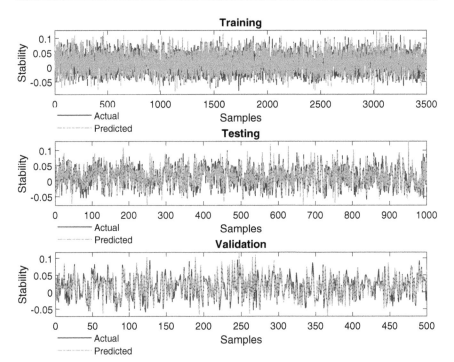

Figure 7.12 Performance of HardTansig function for training, testing, and validation.

depending on the specific problem and the characteristics of the available data.

7.5 CONCLUSION

A fractional feed-forward neural network model for predicting the stability of smart grids has been developed in this chapter. The model utilizes fractional-order tangential activation functions, including commonly used functions like Tansig, HardTansig, LiSHT, and LeCunTanh. These functions improve the accuracy of smart grid stability predictions by incorporating

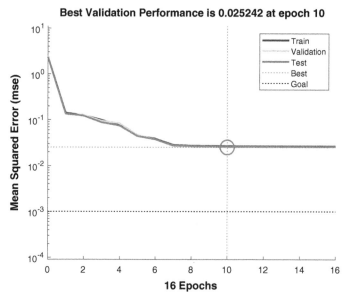

Figure 7.13   MSE plot for training, testing, and validation.

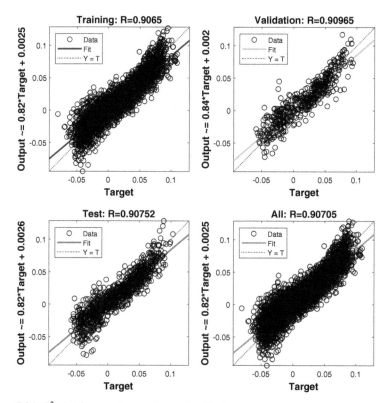

Figure 7.14 R^2 plot for training, testing, and validation.

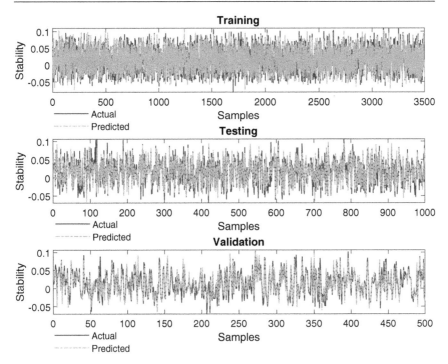

Figure 7.15 Performance of ArchTan function at $\alpha = 0$ for training, testing, and validation.

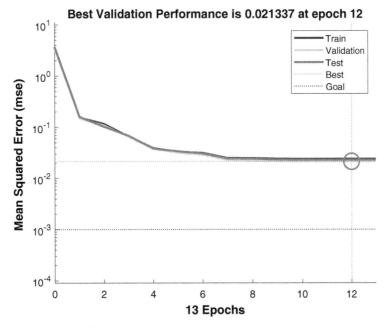

Figure 7.16 MSE plot for training, testing, and validation.

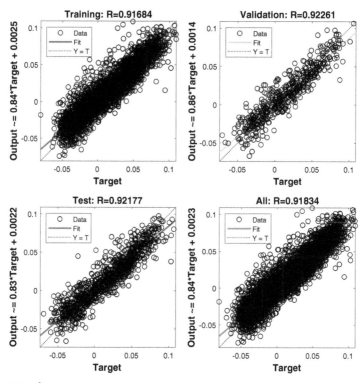

Figure 7.17 R^2 plot for training, testing, and validation.

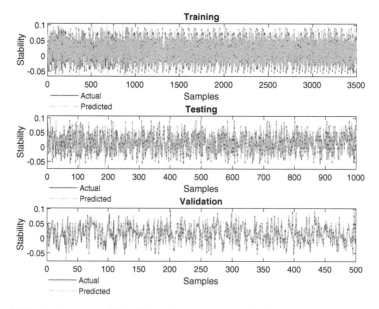

Figure 7.18 Performance of HardTansig function at $\alpha = 0.5$ for training, testing, and validation.

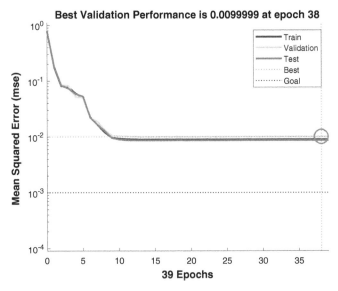

Figure 7.19 MSE plot for training, testing, and validation.

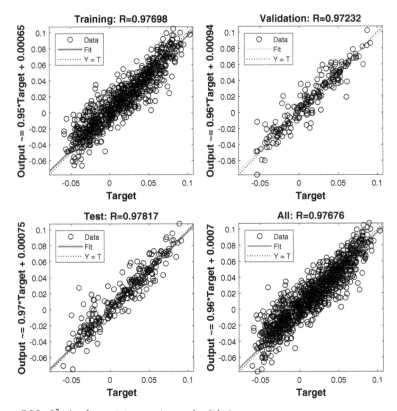

Figure 7.20 R^2 plot for training, testing, and validation.

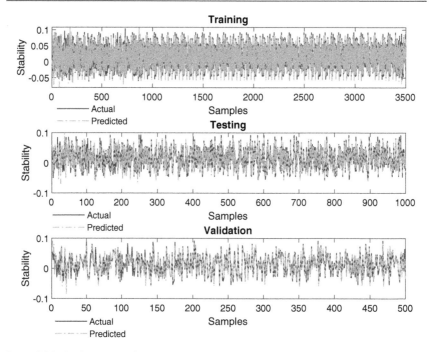

Figure 7.21 Performance of HardTansig function at $\alpha = 0.8$ for training, testing, and validation.

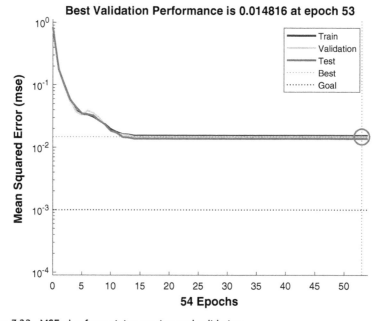

Figure 7.22 MSE plot for training, testing, and validation.

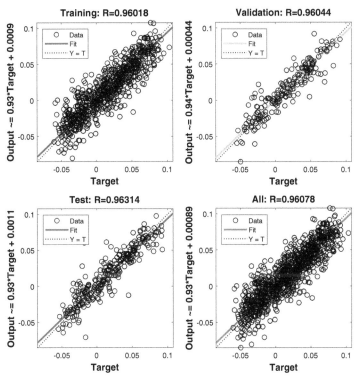

Figure 7.23 R^2 plot for training, testing, and validation.

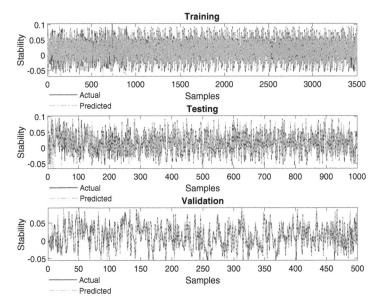

Figure 7.24   Performance of the LeCunTanh function at $\alpha = 0.2$ for training, testing, and validation.

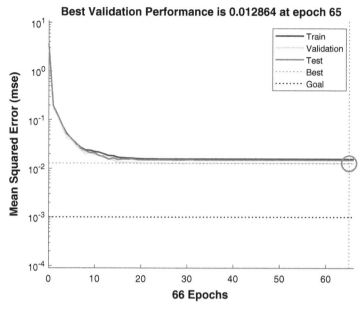

Figure 7.25 MSE plot for training, testing, and validation.

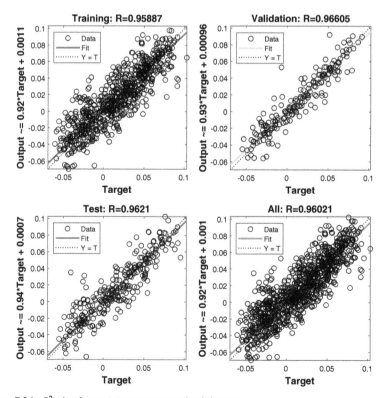

Figure 7.26 R^2 plot for training, testing, and validation.

fractional-order derivatives. To evaluate the effectiveness of the developed functions, simulations were conducted on a smart grid. The simulations involved comparing the stability forecasting results of the developed fractional-order functions with conventional functions at the hidden layer while keeping the purelin function constant at the output layer of the neural network. Performance metrics such as MSE and R^2 were employed to evaluate the stability forecasting accuracy across training, testing, and validation datasets. The results show that the ArchTan function at $\alpha = 0$ exhibited better performance, with high R^2 values of 0.9168, 0.9218, and 0.9226, and low MSE values of 0.0239, 0.0231, and 0.0214 during training, testing, and validation, respectively. Additionally, the HardTansig function at $\alpha = 0.5$ performed best, achieving high R^2 values of 0.9769, 0.9782, and 0.9723, along with low MSE values of 0.0086, 0.0089, and 0.0099 during training, testing, and validation datasets, respectively. These results demonstrate the effectiveness of the developed fractional-order tangential activation functions in accurately forecasting the stability of smart grids.

REFERENCES

1. Hamid Gharavi and Reza Ghafurian. *Smart Grid: The Electric Energy System of the Future*, volume 99. IEEE, Piscataway, NJ, 2011.
2. Kieran McLaughlin, Ivo Friedberg, BooJoong Kang, Peter Maynard, Sakir Sezer, and Gavin McWilliams. Secure communications in smart grid: Networking and protocols. In *Smart Grid Security*, Florian Skopik and Paul Smith, pages 113–148. Elsevier, Amsterdam, Netherlands, 2015.
3. AJ Dinusha Rathnayaka, Vidyasagar M Potdar, Tharam Dillon, and Samitha Kuruppu. Framework to manage multiple goals in community-based energy sharing network in smart grid. *International Journal of Electrical Power & Energy Systems*, 73:615–624, 2015.
4. Fahad Ahmed, Maheen Zahid, Nadeem Javaid, Abdul Basit Majeed Khan, Zahoor Ali Khan, and Zain Murtaza. A deep learning approach towards price forecasting using enhanced convolutional neural network in smart grid. In *Advances in Internet, Data and Web Technologies: The 7th International Conference on Emerging Internet, Data and Web Technologies (EIDWT-2019)*, pages 271–283. Springer, 2019.
5. Maheen Zahid, Fahad Ahmed, Nadeem Javaid, Raza Abid Abbasi, Hafiza Syeda Zainab Kazmi, Atia Javaid, Muhammad Bilal, Mariam Akbar, and Manzoor Ilahi. Electricity price and load forecasting using enhanced convolutional neural network and enhanced support vector regression in smart grids. *Electronics*, 8(2):122, 2019.
6. Faisal Mohammad and Young-Chon Kim. Energy load forecasting model based on deep neural networks for smart grids. *International Journal of System Assurance Engineering and Management*, 11:824–834, 2020.
7. Ye Hong, Yingjie Zhou, Qibin Li, Wenzheng Xu, and Xiujuan Zheng. A deep learning method for short-term residential load forecasting in smart grid. *IEEE Access*, 8:55785–55797, 2020.

8. Jian Li, Daiyu Deng, Junbo Zhao, Dongsheng Cai, Weihao Hu, Man Zhang, and Qi Huang. A novel hybrid short-term load forecasting method of smart grid using mlr and lstm neural network. *IEEE Transactions on Industrial Informatics*, 17(4):2443–2452, 2020.

9. Mamoun Alazab, Suleman Khan, Somayaji Siva Rama Krishnan, Quoc-Viet Pham, M Praveen Kumar Reddy, and Thippa Reddy Gadekallu. A multidirectional lstm model for predicting the stability of a smart grid. *IEEE Access*, 8:85454–85463, 2020.

10. Min Xia, Haidong Shao, Xiandong Ma, and Clarence W de Silva. A stacked gru-rnn-based approach for predicting renewable energy and electricity load for smart grid operation. *IEEE Transactions on Industrial Informatics*, 17(10):7050–7059, 2021.

11. Mohamed Massaoudi, Haitham Abu-Rub, Shady S Refaat, Ines Chihi, and Fakhreddine S Oueslati. Accurate smart-grid stability forecasting based on deep learning: Point and interval estimation method. In *2021 IEEE Kansas Power and Energy Conference (KPEC)*, pages 1–6. IEEE, 2021.

12. Paulo Breviglieri, Türkücan Erdem, and Süleyman Eken. Predicting smart grid stability with optimized deep models. *SN Computer Science*, 2:1–12, 2021.

13. Kishore Bingi and B Rajanarayan Prusty. Neural network-based models for prediction of smart grid stability. In *2021 Innovations in Power and Advanced Computing Technologies (i-PACT)*, pages 1–6. IEEE, 2021.

14. Saeed Mohsen, Mohit Bajaj, Hossam Kotb, Mukesh Pushkarna, Sadam Alphonse, Sherif SM Ghoneim, et al. Efficient artificial neural network for smart grid stability prediction. *International Transactions on Electrical Energy Systems*, 2023.

15. Benjamin Schäfer, Moritz Matthiae, Marc Timme, and Dirk Witthaut. Decentral smart grid control. *New Journal of Physics*, 17(1):015002, 2015.

16. Madiah Binti Omar, Rosdiazli Ibrahim, Rhea Mantri, Jhanavi Chaudhary, Kaushik Ram Selvaraj, and Kishore Bingi. Smart grid stability prediction model using neural networks to handle missing inputs. *Sensors*, 22(12):4342, 2022.

17. Haldun Akoglu. User's guide to correlation coefficients. *Turkish Journal of Emergency Medicine*, 18(3):91–93, 2018.

18. Yann A LeCun and Bottou. Efficient backprop. In *Neural Networks: Tricks of the Trade*, pages 9–48. Springer, Heidelberg, 2012.

19. Megha S Job, Priyanka H Bhateja, Muskan Gupta, Kishore Bingi, and B Rajanarayan Prusty. Fractional rectified linear unit activation function and its variants. *Mathematical Problems in Engineering*, 2022, 2022.

20. Shiv Ram Dubey, Satish Kumar Singh, and Bidyut Baran Chaudhuri. A comprehensive survey and performance analysis of activation functions in deep learning. arXiv preprint arXiv:2109.14545, 2021.

21. Bin Ding, Huimin Qian, and Jun Zhou. Activation functions and their characteristics in deep neural networks. In *2018 Chinese Control and Decision Conference (CCDC)*, pages 1836–1841. IEEE, 2018.

22. Chigozie Nwankpa, Winifred Ijomah, Anthony Gachagan, and Stephen Marshall. Activation functions: Comparison of trends in practice and research for deep learning. arXiv preprint arXiv:1811.03378, 2018.

23. Johannes Lederer. Activation functions in artificial neural networks: A systematic overview. arXiv preprint arXiv:2101.09957, 2021.

24. Sagar Sharma, Simone Sharma, and Anidhya Athaiya. Activation functions in neural networks. *Towards Data Science*, 6(12):310–316, 2017.

Chapter 8

Data-driven optimization framework for microgrid energy management

Mohamed Atef, Moslem Uddin, Md Masud Rana,
Md Rasel Sarkar, and G.M. Shafiullah

8.1 INTRODUCTION

Egypt is currently experiencing a substantial increase in population and a dynamic energy sector. Therefore, the country faces several challenges to provide reliable and sustainable electricity access, specially in regional areas. In recent years, microgrids (MGs) have become a viable option for addressing the aforementioned challenges and providing the country with numerous benefits. Due to their decentralized structure, MGs provide a robust and localized strategy for energy generation, distribution, and management. Effective EM is essential for MGs to efficiently allocate resources, maintain load balance, integrate RESs, facilitate DR, and strengthen grid resilience. Implementing EM strategy facilitates the efficient and reliable operation of MGs, thereby contributing significantly to the development of a sustainable and resilient energy infrastructure.

In recent years, there has been growing interest in MEM, leading to the development of advanced strategies. Gong et al. [2020] proposed an energy management (EM) system based on a stochastic framework for a hybrid AC/DC MG. However, the study did not investigate the technoeconomic benefits of their approach. Shen et al. [2016] proposed a DR-based EM to address uncertainties in wind, solar photovoltaic (PV), and loads. However, the effectiveness of DR relies on customer willingness. Robust techniques, such as those by Bersani et al. [2016], Hussain, Bui, and Kim [2016], Xu, Zou, and Niu [2013], Zhang et al. [2018], have been considered for EM applications in MG systems. However, their computational time requirements for designing uncertainty bounds and solving the problem make them impractical. Thirugnanam et al. [2018] proposed an EM technique based on battery energy storage system (BESS) for MGs, but only considered solar PV among RESs. Incorporating more RESs can help MG utilities minimize energy production costs per kWh by reducing diesel generator (DG) utilization. Liu et al. [2014] demonstrated a novel system operation technique for a small-scale DC MG integrated with RESs and introduced an EM strategy. However, further investigation is needed to verify the effectiveness of this method for AC MGs. Model predictive control-based

DOI: 10.1201/9781003470274-8

MEM has gained renewed interest Dagdougui and Sacile [2013], Ouammi et al. [2015], Parisio et al. [2017]. However, these studies have not directly addressed uncertainty. Scenario-based EM approaches considering system uncertainty have been proposed Hooshmand et al. [2012], Nguyen and Le [2013], Nikmehr, Najafi-Ravadanegh, and Khodaei [2017]. However, these methods require significant computational effort to derive solutions under different probable scenarios.

In the literature review, there are very few studies that address the EM problem in community MGs consisting of PV, DG, BESS, grid connections, and loads. The coordination of these MG components and the technoeconomic analysis in a real scenario have not been investigated yet. This indicates that research on this issue is still in its early stages, with numerous unresolved issues. Therefore, this study proposes an EM technique for coordinating PV, DG, BESS, grid connections, and loads in a community MG. Furthermore, the technoeconomic benefits are investigated. To the best of the authors' knowledge, no other studies have reported on the technoeconomic perspective of EM for a community MG in the Egyptian context, highlighting the main contribution of this study. In summary, the importance and originality of this study lie in the following aspects:

(i) A technoeconomic feasibility assessment is conducted to propose a PV/BESS/DG/grid-based hybrid MG for Sugar Beet Village, Egypt.

(ii) A data-driven EM strategy is introduced for a community MG that relies on RESs. The effectiveness of this framework is evaluated through a case study.

(iii) The analytical justification is provided for the significant capital investment required for installing hybrid MGs compared to relying solely on grid power supply.

(iv) The proposed MG's technoeconomic performance is assessed by comparing scenarios with and without the implementation of the EM strategy.

(v) Recommendations for all stakeholders are outlined to promote significant advancements and effective decision-making within the realms of MEM in a communiity setting.

(vi) Potential areas for future work are directed to advance the field of community-based MEM.

8.2 SITE DESCRIPTION, AVAILABLE RESOURCES, AND LOAD ASSESSMENT

8.2.1 Community under study

Sugar Beet Village is a rural community in the governorate of Elbeheira in the Nile Delta region of Egypt. Sugar beets, a significant agricultural crop in the region, inspired the naming of this community. The village is located near the Nile River and has a population of approximately 10,000 people, the majority of whom are involved in agriculture. The community has a school, a mosque, a health centre, and a market, among other public facilities. Due to the rural location of the community, there is limited access to electricity and other essential infrastructure. However, a reliable energy supply will aid in the development of the agricultural sector in this region, thereby boosting the nation's economy.

8.2.2 Climatic condition

Egypt's Sugar Beet Village has a typical Mediterranean climate characterized by warm summers and moderate winters. The climate is generally dry and sunny throughout the year, with minimal rainfall and high temperatures in the summer. The annual average temperature falls between 20 and 30 °C. July and August are typically the warmest months, with temperatures frequently exceeding 35 °C. In contrast, winters are moderate, with average temperatures between 15 and 20 °C. The region receives minimal rainfall, with the preponderance falling between November and February. In general, the climatic conditions of Sugar Beet Village in Egypt are favourable for agriculture, especially for crops such as sugar beet that flourish in warm, dry climates.

8.2.3 Solar potential

Solar radiation data for the research area was obtained from the National Renewable Energy Laboratory (NREL) prediction of the worldwide energy resources database. The research area lies between 26°49.2′N latitudes and 30°48.1′E longitudes The daily solar radiation values in this area vary between 6.37 and 2.26 kWh/m^2/d. Figure 8.1 illustrates the solar radiation data. Using the monthly average values specific to the research location, a simulation tool generates artificial hourly solar radiation. The tool utilizes the Graham method, taking into account only the latitude and monthly averages provided. Figure 8.1 showcases the solar radiation profile throughout the year.

8.2.4 Load estimation

The village's electricity demand is determined by analysing the energy consumption patterns of appliances and the typical durations for which they are used in the village. The study takes into account households of various sizes, ranging from medium-sized households with three family members to larger households with seven members. The investigation assumes a typical family size of five members. There are a total of 200 households included in the analysis, which equates to approximately 1000 individuals. Three categories are considered for load estimation: households, community facilities, and businesses. For each consumer class, the load of a single user is determined by multiplying the wattage of each appliance by its daily utilization duration.

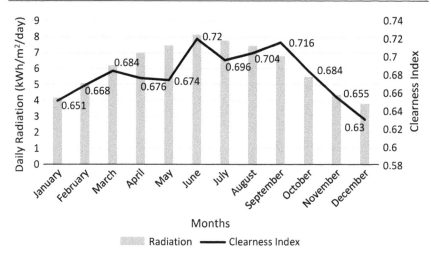

Figure 8.1 Average solar radiation and clearness index for Sugar Beet Village, located in Egypt.

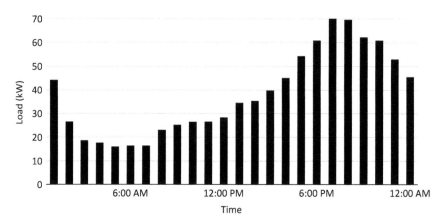

Figure 8.2 Estimated hourly load for Sugar Beet Village, Egypt.

The total village load is then calculated by adding up the individual consumption of all consumer classes. The study estimates a total daily load of 913.655 kWh, with a peak load of 119.57 kWh. This estimate represents the average daily load profile for each weekday of the month and year for all three consumer classes. This load profile is assumed to remain constant throughout the duration of the undertaking. Furthermore, any variations in power generation and consumption at different timescales (hourly, daily, monthly, and seasonal) are considered to be negligible. Table 8.1 provides a detailed breakdown of this load estimation. Additionally, Figure 8.2 presents the estimated hourly load profile for the community.

Table 8.1 Community load estimation – Sugar Beet Village, Alexandria Governorate, Egypt

Load category	Appliances	Qty	Watts (W)	Usage (hr/d)	TCL (d)
School (1)	Bulbs	14	15	5	
	Fan	12	50	6	
	Desktop	1	60	6	5130
	Printer	1	60	1	
	Photocopier	1	60	1	
Health clinic (1)	Bulbs	6	15	6	
	Vaccine refrigerator	1	80	24	3480
	Microscope	1	20	1	
	Electric heater	1	1000	1	
Community mills (1)	Flour mills	1	1000	5	5000
Households (200)	Bulbs (6 × 200)	1200	15	7	
	Roof fan (3 × 200)	600	50	16	
	TV (1 × 200)	200	150	4	894000
	Refrigerator (1 × 200)	200	150	16	
	Mob. charger (5 × 200)	1000	5	4	
	Water pump (1 × 200)	200	500	1	
Small businesses (20)	Bulbs	20	15	3	6045
	charger	20	5	1	

8.3 MODELLING OF MG

The multienergy community MG has the potential to provide a cost-effective solution to meet fluctuating real-time energy demands effectively without any energy deficit. In addition, it has the potential to offer reliable access to electricity in rural areas. Figure 8.3 shows the schematic diagram of the proposed multienergy MG's for Sugar Beet Village, Egypt. Detailed technical specifications and economic information for the components of the MG are summarized in Table 8.2. Each energy source's modeling approach is discussed in subsequent sections.

8.3.1 PV

Flat PV panels were chosen for this study due to their easy availability in the local market. The impact of temperature on the power output of PV modules was taken into consideration during the estimation process. To calculate the module's output, the following equation was utilized:

$$P_{\mathrm{pv}} = P_{\mathrm{pv}}^{\mathrm{r}} \times f_{\mathrm{pv}} \left(\frac{\Psi}{\Psi_{\mathrm{std}}} \right) \left[1 + \alpha^{\mathrm{P}}(T_0 - T_{\mathrm{std}}) \right] \tag{8.1}$$

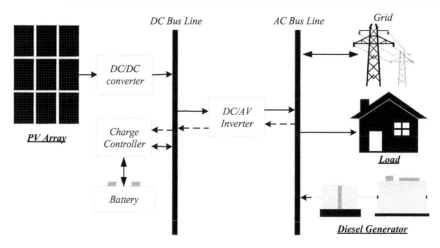

Figure 8.3 Schematic diagram of the proposed MG for Sugar Beet Village, Egypt.

Table 8.2 Technical characteristics and economic data for MG components

MG components	Characteristics	Values	Unit
PV	Nominal power, P_{pv}	1 kW	kW
	Derating factor	80	%
	Capital cost	2,540	$/kW
	Replacement cost	2,540	$/kW
	O&M cost	100	$/kW
	Lifetime	20	Year
DG	Nominal capacity, C_{deg}	60	kW
	Capital cost	800	$/kW
	Replacement cost	800	$/kW
	O&M cost	0.03	$/h/kw
BESS	Nominal capacity, C_{batt}	1	kWh
	Nominal voltage, V_{batt}	24	V
	Roundtrip efficiency, η_{RT}	90	%
	DOD	80	%
	Capital cost	700	$/kW
	Replacement cost	700	$/kW
	O&M cost	10	$/yr/kWh
	Lifetime	10	Year
CON	Nominal capacity	1	kW
	Conversion efficiency, η_{inv}	95	%
	Capital cost	300	$/kW
	Replacement cost	300	$/kW
	O&M cost	0	$/yr
	Lifetime	15	Year

8.3.2 BESS

The battery bank in the system has a nominal capacity of C_{nom} (in Ah) and is capable of discharging up to the predefined maximum depth of discharge (DOD) as determined by the system designer during the optimal sizing process.

$$C_{min} = DOD \times C_{nom} \qquad (8.2)$$

The state of charge (SOC) of the BESS is influenced by the power requirements of the PV system, DG, and loads. Throughout the simulation period, the SOC is accumulated based on these factors, as described below:

$$C_{batt}(t) = C_{batt}(t-1) + \eta_{batt} \left\{ \frac{P_{batt}(t)}{V_{batt}^b} \right\} \times t \qquad (8.3)$$

8.3.3 DG

For this research, a Caterpillar DG with a capacity of 60 kW was employed. The hourly fuel consumption of the DG (k_{con}^f) in litres per hour is modelled using a linear law based on the power output required by the load.

$$k_{con}^f(t) = A_{dg}P_{dg}^r(t) + B_{dg}P_{dg}^o(t) \qquad (8.4)$$

The two coefficients A_{dg} and B_{dg} are provided by the manufacturer.

8.3.4 Power converter

In the proposed MG framework, a power converter is necessary to ensure a continuous flow of power between the system and the load. The rating of the power converter is determined using Equation (8.5).

$$kW_{cov} = kW_{max} \times \eta_{cov} \qquad (8.5)$$

8.4 PROBLEM FORMULATION

The optimization problem formulated for the case study MG with PV, DG, grid, and BESS as follows:

- Objective function:

$$Obj1 = \min\{LCOE\} \qquad (8.6)$$
$$Obj2 = \min\{NPC\} \qquad (8.7)$$
$$Obj3 = \min\{(1 - RL)\} \qquad (8.8)$$

$$Obj4 = \min \{(1 - RF)\} \tag{8.9}$$

$$Obj = k_1 \times Obj1 + k_1 \times Obj2$$
$$+ k_3 \times Obj3 + k_4 \times Obj4 \tag{8.10}$$

- Constraints:

   a. *Energy balance constraint:*

$$P_{pv} + P_{cg} + P_{batt} + P_d = 0 \tag{8.11}$$

   b. *BESS SOC constraint:*
      (i) $SOC_{min} \leq SOC \leq SOC_{max}$
   c. *Reliability constraints:*
      (i)   Unmet load = 0%

The weights $k1, k2, k3,$ and $k4$ are adjusted to reflect the relative importance of each objective.

8.5 PROPOSED EM FRAMEWORK

EM participation is essential for attaining cost-effective energy scheduling and enhancing energy security. The proposed EM framework's power balance equation can be represented as:

$$P_d(t) = P_{cg}(t) + P_{pv}(t) + P_{batt}(t) \tag{8.12}$$

where $P_d(t)$ represents the real power demand of the MG at time t, where t ranges from 1 to N (corresponding to 8760 hours). A flowchart illustrating the proposed EM strategy is presented in Figure 8.4.

8.5.1 Economic dispatch

A DG is employed as a backup generation unit to ensure a reliable energy supply to remote communities during natural disasters, peak demand periods, and localized blackouts. If the power capacity from the grid is zero at any given time t, the DG will be activated to maintain a continuous power supply to the load. Consequently, the power balance equation can be expressed as follows:

$$P_{dg}(t) + P_{pv}(t) + P_{batt}(t) - P_d(t) = 0 \tag{8.13}$$

8.5.2 Application of storage-based DR

The EM block in the system utilizes load, generation, and market information to effectively manage power flow, generation output, utility grid

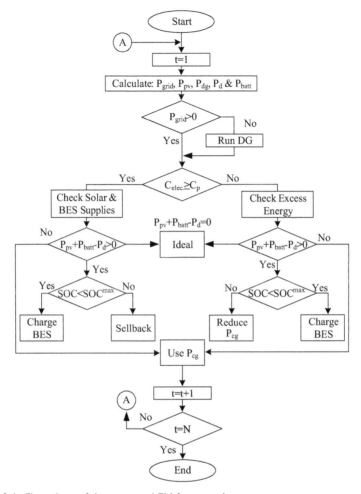

Figure 8.4 Flow chart of the proposed EM framework.

consumption levels, and dispatchable energy sources. The depicted electricity prices (C_{elec}) in Figure 8.5 are categorized as peak price (C_p) and off-peak price (C_{op}). In this study, any electricity price equal to or above 20 cents per kilowatt-hour ($) is considered as the peak price.

Operational mode 1: When $C_{elec.} \geq C_p$, the EM block reduces energy consumption from the utility grid and, if there is excess energy, sells it back to the grid to maximize economic benefits. If the energy surplus during the peak period, calculated as $P_{pv}(t) + P_{batt}(t) - P_d(t)$, is greater than zero, the excess energy is either stored in the BESS for future use if the SOC is below the minimum SOC threshold (SOC_{min}) or sold to the grid. However, if $P_{pv}(t) + P_{batt}(t) - P_d(t)$ is less than zero, the system purchases energy from the grid if available; otherwise, the DG is operated to meet the load demand. In the

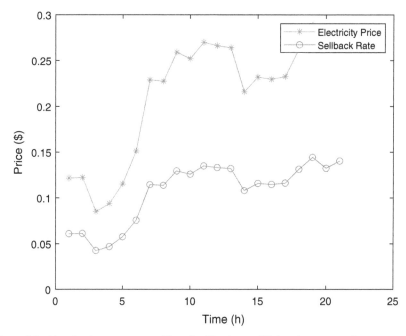

Figure 8.5 Hourly electricity price ($) and sellback rate ($) for the case study community.

scenario where the sum of solar PV power generation (P_{pv}) and BESS power discharge (P_{batt}) equals the real power demand (P_d), the system operates optimally without any transactions involving the purchase or sellback of electricity from/to the grid.

Operational mode 2: When $C_{elec.} \leq C_p$, excess energy is calculated using the following equation:

$$P_{exc}(t) = P_{pv}(t) + P_{bes}(t) - P_d(t) \tag{8.14}$$

In the condition when $P_{exc} > 0$, the BESS will store the excess energy for future use if $SOC < SOC_{min}$. However, EM block denies the BESS to absorb power if $SOC \leq SOC_{min}$. Therefore, the excess energy will be sold to the grid. However, if $P_{exc} < 0$, the system purchases energy from the grid if available; otherwise, the DG is operated to meet the load demand. In the scenario where $P_{exc} = 0$, the system operates optimally without any transactions involving the purchase or sellback of electricity from/to the grid.

8.5.3 Evaluation metrics

This study considers multiple performance metrics to assess the effectiveness of the MG system following the implementation of the EM application.

Table 8.3 Overall optimization results of community MGs

Case	Grid	PV (kW)	DG (kW)	BESS (kWh)	CON (kW)	NPC ($)	LCOE ($/kWh)	OPEX ($)	CAPEX ($)	RF (%)
1	✓	0	0	0	0	867253	0.209	67008	1000	-
2	✓	43.9	60	136	39.1	926397	0.156	50966	267535	17.3
3	✓	6.29	60	8	0.317	723863	0.125	50527	70673	0.266

The metrics included in this study are the net present cost (NPC), levelized cost of electricity (LCOE), fuel consumption, capital expenditure (CAPEX), emission reduction, operational expenditure (OPEX), renewable fraction (RF), and energy supply reliability.

8.6 RESULTS

The optimal EM is a challenging task for community MG with optimal utilization of multienergy sources and energy storage devices considering uncertain environment. This study simulates the grid-connected MG with PV, DG, and BES to quantify technoeconomic benefits of EM. The optimal power system configuration is also determined based on Equation 8.10. The community MG system is modelled with hybrid energies to cater the varying seasonal residential and commercial loads for the project site. In this investigation, the community MG system is designed to provide the minimum requisite operation reserve to ensure the grid reliability.

As part of this research, three different cases are investigated: Case 1 (base), Case 2 (MG with EM), and Case 3 (MG without EM). Case 1 represents the system relying on grid only. Case 2 includes the EM strategy, while Case 3 represents the system without the implementation of an EM strategy. The comparative analysis results are summarized in Table 8.3.

8.6.1 System capacity

In Case 2, the greater PV capacity (43.9 kW) indicates a greater utilization of solar energy resources, resulting in an increase in renewable energy generation and a decrease in reliance on non-renewable sources. In contrast, the DG capacity remains the same (60 kW) in both Case 2 and Case 3, indicating that the EM strategy has no direct effect on the size of the DG. However, the efficient utilization of the DG in Case 2 results in improved system performance, as evidenced by the absence of unmet load in Table 8.4. In a similar vein to PV systems, Case 2 demonstrates a superior capacity of BESS. Compared to Case 3, the BESS has a substantially larger capacity in the EM implementation. This improves energy storage and management,

Table 8.4 Comparative results of the proposed MGs with and without EM application

Scenario	Fuel (L/yr)	Unmet load (kWh/yr)	Capacity shortage (kWh/yr)	EE (%)
MG with EM (Case 2)	80594	0	0	0.293
MG without EM (Case 3)	94673	2205	2787	2.38

allowing the system to store excess energy during periods of high generation and use it during periods of low generation or high demand. As demonstrated in Table 8.4, the system exhibits improved dependability and adaptability.

Power converter capacity in Case 2 is significantly greater than Case 3. Specifically, the values are 39.1 kW and 0.317 kW, respectively. This disparity indicates that the system's management of power flow is more robust and efficient. Under the EM scheme, the increased capacity of the power converter enables the seamless integration of multiple energy sources and precise control of the power flow, ensuring the efficient fulfilment of load requirements.

8.6.2 Economic metrics with RF

In Case 2 of the analysis, the NPC is calculated to be $926,397, as opposed to 723,864 in Case 3. Case 2 has an LCOE of $0.156 per kWh, while Case 3 has an LCOE of $0.125 per kWh. Moreover, the OPEX is estimated to be $50,966 for Case 2 and $70,676 for Case 3. However, the RF for Case 2 is calculated to be 17.3%, whereas Case 3 attained only 0.266%. The higher NPC, LCOE, and CAPEX values in Case 2 indicate increased investment and operational costs associated with the EM strategy. However, these costs are justified by the higher RF (approximately 65 times greater than in Case 3), which represents a better utilization of RESs. The Case 2 demonstrates a stronger commitment to sustainability and reduced reliance on conventional energy sources.

8.6.3 Fuel consumption

The utilization of EM in the system leads to a noteworthy reduction in fuel consumption within the MG compared to the scenario where EM is absent. As depicted in Table 8.4, the incorporation of EM (Case 2) has the potential to decrease annual fuel consumption in the MG by approximately 14,079 litres when compared to the absence of EM (Case 3). These findings highlight the effective implementation of the EM strategy in Case 2, which successfully diminishes dependence on conventional fuel sources and generates significant fuel savings.

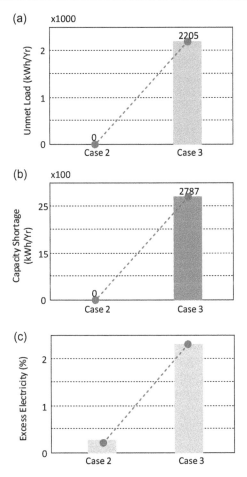

Figure 8.6 Comparative analysis results for case studies: (a) unmet load (kWh/year), (b) capacity shortage (kWh/year), and (c) excess electricity (%).

8.6.4 Unmet load

In Case 2, there is an absence of unmet load, indicating the effective fulfilment of load requirements throughout the year through the implemented EM strategy (as shown in Figue 8.6a). Conversely, Case 3 encounters a substantial unmet load of 2205 kWh/yr. This observation signifies that in the absence of the EM strategy, the system faces challenges in supplying adequate power to meet the demand.

8.6.5 Capacity shortage

Case 2 demonstrates a complete absence of capacity shortage, indicating the adequate design of the system's installed capacity to fulfil load requirements.

Table 8.5 Comparative results of MG's emissions with and without EM

Scenario	CO_2 (kg/yr)	CO (kg/yr)	UH (kg/yr)	PM (kg/yr)	SO_2 (kg/yr)	NO_2 (kg/yr)
MG with EM (Case 2)	268,405	1,434	58.0	5.74	766	237
MG without EM (Case 3)	317,447	1,685	68.2	6.74	910	283

In contrast, Case 3 experiences a significant capacity shortage of 2787 kWh/yr, emphasizing the inadequacy of the system's capacity to meet demand in the absence of the EM strategy. Furthermore, the simulation results illustrated in Figure 8.6b consistently reveal a zero unmet load even under severe conditions. This finding suggests that the MG possesses a substantial operational reserve, ensuring the ability to meet demand at all times.

8.6.6 Excess electricity

Figure 8.6c demonstrates that the MG integrated with EM exhibits a lower proportion of excess electricity than the MG without EM. Specifically, Case 2 exhibits a mere 0.293% of excess electricity, while Case 3 records a higher percentage of 2.38%. These findings highlight the effective optimization of generation and load requirements achieved through the implementation of the EM strategy. Consequently, the utilization of generated electricity becomes more efficient, leading to improved overall system performance.

8.6.7 Emissions

Upon examining the emissions data presented in Section 8.5, a clear distinction emerges when comparing MGs with and without EM. Case 2, which incorporates EM, demonstrates significantly reduced emissions across multiple categories when compared to Case 3, which lacks EM. Specifically, in terms of carbon dioxide emissions, Case 2 shows a reduction of 15.4% (49,042 kg/yr) compared to Case 3. Similarly, carbon monoxide emissions are reduced by 14.8% (251 kg/yr), unburned hydrocarbons by 14.9% (10.2 kg/yr), particulate matter by 14.8% (0.99 kg/yr), sulfur dioxide by 15.6% (144 kg/yr), and nitrogen dioxide by 16.6% (46 kg/yr) in Case 2. These results clearly support the effectiveness of the proposed EM approach in reducing emissions and promoting environmental sustainability in the MG system.

8.6.8 Sensitivity analysis and performance comparison

One of the primary objectives of the proposed EM framework is to ensure the reliability of the MG by establishing the necessary operational reserve. To assess system reliability, a sensitivity analysis is conducted to simulate sudden decreases in PV output and increased load. Specifically, the simulation involves a 20% reduction in PV panel output and a 10% increase in load. The results of the simulation demonstrate the MG's ability to maintain a consistent power supply, without any unmet load, even in challenging scenarios. This result indicates that the MG has a significant operational capacity, ensuring dependable completion of tasks under diverse conditions. These findings are further supported by the information presented in Table 8.4.

8.7 DISCUSSION

The results of the investigation offer valuable insights into the technoeconomic and environmental advantages of implementing an EM strategy in a community MG that incorporates multiple energy sources and energy storage devices. This section discusses the findings of this study.

8.7.1 System capacity enhancement

The Case 2 scenario illustrates the possibility of harnessing increased levels of renewable energy, reducing carbon emissions, and enhancing energy sustainability. This aligns with the global objective of transitioning towards cleaner energy sources.

8.7.2 Effective energy storage

The enhanced capacity of the BESS in Case 2 signifies a notable improvement in energy flexibility, which enables the storage of excess renewable energy. This enhances grid stability and reduces the need for backup from non-renewable sources, thereby mitigating the intermittency associated with renewable sources.

8.7.3 Efficient power flow control

Precise power flow control is instrumental in optimizing the utilization of multiple energy sources and guaranteeing a dependable energy supply. The enhanced capacity of the power converters in Case 2 fosters the incorporation of diverse energy resources, thereby leading to system efficiency.

8.7.4 Economic metrics with RF

In Case 2, the higher expenditures linked to the EM strategy are justified by the substantial rise in RF, underscoring the economic rationale for pursuing renewable energy technologies and energy management practices. This reinforces the long-term advantage of investing in sustainable energy sources.

8.7.5 Fuel consumption reduction

The reduction in fuel consumption is consistent with the environmental objectives of decreasing greenhouse gas emissions and enhancing energy security by relying less on finite fossil fuel resources.

8.7.6 Reliability and load fulfillment

A reliable MG is imperative to guarantee that the energy needs of the community are fulfilled. The EM strategy operates as a safety net against power interruptions, and improves the overall stability of the energy system.

8.7.7 Emissions reduction

Reducing emissions is of paramount concern for addressing climate change and improving air quality. The EM strategy is vital for achieving a more sustainable and clean energy system.

8.7.8 Sensitivity analysis

The maintenance of MG stability relies heavily on its capability to adapt to unforeseen changes in both generation and load. The implementation of the EM strategy significantly improved the ability of MGs to respond to variations and disturbances.

8.8 RECOMMENDATIONS FOR STAKEHOLDERS

This section provides insightful recommendations for all stakeholders, including researchers, policymakers, and community members, which will aid in promoting significant advancements and effective decision-making within the realms of community-based MEM.

- Comprehensive stakeholder engagement: Engages a wide range of stakeholders including local residents, utility providers, government agencies, and private sector entities to ensure diverse perspectives and collective input. This holistic approach promotes the development of MEM strategies that are inclusive and consider the needs and aspirations of the entire community.

- Invest in sdvanced EM technologies: Communities and organizations should contemplate resource allocation for the acquisition of cutting-edge EM technologies and control strategies to maximize energy production, storage, and distribution. It is imperative to prioritize research and development to maintain leadership positions at the forefront of EM innovation.
- Promote community engagement: Encouraging active community participation in the planning and operation of MGs. Promote education on the advantages of MGs and EM to ensure widespread acceptance and cooperation.
- Develop regulatory support: Policymakers should enact regulatory frameworks that encourage the development of community MGs and EM strategies. Such frameworks should prioritize sustainability, resilience, and affordability to support the growth of these initiatives.
- Promote education and training: Establish educational programmes and training initiatives to impart the necessary knowledge and expertise to communities and professionals to manage and maintain MGs competently.
- Invest in grid-forming technologies: Contemplate the deployment of grid-forming technologies, particularly in locations with unreliable grid connections, to improve grid stability and resilience. It is prudent to consider investing in grid-forming technologies.
- Collaboration across sectors: Promote inter-sectorial collaboration by encouraging the formation of multidisciplinary teams comprising academia, industry, government agencies, and local communities with the shared objective of advancing research and development in the field of MEM.
- Stay-informed: Participate in conferences, workshops, and knowledge-sharing platforms to stay-informed about emerging trends, best practices, and technological advancements in the fields of MEM.

8.9 FUTURE DIRECTIONS

The findings of this study open various prospective avenues for further research and advancement in the field of community MGs and EM. This section highlights potential directions for future work.

- Advanced EM algorithms: Further research in the field of MEM should focus on the development and implementation of advanced EM algorithms and control strategies. This may involve utilizing machine learning and artificial intelligence techniques to optimize energy generation, storage, and distribution in real time while considering dynamic factors, such as weather patterns and user behaviour.

- Integration of energy markets: Future studies could explore the integration of community MGs into larger energy markets and grid systems through peer-to-peer energy-trading platforms or participation in DR programmes to enhance energy flexibility and economic benefits.
- Resilience and cybersecurity: Improving the resilience of community MGs, particularly in response to natural disasters and cyber threats, should be a top priority in future research. Therefore, it is essential to implement robust cybersecurity measures and disaster recovery plans to ensure continuous operation.
- Smart grid integration: Investigating the incorporation of community MGs with advanced smart grid technologies, such as smart meters, sensors, and sophisticated grid management systems, has the potential to enhance real-time monitoring and control capabilities.
- Environmental impact assessment: A comprehensive assessment of the long-term environmental impacts of EM strategies utilized in community MGs should be undertaken as a future extension of this research. This will enable quantification of carbon emissions and other pollutants over extended periods.
- Regulatory frameworks: Future work can explore the formulation of regulatory frameworks and policies that foster the integration of community MGs and EM strategies. Collaboration with policymakers to establish incentives for sustainable and resilient energy systems is a crucial aspect of this endeavour.
- Energy storage economics: In light of the findings of this research, future work may consider conducting an economic analysis of various energy storage technologies and their potential for cost reduction over time. Moreover, it is advisable to explore the viability of employing recycled or second-life batteries for energy storage in the MGs.
- Case studies and demonstrations: Further research may explore real-world applications and demonstrations of community-based MEM in various geographical and socio-economic settings to evaluate the scalability and adaptability of EM solutions.
- MG interconnection: Future studies could investigate the interconnection of multiple community MGs to form larger energy networks. Examining the challenges and potential advantages of creating interconnected MG clusters is an area of inquiry that should be pursued in future studies.
- Life cycle assessment: Conducting life cycle assessments of MG components and technologies is a critical aspect of ensuring their sustainability, as it allows for a comprehensive understanding of their environmental impact across all stages of their life cycle, from production to disposal. This information can then be used to identify areas for improvement and to implement strategies to enhance the sustainability of these components and technologies.

8.10 CONCLUSION

This study introduces a data-driven optimization framework for MEM considering DR and generation uncertainties. Findings reported in this study shed a new light on supplying secure, reliable, and affordable power in Egypt's regional and remote areas. The technoeconomic analysis highlights the benefits of incorporating EM strategy in community MG. It is found that proposed technique increased the penetration of renewable energy by about 17% which will significantly contribute to reduce carbon emissions. The comparative assessment shows that EM ensure zero unmet load in MG. It verifies that EM can provide reliable energy for the community in the event of natural disasters, during peak demand and localized blackout.

The current study forms a basis of MEM, however, the sophisticated EM techniques are not explored. Therefore, it would be interesting to include the advanced EM technique as future extension of this study.

REFERENCES

Bersani, Chiara, Hanane Dagdougui, Ahmed Ouammi, and Roberto Sacile. 2016. "Distributed robust control of the power flows in a team of cooperating microgrids." *IEEE Transactions on Control Systems Technology* 25 (4): 1473–1479.

Dagdougui, Hanane, and Roberto Sacile. 2013. "Decentralized control of the power flows in a network of smart microgrids modeled as a team of cooperative agents." *IEEE Transactions on Control Systems Technology* 22 (2): 510–519.

Gong, Xuan, Feifei Dong, Mohamed A Mohamed, Omer M Abdalla, and Ziad M Ali. 2020. "A secured energy management architecture for smart hybrid microgrids considering PEM-fuel cell and electric vehicles." *IEEE Access* 8: 47807–47823.

Hooshmand, Ali, Mohammad H Poursaeidi, Javad Mohammadpour, Heidar A Malki, and Karolos Grigoriads. 2012. "Stochastic model predictive control method for microgrid management." In *2012 IEEE PES Innovative Smart Grid Technologies (ISGT)*, 1–7. IEEE.

Hussain, Akhtar, Van-Hai Bui, and Hak-Man Kim. 2016. "Robust optimization-based scheduling of multi-microgrids considering uncertainties." *Energies* 9 (4): 278.

Liu, Baoquan, Fang Zhuo, Yixin Zhu, and Hao Yi. 2014. "System operation and energy management of a renewable energy-based DC micro-grid for high penetration depth application." *IEEE Transactions on Smart Grid* 6 (3): 1147–1155.

Nguyen, Duong Tung, and Long Bao Le. 2013. "Optimal energy management for cooperative microgrids with renewable energy resources." In *2013 IEEE International Conference on Smart Grid Communications (SmartGridComm)*, 678–683. IEEE.

Nikmehr, Nima, Sajad Najafi-Ravadanegh, and Amin Khodaei. 2017. "Probabilistic optimal scheduling of networked microgrids considering time-based demand response programs under uncertainty." *Applied Energy* 198: 267–279.

Ouammi, Ahmed, Hanane Dagdougui, Louis Dessaint, and Roberto Sacile. 2015. "Coordinated model predictive-based power flows control in a cooperative network of smart microgrids." *IEEE Transactions on Smart Grid* 6 (5): 2233–2244.

Parisio, Alessandra, Christian Wiezorek, Timo Kyntäjä, Joonas Elo, Kai Strunz, and Karl Henrik Johansson. 2017. "Cooperative MPC-based energy management for networked microgrids." *IEEE Transactions on Smart Grid* 8 (6): 3066–3074.

Shen, Jingshuang, Chuanwen Jiang, Yangyang Liu, and Jie Qian. 2016. "A microgrid energy management system with demand response for providing grid peak shaving." *Electric Power Components and Systems* 44 (8): 843–852.

Thirugnanam, Kannan, See Kim Kerk, Chau Yuen, Nian Liu, and Meng Zhang. 2018. "Energy management for renewable microgrid in reducing diesel generators usage with multiple types of battery." *IEEE Transactions on Industrial Electronics* 65 (8): 6772–6786.

Xu, Jun, Yuanyuan Zou, and Yugang Niu. 2013. "Distributed predictive control for energy management of multi-microgrids systems." *IFAC Proceedings Volumes* 46 (13): 551–556.

Zhang, Bingying, Qiqiang Li, Luhao Wang, and Wei Feng. 2018. "Robust optimization for energy transactions in multi-microgrids under uncertainty." *Applied Energy* 217: 346–360.

Chapter 9

Optimization of controllers for sustained building

Gaurav Kumar

9.1 INTRODUCTION

The aim of using a semi-active control system is to improve the structure's response by mitigating the effects of dynamic loadings, including earthquakes. Because of non-linear actuator dynamics, resonance conditions, dynamic coupling, uncertainties, and measurement limitations, this is a challenging task. For protecting structures from seismic and wind loadings, numerous controllers have been utilized for semi-active control schemes. The efficiency of these controllers is good for certain structures but not so good for others. To provide an appropriate command signal to the magnetorheological damper (MRD), a realizable, simple, fault-tolerant, optimal, and robust controller must be developed.

Dyke et al. (2002) discussed the passive ON/OFF controllers [1]. These controllers possess only two states and are easy to implement with the limitation of having only one level of voltage, regardless of the fact that whether the structure is moving away from or towards the centre. Agrawal and Cha (2013) proposed two new methods, namely simple passive control (SPC) and decentralized output feedback polynomial control (DOFPC) [2]. The authors discovered that the DOFPC controller outperformed the passive ON/OFF controller. A quasi-bang-bang controller was also proposed, in which the voltage to the MRD is decided by two different rules. These rules are decided by the structure's reference position. Here, the intermediate voltage levels between the centre and the extreme have been ignored. As a solution, a modified quasi-bang-bang controller approach was proposed. The variable weights in this control law are like a fuzzy logic controller (FLC). This controller's weights are constant and decided by trial and error, which is a disadvantage [3].

Many researchers used proportional-integral-derivative (PID) family controllers for structure control and compared their performance to that of more advanced controllers such as sliding mode controllers (SMC) or FLC [4–6]. According to these studies, PID controllers can be more efficient in hybrid form, i.e., PID with SMC or with FLC. Guclu (2006) designed a PID controller and a sliding mode controller (SMC) to reduce the vibration

DOI: 10.1201/9781003470274-9

of a four-degree-of-freedom structure. The PID controller's efficiency was compared to that of the SMC. The author compared the results using time histories for the first and third floors, specifically the earthquake that occurred in 1999 in Marmara, Turkey [7]. Two proportional-derivative (PD) controllers were used by R. Guclu et al. (2008) to control two actuators installed on the first and top floors of a 15-story structure model. On the other hand, the performance of the PID family controllers was found to be unsatisfactory because proper tuning of the PID gain was difficult [8].

Further, the H-infinity control method is a popular, robust linear controller. The H-infinity represents the Hardy space as defined by the infinity norm. To solve the optimization problem, the authors implement a numerically efficient solution algorithm. The authors also discovered that the H-infinity control algorithm performs admirably in multi-input multi-output (MIMO) systems. Liu et al. (2015) considered various time delays in their work [9]. The H-infinity controller is created by employing a matrix inequality and parameter adjustment method. The SMC is regarded as a non-linear control algorithm. It is an excellent choice for structural control because it is resistant to model uncertainties and extremely robust. Yakut et al. (2011) presented a hybrid approach using SMC with neural network [10]. The hybrid controller has beneficial characteristics of both, the robustness of SMC and the flexibility of neural network. The other advantage of using neural network is to mitigate the chattering effect of SMC. Further, the authors also presented the fuzzy logic concept to avoid the chattering effect in SMC [11]. The resulting controller is known as the fuzzy sliding mode controller (FSMC). The authors created FSMC to reduce the chattering effect of the SMC while supporting the SMC's robustness and insensitivity to parameter changes. The authors found that the efficiency of SMC is satisfactory, but the chattering effect is caused by imperfections in the sliding surface due to high-frequency switching. This may cause damage to mechanical components, such as actuators [2], [12–15]. The chattering effect is a significant issue in the SMC algorithm and should be avoided. According to the reported literature [16–18], this can be accomplished in two ways, namely, by appropriately smoothing the control force. Sliding mode control is achieved by employing a continuous SMC algorithm.

The fuzzy logic controller (FLC) is recognized as a model-free approach for structural control. FLC design entails the intelligent selection of input and output variables, data manipulation methods, membership functions, and rule-based design. To control seismic vibrations, Ramaswamy et al. (2001) created an FLC for active tuned mass dampers [19]. Choi et al. (2004) presented a study that used a semi-active fuzzy control technique on the ground floor of a three-story structure, resulting in a decrease in seismic response [20]. Choi et al. (2005) proposed an FLC based on modern time-domain control theory for structural seismic vibration mitigation. The authors investigate the observer capability of the Kalman filter for state estimation. In addition, the authors used a low-pass filter to eliminate the spillover issue [21]. Das et al. (2012) proposed an FLC-based algorithm for mitigation of seismic vibrations using the semi-active control scheme [22]. The authors fuzzified the MRD characteristics, removing the need for mechanical modelling of the MRD. However, the FLC has some drawbacks in parameter determination, such as membership functions, control rules, and insufficient stability analysis. In addition, some researchers worked on a hybrid approach to designing the controller with FLC [23–30]. Also, the FLC and neural network (NN) controllers do not consider feedback from the actuator (MRD), and these controllers rely solely on structural response measurements, which are difficult to obtain accurately during a seismic event.

Furthermore, the linear quadratic regulator (LQR) controller is a well-known and well-studied controller. In optimal control theory, a cost function must be minimized to achieve the desired or optimum results. This cost function is determined by the controller and system parameters. To determine the control signal (voltage or current) for the MRD, Dyke et al. (1996) proposed the LQR controller in conjunction with the on-off switch-based controller [31]. Due to the highly non-linear nature of the MRD, which is difficult to model precisely, and it is difficult to maintain the relationship between the input voltage and output force of the MRD. As a result, most of the proposed control strategies modify the voltage through ON-OFF rules rather than using a model. This controller became well known in structural control and is commonly referred to as the "clipped-optimal controller." Using the damper's force as feedback, the authors created a command signal (voltage) for the MRD using the LQR controller. The command signal (voltage) was set using the clipped control law by comparing the desired force to the force of the available damper [32–34].

In the presence of this noise, the system states are unknown for the application of the control action. As a result, an observer known as a Kalman filter is used to estimate the system's states. Linear quadratic Gaussian (LQG) refers to the combination of the Kalman observer and the LQR controller. Jansen et al. (2002) compared the performance of controllers such as the Lyapunov controller, decentralized bang-bang controller, and moderated homogeneous friction procedure to the performance of the clipped-optimal LQG controller used in a semi-active control scheme [35]. In this study, clipped-optimal LQG/LQR controllers were found to be the most effective. However, determining the optimal weighting matrix for optimal performance remains a research topic. Panariello et al. (1997) proposed an algorithm for carrying up-to-date weighting matrices for the gain of the LQR controller from a database of documented earthquake excitations in this direction. The limitation of the preceding studies is the lack of an offline repository of known earthquakes [36].

Alavinasab et al. (2006) present an energy-based approach to determining the LQR controller's gain matrices. The authors worked to eliminate the need for the trial-and-error method of determining suitable gain matrices [37]. Basu et al. (2008) developed the modified time variable LQR (TVLQR) method, which involves updating weighting matrices with a constant multiplier using discrete wavelet transform (DWT) analysis. Although the weighting matrices in this method vary at resonance conditions, the constant multiplier was determined offline. As a result, offline data was still required [38]. Amini et al. (2013) presented a novel technique for determining the best control forces for an active tuned mass damper to solve this problem. This technique employed three distinct procedures: DWT, particle swarm optimization (PSO), and LQR [39].

The aim of this work is to create an optimized LQG controller by combining a maximum dominant period $\left(\tau_p^{\max}\right)$ approach with PSO in three steps. First, adaptive LQG controllers are developed by modifying their parameters in real time using PSO-$\tau_p^{\max}$ approaches. Second, the proposed controllers' performance is investigated using numerical simulations on a scaled three-story building with an MRD between the ground and first floors. Concurrently, the structural responses produced by the widely used LQR/LQG-based clipped-optimal controller are compared to the responses produced by the proposed controllers.

9.2 DEVELOPMENT OF MODIFIED LQG CONTROLLER USING THE PSO-τ_p^{MAX} APPROACH

A basic mathematical understanding of the LQG controller is presented before the modification of LQG. This controller is advised to be used in circumstances where uncertainties and noise are present as the states of the systems may not be available all the time as assumed in the LQR controller.

Assume a linear time invariant (LTI) system represented by Equations (9.1) and (9.2)

$$\dot{z} = Az + Bf + Ew \qquad (9.1)$$
$$y = Cz + Df + v \qquad (9.2)$$

where w and v are the disturbance input and measurement error, respectively. Both are assumed to be uncorrelated white Gaussian random processes with zero means. For this system, the cost function is defined as given in Equation (9.3):

$$J_i(z, u) = \frac{Lim}{t \to \infty} \left[\int_0^t \left(z^T Q_i z(t) + u^T R_i u(t) \right) d(t) \right] \qquad (9.3)$$

where w and v are the disturbance input and measurement error, respectively. Both are assumed to be uncorrelated white Gaussian random processes

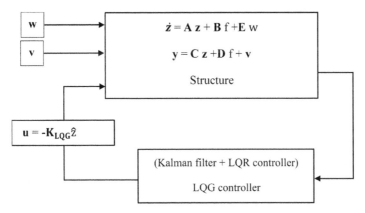

Figure 9.1   The block diagram of the LQG controller.

with zero means. For this system, the cost function is defined as given in Equation (9.3).

$$\dot{\widehat{z}} = A\widehat{z} + Bu + L_{Kal}\left(y - C\widehat{z} - Du\right) \qquad (9.4)$$

$$u = -K_{LQR}\widehat{z} \qquad (9.5)$$

Here, z is the observed state or the next state. As described earlier, the LQG controller is the combination of the LQR controller and the Kalman filter; the Kalman filter gain, L_{Kal}, and the LQR controller gain, K_{LQR}, are calculated separately using the algebraic Ricatti equation. These gains are given independently by Equations (9.6) and (9.7).

$$L_{Kal} = R^{-1}B^{T}P_{LQR} \qquad (9.6)$$

$$K_{LQR} = P_{Kal}V^{-1}C^{T} \qquad (9.7)$$

The Kalman filter is used to design an observer by measuring the available data. This observer reduces the spread of the estimated error probability density in the process. The block diagram for the LQG controller is shown in Figure 9.1.

Further, coming to the methodology to modify the LQG using PSO and τ_p^{max} approach, it is understood that the structure's response reflects similar properties of the earthquake excitation. So, the entire duration of the response $(0, t_i)$ is divided further into smaller time windows, with the ith window being (t_{i-1}, t_i). Largest predominant period τ_p^{max} is used to find the dominant frequency for each time window. This keeps the system always in the time domain, and thus the system becomes inherently fast. Originally, the idea of the largest predominant period τ_p was first introduced by Nakamura [40] to classify large and small earthquakes based on frequency content present in the earthquake signal. The parameter τ_p can be calculated from the acceleration time series for each time step in real time according to the following relations given in Equations (9.8–9.10).

$$\tau_{p,i} = 2\pi\sqrt{\frac{V_i}{A_i}} \tag{9.8}$$

$$V_i = aV_{i-1} + v_i^2 \tag{9.9}$$

$$A_i = aA_{i-1} + \left(\frac{dv}{dt}\right)_i^2 \tag{9.10}$$

Here, v_i is the recorded ground velocity, V_i is the smoothed ground velocity squared, A_i is the smoothed acceleration squared and the smoothing parameter a is having a value between 0 and 1. Largest predominant period τ_p^{max} is the maximum value of τ_p in the selected time window. Thus, Equation (9.11) can obtain the maximum dominant frequency of a selected time window.

$$f_d = \frac{1}{\tau_p^{max}} \tag{9.11}$$

This dominant frequency decides the quasi-resonance stances where the value of **R** is to be changed. Here, the PSO algorithm is used to find the optimal value of **R** that gives the optimum structural response with lesser control effort. PSO algorithm helps to find weighting matrices **R** on the quasi-resonant bands. The benefit of this specific local optimal solution is that it can change the estimation of matrix **R** on an odd frequency at which quasi-resonance occurs, unlike the clipped-optimal LQR which has a global value of **R** during an earthquake. The cost function to be minimized for this modified LQR problem is formulated by having state weighting matrix $\mathbf{Q_i}$ and control weighting matrix $\mathbf{R_i}$ for ith window and is given in Equation (9.12):

$$J_i(x, u) = \int_0^t \left(x^T Q_i x\,(t) + u^T R_i u\,(t)\right) dt \tag{9.12}$$

The result of this modified optimal control problem with cost function J_i leads to a control law given in Equation (9.13):

$$u = -G_i x \tag{9.13}$$

The solution of the Ricatti matrix differential equation for every windowed interval gives the gain matrix G_i and the anticipated control force required to counter the effect of quasi-resonance can be found by applying this gain of the ith window. The flow chart of the development of the adaptive LQR controller is shown in Figure 9.2. In this first, the earthquake excitation is loaded and divided in 1 sec wide (t_w) small window. The seismic

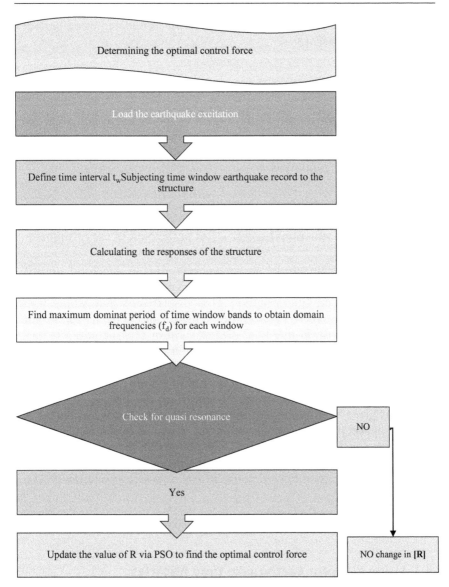

Figure 9.2 The flow chart of the development of adaptive LQR controller using PSO-τ_p^{max} approach.

responses of the structure have been calculated. These responses were used to calculate the domain frequency of each time window. This domain frequency will be compared with the natural frequency of the structure to check the resonance between them. At resonance, the magnitudes of the structural responses are the maximum which may lead to maximum damage to the structure. At this point, the maximum counterforce is required to minimize the damage. Hence, the control weighting matrix is updated using particle swarm optimization (PSO).

9.3 RESULTS AND DISCUSSION

A comprehensive performance analysis of the proposed controllers is carried out by comparing the structural responses of the three-story test structure obtained using the proposed controller and the conventional LQG controller under the following conditions:

(i)   Using different earthquake time histories.
(ii) Using an earthquake recorded in different soil conditions.
(iii) Considering a situation if power is lost at the peak of the earthquake.

There exist two main regulatory control objectives in structural control, namely acceleration mitigation and displacement mitigation. Acceleration mitigation is a serviceability criterion while displacement mitigation deals with structural integrity. The acceleration criterion allows higher robustness for the control algorithm due to the lesser concern of structural integrity. Though acceleration mitigation is important, displacement mitigation is a prevalent concern during earthquake excitations because structural integrity is at stake. For structural integrity, it is essential to minimize stresses and strains in structural members. Therefore, in the present discussion, emphasis is given to displacement mitigation. Further, a new parameter of the performance analysis, cumulative energy, confined in the displacement signal of the top floor is introduced. This parameter gives the maximum of the disruptive energy content of the displacement signal. The cumulative energy (W) for any continuous-time signal $x(t)$ is given by Equation (9.14):

$$W = \int_0^t |x(t)|^2 \, dt \tag{9.14}$$

9.3.1 Using different earthquake time histories

For analysis under this condition, the following three earthquake time histories are used.

a. 1940 El-Centro Valley earthquake
b. 1999 Chi-Chi Nantou County Taiwan earthquake
c. 1999 Gebze Turkey earthquake

Figure 9.3(a) displays the displacement response of the uncontrolled structure, while Figure 9.3(b) compares the uncontrolled displacement response

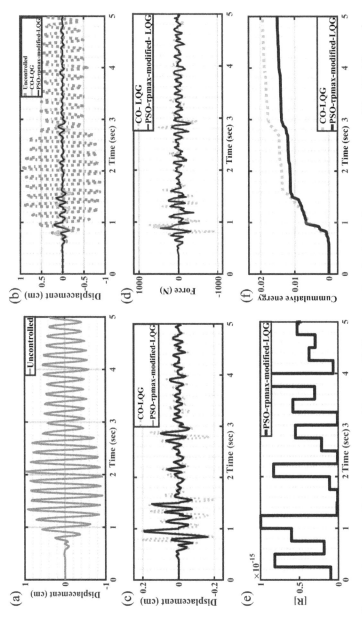

Figure 9.3 Structural responses for the structure subjected to El-Centro earthquake: (a) displacement response of the third floor of uncontrolled structure; (b) comparison of uncontrolled and controlled responses of the third floor using CO-LQG and PSO-τ_p^{max}-modified-LQG algorithms; (c) comparison of controlled responses of the third floor using CO-LQG and PSO-τ_p^{max}-modified-LQG algorithms; (d) control forces for the CO-LQG and the PSO-τ_p^{max}-modified-LQG; (e) variation of **R** with time; and (f) comparison of cumulative energies of the third floor's displacement by applying CO-LQG and PSO-τ_p^{max}-modified-LQG.

with the responses obtained using the CO-LQG and PSO-$\tau_p^{\max}$-modified-LQG controllers. Visual inspection of Figure 9.3(b) indicates a reduction in the displacement response. According to Table 9.1, this reduction in peak values is 78% with CO-LQG and 82% with the PSO-$\tau_p^{\max}$-modified-LQG controller. Furthermore, Figure 9.3(c) presents a comparison of the displacement achieved with the CO-LQG and PSO-$\tau_p^{\max}$-modified-LQG controllers, demonstrating consistent displacement reduction throughout the time history. Table 9.1 shows that the proposed controller achieves a 15% reduction in peak values of relative displacement for the first floor, 21% for the second floor, and 22% for the third floor compared to CO-LQG. Figure 9.3(e) exhibits the adaptive variation in R, where R remains constant for CO-LQG but shows variations in the proposed algorithm due to quasi-resonance. The proposed control algorithm achieves a 29% reduction in peak values of inter-story drift between the first and second floors, and a 33% reduction between the second and third floors compared to CO-LQG. Table 9.1 presents the reduction in peak values of absolute acceleration, indicating a 28% reduction for the first floor, 46% for the second floor, and 27% for the third floor with the proposed algorithm compared to CO-LQG. Importantly, all these reductions in structural responses are achieved using less control force, as depicted in Figure 9.3(d). The proposed controller utilizes 24% less force (peak value) to achieve these results compared to CO-LQG. Finally, Figure 9.3(f) illustrates the energy confined in the controlled signal of the relative displacement of the third floor with CO-LQG and the PSO-$\tau_p^{\max}$-modified-LQG.

The discussions regarding the Chi-Chi and Gebze earthquakes are presented, with specific figures illustrating the displacement response of the uncontrolled structure and a comparison between different control methods. In Figure 9.4(a), the displacement response of the third floor of the uncontrolled structure during the Chi-Chi earthquake is shown. Figure 9.4(b) compares the uncontrolled displacement response with the response obtained using the CO-LQG and PSO-$\tau_p^{\max}$-modified-LQG controllers. Visual inspection of Figure 9.4(b) suggests a reduction in the displacement response when using the proposed controllers. Similar comparisons are shown in Figure 9.4(c) for the Chi-Chi earthquake and Figure 9.5(c) for the Gebze earthquake. The results from Table 9.1 indicate the percentage reduction in peak values of relative displacement achieved by the proposed controller compared to CO-LQG. Under the Chi-Chi earthquake, the proposed controller achieved a reduction of 26% for the first floor, 23% for the second floor, and 20% for the third floor. For the Gebze earthquake, the reductions were 6% for the first floor, 18% for the second floor, and 22% for the third floor. The variations of the control weighting matrix $\mathbf{R}$ are shown in Figure 9.4(e) for the Chi-Chi earthquake and Figure 9.5(e) for the Gebze earthquake. Additionally, the inter-story drift for the Chi-Chi

Table 9.1 Peak responses of the structure due to conventional CO-LQG controller and PSO-τ_p^{max}-modified LQG controller

Control algorithm	El-Centro earthquake			Chi-Chi earthquake			Gebze earthquake		
	Uncontrolled	CO-LQG	PSO-τ_p^{max}-modified LQG	Uncontrolled	CO-LQG	PSO-τ_p^{max}-modified LQG	Uncontrolled	CO-LQG	PSO-τ_p^{max}-modified LQG
Displacement (cm)	0.55	0.12	0.10	0.14	0.02	0.015	0.074	0.0180	0.017
	0.83	0.19	0.15	0.22	0.04	0.031	0.117	0.0353	0.029
	0.97	0.22	0.17	0.27	0.05	0.040	0.138	0.0513	0.040
Inter-story drift (i_d) (cm)	0.55	0.12	0.10	0.14	0.02	0.015	0.074	0.018	0.017
	0.29	0.07	0.05	0.08	0.02	0.016	0.042	0.017	0.012
	0.14	0.03	0.02	0.05	0.01	0.009	0.022	0.016	0.011
Acceleration (cm/s²)	870	733	526	181	98	48	126	91	47
	1070	755	410	268	81	60	150	74	61
	1400	723	525	317	97	84	185	113	101
Force (N)	0	971	736	0	1178	1098	0	1278	1167

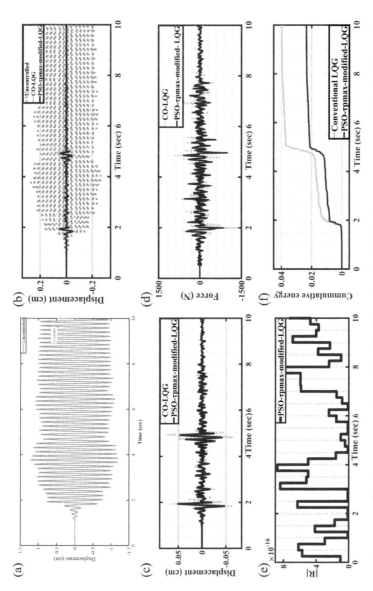

Figure 9.4 Structural responses for the structure subjected to Chi-Chi earthquake: (a) displacement response of the third floor of uncontrolled structure; (b) comparison of controlled responses of the third floor using CO-LQG and PSO-τ_p^{max}-modified-LQG algorithms; (c) comparison of uncontrolled and controlled responses of the third floor using CO-LQG and PSO-τ_p^{max}-modified-LQG algorithms; (d) control forces for the CO-LQG and the PSO-τ_p^{max}-modified-LQG; (e) variation of **R** with time; and (f) comparison of cumulative energies of the third floor's displacement by applying CO-LQG and PSO-τ_p^{max}-modified-LQG.

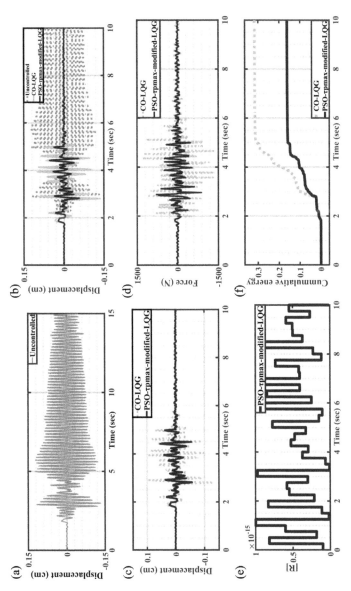

Figure 9.5 Structural responses for the structure subjected to Gebze earthquake: (a) displacement response of the third floor of uncontrolled structure; (b) comparison of controlled responses of the third floor using CO-LQG and PSO-τ_p^{max}-modified-LQG algorithms; (c) comparison of uncontrolled and controlled responses of the third floor using CO-LQG and PSO-τ_p^{max}-modified-LQG algorithms; (d) control forces for the CO-LQG and the PSO-τ_p^{max}-modified-LQG; (e) variation of **R** with time; and (f) comparison of cumulative energies of the third floor's displacement by applying CO-LQG and PSO-τ_p^{max}-modified-LQG.

earthquake showed a reduction of 20% between the first and second floors, and 10% between the second and third floors according to Table 9.1. For the Gebze earthquake, the reduction was 31% for both inter-story drifts (first-second floor and second-third floor. Analysing the performance of the proposed controller, comparisons were made with the CO-LQG (clipped-optimal linear quadratic Gaussian) controller for two different earthquakes: Chi-Chi and Gebze. Table 9.1 provides a summary of the results obtained.

For the Chi-Chi earthquake, the proposed controller demonstrated a significant reduction in inter-story drift. Specifically, there was a 31% reduction between the first and second floors, as well as between the second and third floors, compared to the CO-LQG controller. Table 9.1 also presents the absolute accelerations of all floors during both earthquakes. It can be observed that the proposed algorithm achieved notable reductions in peak acceleration values. Compared to the CO-LQG controller, there was a 51% reduction for the first floor, 25% reduction for the second floor, and 13% reduction for the third floor during the Chi-Chi earthquake. Similarly, for the Gebze earthquake, reductions of 48%, 17%, and 10% were achieved for the first, second, and third floors, respectively, by the proposed control algorithm.

To further illustrate the differences between the controllers, Figure 9.4(d) depicts the time histories of the control force for the Chi-Chi earthquake, while Figure 9.5(d) shows the same for the Gebze earthquake. It can be observed that the proposed controller required less force to achieve the results. Additionally, the cumulative energies of the displacement for the third floor were compared between the CO-LQG and the PSO-τ_p^{max}-modified-LQG controllers. These comparisons are shown in Figure 9.4(f) for the Chi-Chi earthquake and Figure 9.5(f) for the Gebze earthquake. Overall, the findings indicate that the proposed controller outperforms the CO-LQG controller in terms of inter-story drift reduction, peak acceleration reduction, and control force utilization. These results demonstrate the effectiveness and efficiency of the proposed algorithm in mitigating the effects of the Chi-Chi and Gebze earthquakes on the structure.

9.3.2 Using an earthquake recorded in different soil conditions

This earthquake record is taken from the Kyoshin network (K-NET). The soil type is determined according to the Federal Emergency Management Agency (FEMA)-356 based on the shear wave velocity (v_s). The performance analysis of the proposed controller is carried out for the structure subjected to the hard, medium, and soft soil. For the performance assessment in hard soil, the uncontrolled displacement response of the third floor of the structure is considered in Figure 9.6(a).

Figure 9.6(b) provides a comparison of the displacement responses of the third floor in an uncontrolled structure versus a semi-actively controlled

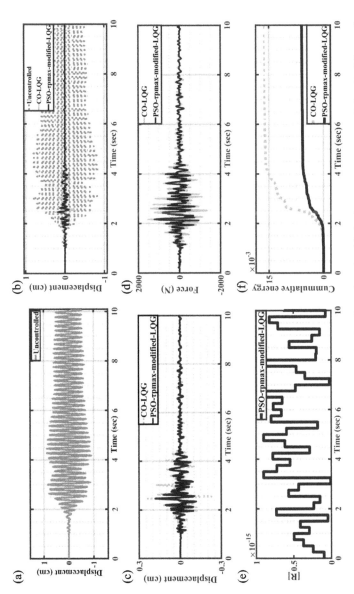

Figure 9.6 Structural responses for the structure subjected to hard soil earthquake: (a) displacement response of the third floor of uncontrolled structure; (b) comparison of controlled responses of the third floor using CO-LQG and PSO-τ_p^{max}-modified-LQG algorithms; (c) comparison of uncontrolled and controlled responses of the third floor using CO-LQG and PSO-τ_p^{max}-modified-LQG algorithms; (d) control forces for the CO-LQG and the PSO-τ_p^{max}-modified-LQG algorithm; (e) variation of **R** with time; (f) comparison of cumulative energies of the third floor's displacement by applying CO-LQG and PSO-τ_p^{max}-modified-LQG.

structure using two different control algorithms: CO-LQG and PSO-τ_p^{max}-modified-LQG. The purpose of this comparison is to evaluate the effectiveness of these control algorithms in mitigating the displacement response during a seismic event. The results show that both control algorithms significantly reduce the peak value of the displacement response compared to the uncontrolled structure. Specifically, CO-LQG achieves a 72% reduction, while the proposed PSO-τ_p^{max}–modified-LQG achieves an 80% reduction. Additionally, Figure 9.6(c) displays a comparison of the displacement response between CO-LQG and PSO-τ_p^{max}-modified-LQG. This comparison specifically focuses on the relative displacement response of the structure. The results demonstrate that the proposed PSO-τ_p^{max}-modified-LQG controller effectively reduces the relative displacement response. Table 9.2 further supports these findings by quantifying the reduction achieved by each controller. The proposed PSO-τ_p^{max}–modified-LQG controller outperforms CO-LQG by achieving a greater reduction in peak values of relative displacement: 46% for the first floor, 33% for the second floor, and 28% for the third floor. Overall, these findings highlight the efficacy of the proposed PSO-τ_p^{max}-modified-LQG control algorithm in reducing the displacement response of the structure, particularly in terms of relative displacement. The results demonstrate its superiority over the CO-LQG controller in mitigating the impact of seismic events.

The results presented in Table 9.2 demonstrate the impact of using the PSO-τ_p^{max}-modified-LQG controller and CO-LQG in the semi-active control scheme. The inter-story drift is reduced by 12% for the first-second floor and 25% for the second-third floor when applying the proposed controller. However, the reduction in absolute acceleration using the proposed controller is moderate compared to CO-LQG, with reductions of 4%, 2%, and 14% for the first, second, and third floors, respectively. Interestingly, the proposed controller achieves these reductions using 20% less force than the CO-LQG controller, as depicted in Figure 9.6(d) which compares the time histories of the forces used by both controllers. Figure 9.6(e) illustrates the variations of the control weighting matrix **R**, while Figure 9.6(f) compares the cumulative energy of the displacement. The comparison of cumulative energy indicates that the displacement signal of the third floor has less energy when using the proposed controller, thereby ensuring structural integrity.

For earthquakes recorded in medium soil, Figure 9.7(b) shows a comparison of the displacement time histories of an uncontrolled structure and controlled structures employing CO-LQG and the proposed control algorithm. Figure 9.7(c) further highlights the superiority of the proposed controller over CO-LQG by comparing the displacement responses over time. Referring to Table 9.2, the proposed controller achieves significant reductions in displacement compared to CO-LQG, with reductions of 53%, 47%, and 43% for the first, second, and third floors, respectively. Additionally, the inter-story drift is reduced by 14% and 17% for the first-second

Table 9.2 Peak responses due to CO-LQG and PSO-τ_p^{max}-modified-LQG for structure subjected to earthquakes recorded in different soil conditions

Control algorithm	Earthquake (hard rock)			Earthquake (medium soil)			Earthquake (soft soil)		
	Uncontrolled	CO-LQG	PSO-τ_p^{max}-modified-LQG	Uncontrolled	CO-LQG	PSO-τ_p^{max}-modified-LQG	Uncontrolled	CO-LQG	PSO-τ_p^{max}-modified-LQG
Displacement (cm)	0.66	0.13	0.07	0.60	0.38	0.18	0.99	0.22	0.15
	0.80	0.22	0.15	0.93	0.45	0.24	1.26	0.55	0.39
	0.89	0.25	0.18	1.20	0.51	0.29	1.53	0.76	0.49
Inter-story drift (i_d) (cm)	0.66	0.13	0.07	0.60	0.38	0.18	0.99	0.22	0.15
	0.14	0.09	0.08	0.33	0.07	0.06	0.27	0.33	0.24
	0.09	0.04	0.03	0.27	0.06	0.05	0.27	0.21	0.10
Acceleration (cm/s^2)	1167	512	493	830	615	520	852	580	540
	1287	570	561	1018	702	602	1217	770	660
	1356	854	735	1157	970	840	1299	904	814
Force (N)	–	1533	1224	–	1642	1129	–	1690	1367

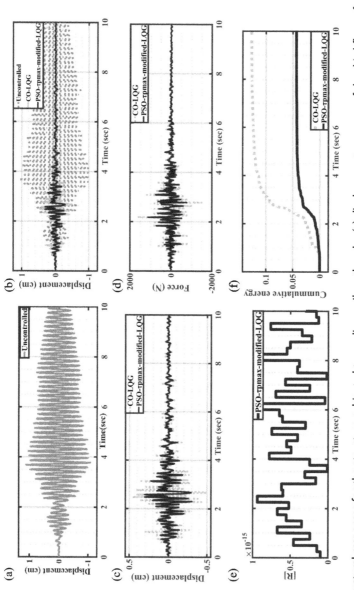

Figure 9.7 Structural responses for the structure subjected to medium soil earthquake: (a) displacement response of the third floor of uncontrolled structure; (b) comparison of controlled responses of the third floor using CO-LQG and PSO-τ_p^{max}-modified-LQG algorithms; (c) comparison of uncontrolled and controlled responses of the third floor using CO-LQG and PSO-τ_p^{max}-modified-LQG algorithms; (d) control forces for the CO-LQG and the PSO-τ_p^{max}-modified-LQG algorithm; (e) variation of **R** with time; and (f) comparison of cumulative energies of the third floor's displacement by applying CO-LQG and PSO-τ_p^{max}-modified-LQG.

floor and second-third floor, respectively, using the proposed controller. The proposed controller also decreases absolute accelerations by 15%, 14%, and 13% for the first, second, and third floors, respectively, compared to CO-LQG. Notably, these reductions are achieved using 31% less force than CO-LQG, as shown in Figure 9.7(d). Figure 9.7(e) displays the variations in the control weighting matrix $\mathbf{R}$, while Figure 9.7(f) compares the cumulative energies of the displacement, affirming that the displacement signal obtained using the proposed controller has lower destructive energy.

Figure 9.8(a) displays the displacement response of the third floor of an uncontrolled structure when subjected to earthquakes recorded in soft soil. To mitigate this displacement, a semi-active control scheme is employed. Figure 9.8(b) compares the time histories of the displacement response between the uncontrolled structure using CO-LQG and the proposed controller, demonstrating the effectiveness of the semi-active control scheme. Table 9.2 shows that the proposed controller reduces the displacement by 32% for the first floor, 29% for the second floor, and 36% for the third floor compared to CO-LQG. Additionally, inter-story drifts between the first-second and second-third floors are reduced by 27% and 52%, respectively, compared to CO-LQG. Accelerations for the first, second, and third floors are reduced by 7%, 14%, and 10%, respectively. These reductions in structural responses are achieved with 19% less force compared to CO-LQG. Figure 9.8(d) provides a comparison of the time histories between CO-LQG and PSO-τ_p^{max}-modified-LQG to validate the results. Furthermore, Figure 9.8(e) illustrates the variation of the control weighting matrix $\mathbf{R}$, which is determined by the PSO algorithm based on quasi-resonance between the natural frequency of the structure and the dominant frequencies of each time window for the earthquake. In quasi-resonance, larger forces are required to control increased vibrations, thus a lower value of weighting matrix $\mathbf{R}$ is determined. Figure 9.8(f) depicts the cumulative energy content of the displacement signal of the third floor obtained using the proposed controller.

9.3.3 Effect of the power cut-off at the peak of the earthquake

In this analysis, a hypothetical scenario is considered where a power outage coincides with the peak of an earthquake event. The El-Centro earthquake is used for simulation purposes. Specifically, the comparison focuses on the relative displacement of the third floor between an uncontrolled structure and a structure controlled using the PSO-τ_p^{max}-modified-LQG method, when power loss occurs at 0.9 sec into the El-Centro time history. Figure 9.9(a) illustrates the comparison of displacement between the third floor of an uncontrolled building and a controlled structure using the PSO-τ_p^{max}m-modified-LQG method, under the assumption of a continuous power supply that suddenly disappears at the peak of the earthquake. Figure 9.9(a) provides additional details.

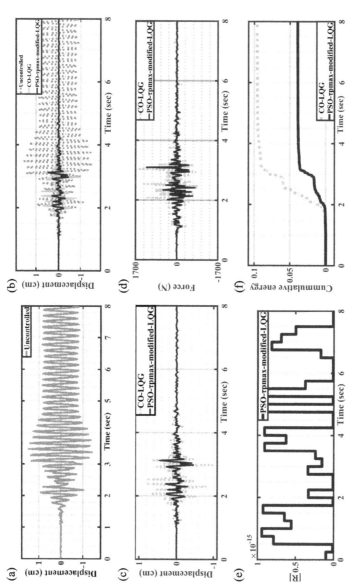

Figure 9.8 Structural responses for the structure subjected to soft soil earthquake; (a) displacement response of the third floor of uncontrolled structure; (b) comparison of controlled responses of the third floor using CO-LQG and PSO-τ_p^{max}-modified-LQG algorithms; (c) comparison of uncontrolled and controlled responses of the third floor using CO-LQG and PSO-τ_p^{max}-modified-LQG algorithms; (d) control forces for the CO-LQG and the PSO-τ_p^{max}-modified-LQG algorithm; (e) variation of **R** with time; and (f) comparison of cumulative energies of the third floor's displacement by applying CO-LQG and PSO-τ_p^{max}-modified-LQG.

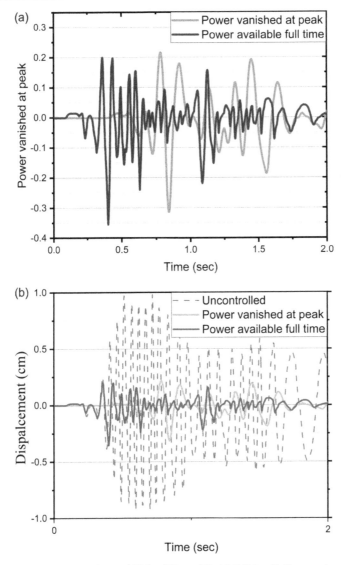

Figure 9.9 Performance analysis of PSO-τ_p^{max}-modified-LQG for El-Centro time history, considering a situation if the power goes off during the peak of the earthquake (a) comparison of the third floor's displacement of uncontrolled structure with the PSO-τ_p^{max}-modified-LQG controlled displacement when power is available for full time and cut-off during the peak of the earthquake.

9.3.3.1 Effect of placing MRD at different floors

This analysis is carried out by placing the MRD within the three-story structure on (a) ground floor, (b) first floor, and (c) second floor, respectively.

For each case, the structure is subjected to the three different earthquakes, namely the El-Centro earthquake, the Chi-Chi earthquake, and the Gebze earthquake.

For the El-Centro earthquake, the maximum percentage reduction in the relative displacement for every floor of the structure is shown in Figure 9.10(a). The percentage reduction in third floor's relative displacement is 69%, 62%, and 58% whereas 74%, 66%, and 64% in the second floor's displacement and 76%, 67%, and 62% on the first floor's displacement when the damper is kept on the ground, first, and second floor, respectively. It can be seen in Figure 9.10(b) that the percentage reduction in the inter-story drift between the first-second floor is 69%, 65%, and 58%, the percentage reduction between the second-third floor is 41%, 34%, and 19%, whereas for the first floor, the percentage reduction is 76%, 67%, and 62% when the damper is kept on the ground, first, and second floor, respectively.

It can be seen in Figure 9.10(c) that the percentage reduction in the third floor's absolute acceleration is 62%, 61%, and 57%, the percentage reduction in the second floor's absolute acceleration is 51%, 50%, and 49%, and for the first floor, reduction is 52%, 51%, and 50% when the damper is kept on the ground, first, and second floor, respectively. For the Chi-Chi earthquake, the percentage reductions in the structural responses are shown in Figure 9.11.

From the observations from Figure 9.11(a), the percentage reduction on the third floor's relative displacement is 81%, 70%, and 44%, for the second floor it is 82%, 68%, and 50%, whereas the percentage reduction in first floor's displacement is 86%, 64%, and 57% when the damper is kept on the ground, first, and second floor, respectively. Observing Figure 9.11(b), the percentage reduction in the inter-story drift between the first-second floor is 75%, 69%, and 50%, between the second-third floor, it is 72%, 60%, and 40%, whereas for the first floor, it is 86%, 64%, and 57% when the damper is kept on the ground, first, and second floor, respectively. Figure 9.11(c) reveals that the percentage reduction on the third floor's absolute acceleration is 69%, 62%, and 54%, for the second floor, it is 70%, 63%, and 53%, and for the first floor, the percentage reduction is 73%, 69%, and 62% when the damper is kept on the ground, first, and second floor, respectively.

Further, for the Gebze earthquake, the percentage reduction on the third floor's relative displacement is 64%, 57%, and 46%, for the second floor's relative displacement is 66%, 59%, and 51%, whereas percentage reduction in the first floor's relative displacement is 53%, 46%, and 58% when the damper is kept on ground, first, and second floor, respectively, as can be seen in Figure 9.12(a). Observing Figure 9.12(b), the percentage reduction in the inter-story drift between the first-second floor is 52%, 45%, and 38%, between the second-third floor, it is 55%, 41%, and 36%, whereas for the first floor, it is 73%, 64%, and 58% when the damper is kept on the ground, first, and second floor, respectively.

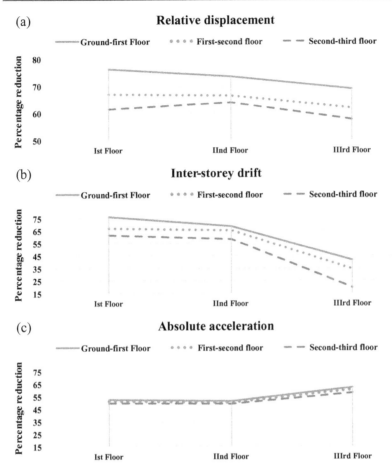

Figure 9.10 Percentage reductions in the structural responses using PSO-τ_p^{max}-modified-LQG in the structure subjected to the El-Centro earthquake by placing MRD at different floors: (a) relative displacement; (b) inter-storey drift; and (c) absolute acceleration.

It can be seen in Figure 9.12(c) that the percentage reduction in the third floor's absolute acceleration is 39%, 36%, and 33%, for the second floor, it is 39%, 37%, 35%, and for the first floor, the percentage reduction is 73%, 69%, and 62% when the damper is kept on the ground, first, and second floor, respectively. Based on the above discussion, it is concluded that the best location to place an MRD on the ground floor in a three-storey structure to achieve maximum reduction in the structural responses.

9.4 CONCLUSION

This study delves into the fascinating world of the PSO-τ_p^{max}-modified-LQG controller, exploring its development process and the remarkable results it

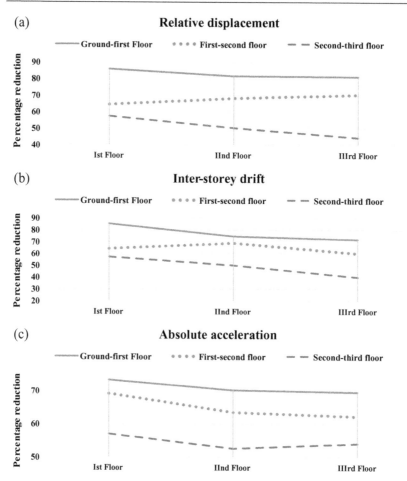

Figure 9.11   Percentage reductions in the structural responses using PSO-τ_p^{max}-modified-LQG in the structure subjected to the Chi-Chi earthquake by placing MRD at different floors: (a) relative displacement; (b) inter-storey drift; and (c) absolute acceleration.

yields. By employing an ingenious technique, we adjust the control weighting matrix **R** through the PSO-τ_p^{max}-algorithm within small-time windows, specifically when quasi-resonance occurs. This transformative approach breathes new life into the traditional LQG controller, paving the way for the creation of this remarkable controller. During seismic events, the updated values of **R** dynamically provide the optimal control force necessary to tackle the challenges posed by earthquakes. What sets our study apart is the utilization of the PSO-τ_p^{max}-algorithm to estimate quasi-resonance between the fundamental frequencies and the earthquake. Unlike previous research, which relied on frequency/time–frequency domain analysis, we evaluate the

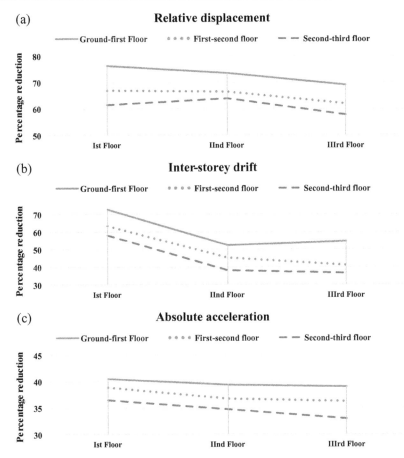

Figure 9.12 Percentage reductions in the structural responses using PSO-τ_p^{max}-modified-LQG in the structure subjected to the Gebze earthquake by placing MRD at different floors: (a) relative displacement; (b) inter-storey drift; and (c) absolute acceleration.

signal in the time domain itself, transcending the limitations of FFT, STFT, DWT, and similar methods.

The specialty of this approach lies in its simplicity and adaptability. Operating exclusively in the time domain, our controller leverages the PSO algorithm to determine the gain matrices in a flexible manner. In contrast to conventional LQG controllers, where the gain matrix remains unchanged, our approach adjusts the gain matrices for each time window, seamlessly adapting to the evolving conditions using the power of PSO. To put our PSO-τ_p^{max}-modified-LQG controller to the test, a prototype three-story structure equipped with a single MRD is subjected to various scenarios. The results are nothing short of astounding. The suggested controllers outperform the traditional LQG controller by a significant margin, demonstrating their superiority in regulating the response of the structure.

Intriguingly, the simulation of different seismic events occurring in diverse soil conditions is shown, and even considering a scenario where a power outage coincides with the peak of seismic activity has also been discussed. Through it all, the developed controller remains steadfast, showcasing its adaptability and robustness. With its exceptional capacity to account for quasi-resonance by manipulating the $\mathbf{R}$ matrix, our PSO-τ_p^{max}-modified-LQG controller has become a favoured choice for vibration control. Its inherent flexibility and innovative design offer a promising solution to the challenges posed by seismic vibrations, propelling us into a future where structures can withstand and adapt to the forces of nature with unparalleled efficiency.

Furthermore, it is observed that the MRD must be placed on the ground floor to achieve the maximum efficiency.

The fellow researchers may choose to work on the following topics in the future.

i. The time delay between the seismic excitation and application of the counter-control force is a limitation of this study. Research may be carried out to further reduce this time delay.
ii. Though the PSO is a very popular heuristic approach for optimization, it takes considerable time to find the optimized results. Other approaches may be explored to reduce the processing time without compromising the outcomes.

REFERENCES

1. B. Spencer, S. Dyke, M. Sain, and M. Carlson, "Phenomenological model for magnetorheological dampers," *J Eng Mech*, vol. 123, no. 3, pp. 230–238, 1997, doi: 10.1061/(ASCE)0733-9399(1997)123:3(230).
2. G. Kumar, R. Kumar, and A. Kumar, "A review of the controllers for structural control," *Arch Comput Methods Eng*, vol. 30, pp. 3977–4000, May 2023, doi: 10.1007/s11831-023-09931-y.
3. G. Kumar, A. Kumar, and R. S. Jakka, "The particle swarm modified quasi bang-bang controller for seismic vibration control," *Ocean Engineering*, vol. 166, pp. 105–116, 2018, doi: 10.1016/j.oceaneng.2018.08.002.
4. S. Y. Zhang and X. M. Wang, "Study of Fuzzy-PID control in MATLAB for two-phase hybrid stepping motor," in *Energy Research and Power Engineering*, in Applied Mechanics and Materials, vol. 341. Trans Tech Publications, 2013, pp. 664–667. doi: 10.4028/www.scientific.net/AMM.341-342.664.
5. S. Gad, H. Metered, A. Bassuiny, and A. M. Abdel Ghany, "Multi-objective genetic algorithm fractional-order PID controller for semi-active magnetorheologically damped seat suspension," *J Vib Control*, vol. 23, no. 8, pp. 1248–1266, Jun. 2015, doi: 10.1177/1077546315591620.

6. M. H. Ab Talib et al., "Vibration control of semi-active suspension system using PID controller with advanced firefly algorithm and particle swarm optimization," *J Ambient Intell Humaniz Comput*, vol. 12, no. 1, pp. 1119–1137, 2021, doi: 10.1007/s12652-020-02158-w.

7. R. Guclu, "Sliding mode and PID control of a structural system against earthquake," *Math Comput Model*, vol. 44, no. 1, pp. 210–217, 2006, doi: 10.1016/j.mcm.2006.01.014.

8. R. Guclu and H. Yazici, "Vibration control of a structure with ATMD against earthquake using fuzzy logic controllers," *J Sound Vib*, vol. 318, no. 1, pp. 36–49, 2008, doi: 10.1016/j.jsv.2008.03.058.

9. K. Liu, L. Chen, and G. Cai, "H∞ control of a building structure with time-varying delay," *Adv Struct Eng*, vol. 18, no. 5, pp. 643–657, 2015, doi: 10.1260/1369-4332.18.5.643.

10. O. Yakut and H. Alli, "Neural based sliding-mode control with moving sliding surface for the seismic isolation of structures," *J. Vib Control*, vol. 17, no. 14, pp. 2103–2116, 2011, doi: 10.1177/1077546310395964.

11. H. Alli and O. Yakut, "Fuzzy sliding-mode control of structures," *Eng Struct*, vol. 27, no. 2, pp. 277–284, 2005, doi: 10.1016/j.engstruct.2004.10.007.

12. Y. Chu, J. Fei, and S. Hou, "Adaptive global sliding-mode control for dynamic systems using double hidden layer recurrent neural network structure," *IEEE Trans Neural Netw Learn Syst*, vol. 31, no. 4, pp. 1297–1309, Apr. 2020, doi: 10.1109/TNNLS.2019.2919676.

13. Y. Chu, J. Fei, and S. Hou, "Adaptive global sliding-mode control for dynamic," *IEEE Trans Neural Netw Learn Syst*, vol. 31, no. 4, pp. 1–13, 2019.

14. M. Allen, F. Bernelli-Zazzera, and R. Scattolini, "Sliding mode control of a large flexible space structure," *Control Eng Pract*, vol. 8, no. 8, pp. 861–871, 2000, doi: 10.1016/S0967-0661(00)00004-6.

15. V. Utkin, "Variable structure systems with sliding modes," *IEEE Trans Automat Contr*, vol. 22, no. 2, pp. 212–222, 1977, doi: 10.1109/TAC.1977.1101446.

16. S. A. Chen, J. C. Wang, M. Yao, and Y. B. Kim, "Improved optimal sliding mode control for a non-linear vehicle active suspension system," *J Sound Vib*, vol. 395, pp. 1–25, 2017, doi: 10.1016/j.jsv.2017.02.017.

17. Q. P. Ha, M. T. Nguyen, J. Li, and N. M. Kwok, "Smart structures with current-driven MR dampers: modeling and second-order sliding mode control," *IEEE/ASME Transactions on Mechatronics*, vol. 18, no. 6, pp. 1702–1712, 2013, doi: 10.1109/TMECH.2013.2280282.

18. B. Zhao, X. Lu, M. Wu, and Z. Mei, "Sliding mode control of buildings with base-isolation hybrid protective system," *Earthq Eng Struct Dyn*, vol. 29, no. 3, pp. 315–326, 2000, doi: 10.1002/(SICI)1096-9845(200003)29.

19. A. Ahlawat and A. Ramaswamy, "Multiobjective optimal structural vibration control using fuzzy logic control system," *J Struct Eng*, vol. 127, no. 11, pp. 1330–1337, 2001, doi: 10.1061/(ASCE)0733-9445(2001)127:11(1330).

20. K. M. Choi, S. W. Cho, H. J. Jung, and I. W. Lee, "Semi-active fuzzy control for seismic response reduction using magnetorheological dampers," *Earthq Eng Struct Dyn*, vol. 33, no. 6, pp. 723–736, 2004, doi: 10.1002/eqe.372.

21. K.-M. Choi, S.-W. Cho, D.-O. Kim, and I.-W. Lee, "Active control for seismic response reduction using modal-fuzzy approach," *Int J Solids Struct*, vol. 42, no. 16, pp. 4779–4794, 2005, doi: 10.1016/j.ijsolstr.2005.01.018.

22. D. Das, T. K. Datta, and A. Madan, "Semiactive fuzzy control of the seismic response of building frames with MR dampers," *Earthq Eng Struct Dyn*, vol. 41, no. 1, pp. 99–118, 2012, doi: 10.1002/eqe.1120.

23. H. Pang, F. Liu, and Z. Xu, "Variable universe fuzzy control for vehicle semi-active suspension system with MR damper combining fuzzy neural network and particle swarm optimization," *Neurocomputing*, vol. 306, pp. 130–140, 2018, doi: 10.1016/j.neucom.2018.04.055.

24. L. Zhou, C. C. Chang, and L. X. Wang, "Adaptive fuzzy control for nonlinear building-magnetorheological damper system," *J Struct Eng*, vol. 129, no. 7, pp. 905–913, 2003, doi: 10.1061/(ASCE)0733-9445(2003)129:7(905).

25. Y. Solgi and S. Ganjefar, "Variable structure fuzzy wavelet neural network controller for complex nonlinear systems," *Appl Soft Comput*, vol. 64, pp. 674–685, Mar. 2018, doi: 10.1016/J.ASOC.2017.12.028.

26. S. F. Ali and A. Ramaswamy, "Optimal fuzzy logic control for MDOF structural systems using evolutionary algorithms," *Eng Appl Artif Intell*, vol. 22, no. 3, pp. 407–419, 2009, doi: 10.1016/j.engappai.2008.09.004.

27. A. R. M. Rao and K. Sivasubramanian, "Multi-objective optimal design of fuzzy logic controller using a self configurable swarm intelligence algorithm," *Comput Struct*, vol. 86, no. 23, pp. 2141–2154, 2008, doi: 10.1016/j.compstruc.2008.06.005.

28. K. Takin, R. Doroudi, and S. Doroudi, "Vibration control of structure by optimising the placement of semi-active dampers and fuzzy logic controllers," *Aust J Struct Eng*, vol. 22, no. 3, pp. 222–235, 2021, doi: 10.1080/13287982.2021.1957198.

29. X. B. Nguyen, T. Komatsuzaki, Y. Iwata, and H. Asanuma, "Modeling and semi-active fuzzy control of magnetorheological elastomer-based isolator for seismic response reduction," *Mech Syst Signal Process*, vol. 101, pp. 449–466, Feb. 2018, doi: 10.1016/J.YMSSP.2017.08.040.

30. X. Tang, H. Du, S. Sun, D. Ning, Z. Xing, and W. Li, "Takagi-Sugeno fuzzy control for semi-active vehicle suspension with a magnetorheological damper and experimental validation," *IEEE/ASME Transactions on Mechatronics*, vol. 22, no. 1, pp. 291–300, 2017, doi: 10.1109/TMECH.2016.2619361.

31. S. J. Dyke, B. F. Spencer Jr, M. K. Sain, and J. D. Carlson, "Modeling and control of magnetorheological dampers for seismic response reduction," *Smart Mater Struct*, vol. 5, no. 5, p. 565, 1996, doi: http://stacks.iop.org/0964-1726/5/i=5/a=006.

32. G. Kumar and A. Kumar, "Fourier transform and particle swarm optimization based modified LQR algorithm for mitigation of vibrations using magnetorheological dampers," *Smart Mater Struct*, vol. 26, no. 11, p. 115013, Oct. 2017, doi: 10.1088/1361-665X/aa8681.

33. G. Kumar, R. Kumar, A. Kumar, and B. Mohan Singh, "Development of modified LQG controller for mitigation of seismic vibrations using swarm intelligence," *Int J Autom Control*, vol. 17, no. 1, pp. 19–42, 2023, doi: 10.1504/IJAAC.2023.10049079.

34. G. Kumar, A. Kumar, and R. S. Jakka, "An adaptive LQR controller based on PSO and maximum predominant frequency approach for semi-active control scheme using MR damper," *Mech Ind*, vol. 19, no. 1, p. 109, 2018, doi: 10.1051/meca/2018018.

35. L. M. Jansen and S. J. Dyke, "Semiactive control strategies for MR dampers: Comparative study," *J Eng Mech*, vol. 126, no. 8, pp. 795–803, 2002, doi: 10.1061/(asce)0733-9399(2000)126:8(795).
36. G. F. Panariello, R. Betti, and R. W. Longman, "Optimal structural control via training on ensemble of earthquakes," *J Eng Mech*, vol. 123, no. 11, pp. 1170–1179, 1997, doi: 10.1061/(ASCE)0733-9399(1997)123:11(1170).
37. A. Alavinasab, H. Moharrami, and A. Khajepour, "Active control of structures using energy-based LQR method," *Comput-Aided Civ Infrastruct Eng*, vol. 21, no. 8, pp. 605–611, 2006, doi: 10.1111/j.1467-8667.2006.00460.x.
38. B. Basu and S. Nagarajaiah, "A wavelet-based time-varying adaptive LQR algorithm for structural control," *Eng Struct*, vol. 30, pp. 2470–2477, 2008, doi: 10.1016/j.engstruct.2008.01.011.
39. F. Amini, N. K. Hazaveh, and A. A. Rad, "Wavelet PSO-based LQR algorithm for optimal structural control using active tuned mass dampers," *Comput-Aided Civ Infrastruct Eng*, vol. 28, no. 7, pp. 542–557, 2013, doi: 10.1111/mice.12017.
40. Y. Nakamura and J. Saita, "UrEDAS, the earthquake warning system: today and tomorrow," in *Earthquake Early Warning Systems*, Berlin, Heidelberg: Springer, 2007, pp. 249–281. doi: 10.1007/978-3-540-72241-0_13.

Chapter 10

Intelligent data-driven approach for fractional-order wireless power transfer system

Arshaque Ali, Ashneel Kumar, Utkal Mehta,
and Maurizio Cirrincione

10.1 INTRODUCTION

In the current era of technology, people are dependent on portable devices and gadgets for daily life, but charging these devices via tethered connections can be inconvenient. Recently, wireless power transfer (WPT) technologies have made it possible to live in a world where charging devices is as easy as placing them near a power source. This wireless charging technology is available for smartphones, smartwatches, and electric toothbrushes, but it cannot handle charging larger batteries such as those in electric vehicles. The existing technology also requires precise orientation and distance between the charging and receiving coils, making it inefficient if the conditions are not met [1]. The magnetic resonance method (MRC) overcomes the issue of efficiency loss caused by the distance between the power transmission and the power reception coils. However, the transfer efficiency and output power are extremely sensitive to the resonant frequency; if the operating frequency deviates outside the resonant frequency range or if the system is affected by metallic or external electromagnetic fields, the system's efficiency will plummet drastically [2]. To address these concerns, this chapter proposes the MRC method in conjunction with a fractional-order capacitor (FOC) to improve system stability. The fractional-order components can be used to make the system more flexible and robust. The fractional order (i.e., α) can be between 0 and 2; $\alpha < 1$ indicates a passive component with positive resistive losses while $\alpha > 1$ indicates an active component with negative resistive losses. The proposed WPT setup employs a FOC with $\alpha < 1$ to obtain enhanced transfer characteristics when compared to a classical WPT. Furthermore, a data-driven approach is considered to obtain information on system performance and component values. Load modelling using optimization has been evaluated for three different cases, and the results were analysed to determine the most suitable topology for experimental verification.

DOI: 10.1201/9781003470274-10

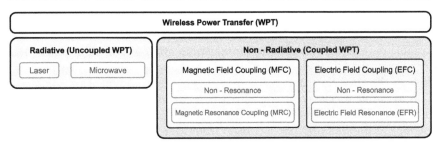

Figure 10.1   Categories of WPT.

10.2 WPT SYSTEM

The WPT system refers to the transfer of electrical energy from a power source to a receiving device without any physical connection. The theory and laws behind WPT are based on electromagnetic fields and electromagnetic induction. Electromagnetic fields are created by the flow of electrical current, and these fields can be used to transfer energy wirelessly. When a current is passed through a coil, it creates a magnetic field around the coil. This magnetic field can then induce a current in another nearby coil, which in turn creates an electrical potential difference and causes a flow of current. The main law that governs WPT is Faraday's law of electromagnetic induction. This law states that a change in magnetic flux through a coil of wire induces an electromotive force (EMF) in the coil, which can be used to generate an electrical current. The magnitude of the induced EMF is proportional to the rate of change of the magnetic flux. Another important law that applies to WPT is Maxwell's equation, which describes the behaviour of electromagnetic fields and their interaction with electric charges. These equations are used to design and analyse the performance of WPT systems.

10.2.1 Classification of WPT systems

The WPT operating principles can be divided into two subcategories: radiative and non-radiative. The radiative category, also known as "uncoupled WPT," deals with the far-field transmission of power using microwaves/lasers and achieves a good transfer distance (up to a few metres) with low efficiency. The non-radiative category, also known as "coupled WPT," is more suitable for near-field transmission of power and uses two types of coupling: magnetic field coupling (MFC) or electric field coupling (EFC). Despite transfer distance limitations, coupled WPT has advanced significantly due to improved efficiency [3]. Under MFC and EFC, there are two coupling techniques for each: non-resonance and resonance. These categorizations of WPT can be seen easily in Figure 10.1.

In the early 1990s, the electromagnetic induction technique (the non-resonance method under MFC) was widely used to charge batteries in portable devices such as electric toothbrushes and cordless telephones [4]. Even today, the Qi wireless charging standard implemented in smartphones employs the same electromagnetic induction concept, and these are commercially available wireless charging devices for charging low-power devices [5]. The MRC method, which has recently gained popularity under magnetic coupling, is another approach. A team from MIT's Departments of Physics, Electrical Engineering, and Computer Science and ISN used the MRC method to demonstrate the transfer of 60 W of power over 2 m. When the transfer distance is increased, the MRC method has been shown to resolve the issue of low efficiencies. MRC has been shown to maintain transfer efficiency as the transfer distance increases gradually, but once the resonant frequency of the receiving coil deviates from the resonant frequency of the transmitting coil, the transfer efficiency suffers greatly. By positioning the transmitting and receiving coils at an optimal distance apart, the magnetic resonance technique achieves and maintains maximum transmission efficiency. The distinction between electromagnetic induction and magnetic resonance coupling is determined by whether resonance is used.

10.2.2 Magnetic resonance coupling (MRC)

The extent of magnetic coupling between the power transmission and reception sides is expressed by the coupling coefficient, denoted by k. Assuming that the inductances of the transmitting and receiving coils are L_1 and L_2, respectively, with the mutual inductance as M, the coupling coefficient can be computed as

$$k = \frac{M}{\sqrt{L_1 L_2}} \tag{10.1}$$

This value can only be within the range; $0 \leq k \leq 1$ and is ideally equal to 1, indicative of a 100% transmission efficiency in the absence of leakage flux. It is expected that a WPT system employing the MRC method will achieve a high transfer efficiency even with a low coupling coefficient. The S–S topology produces higher efficiency with a small load [6]. The MRC method can be employed in the WPT system using four topologies; Series–Series (S–S), Series–Parallel (S–P), Parallel–Series (P–S), and Parallel–Parallel (P–P). The topologies define the connection of the capacitor in the primary and secondary circuits of the WPT system. Denoted by two letters (S for series and P for parallel), the first letter specifies the primary side capacitor connection, while the second letter specifies the secondary side capacitor connection. The topologies are depicted in Figure 10.2 for WPT circuits.

Each of these topologies has sets of advantages and disadvantages that are associated with the MRC WPT. The efficiency of the S–S topology

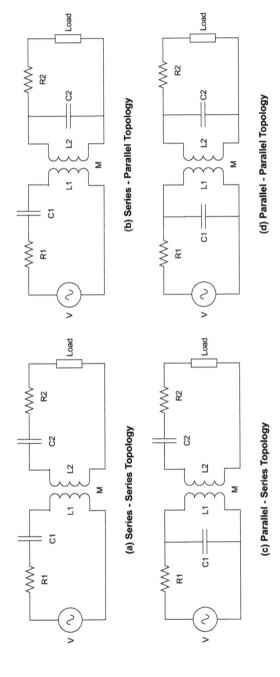

(a) Series - Series Topology

(b) Series - Parallel Topology

(c) Parallel - Series Topology

(d) Parallel - Parallel Topology

Figure 10.2 WPT circuit topologies under the MRC method.

decreased as the load grew, indicating that this setup performs better with smaller loads. The S–S topology has a number of advantages, including its suitability for small load resistances, its ability to handle high-frequency changes while maintaining efficiency, and the fact that its efficiency improves with the coupling coefficient. However, the downsides of the S–S topology include frequency splitting when the distance between the transmission and reception coils is too small and a loss in efficiency as the load resistance increases. At the natural resonant frequency, the input impedance for S–S and S–P topologies is very low, allowing a large amount of input current to flow through the primary coil inductance, resulting in a maximum magnetic field around the coil and, consequently, an adequate induced voltage and current produced in the secondary coil to recharge the battery. For P–S and P–P topologies, however, high input impedance at natural resonant frequency allows a very small current to pass through the main coil inductance, resulting in low induced voltage and current at the secondary, which are insufficient to recharge the battery. The important topologies discussed above were also considered in reference [7] and are tabulated in Table 10.1 with the benefits and drawbacks of each. The qualitative analysis provided by Wang et al. proves useful for the selection of the correct topology for the implementation of a WPT circuit for a specified task. Simply put, the topology that gives the best combination of transfer power and transfer efficiency for the MRC method can be determined using Table 10.2.

The analysis also sheds light on an important phenomenon mentioned earlier, termed "frequency splitting," which occurs when transfer power varies with frequency and splits into two peak values when the coupling coefficient is large enough. The system efficiency is the greatest at the natural resonant frequency, while the transfer power is greatest at the two splitting frequencies [8]. This statement is supported by the maximum power transfer theorem, which states that maximum transfer power and efficiency cannot be reached simultaneously. Consequently, S–S and S–P topologies provide substantially more efficient power transfer than P–S and P–P topologies.

10.3 FRACTIONAL-ORDER CAPACITOR (FOC) APPROXIMATION

A FOC is a capacitor modelled by fractional calculus, and its current–voltage relationship is defined by Equation (10.2) as

$$i(t) = C_\alpha \, \frac{d^\alpha}{dt^\alpha} \, v(t) \tag{10.2}$$

where $\frac{d^\alpha}{dt^\alpha}$ is termed the fractional-order derivative operator, C_α is the pseudocapacitance value, and α is the order in the range of 0 to 2. The

Table 10.1   Merits and demerits of common MRC topologies

Topology	Merits	Demerits
S–S	• Suited for small load resistances • Withstands large frequency fluctuations • Efficiency increases with coupling coefficient	• Frequency splitting • Efficiency decreases with increase in load resistance
S–P	• Suited for large load resistances • Efficiency increases with coupling coefficient	• Efficiency decreases with decrease in load resistance
P–S	• Suited for small load resistances • Efficiency increases with coupling coefficient	• Small load power and current • Resonant frequency is affected by mutual inductance
P–P	• Suited for large load resistances • Efficiency increases with coupling coefficient	• Small load power and current • Resonant frequency is affected by mutual inductance

Table 10.2   Criteria for WPT topology selection

Condition	Secondary circuit	Primary circuit
$R_L > \left(\frac{L_2}{C_2}\right)^{\frac{1}{2}}$	**Parallel**	Compare both topologies, if: • Large load power → **Series** (with parameter optimization) • Small load power → **Parallel**
$R_L < \left(\frac{L_2}{C_2}\right)^{\frac{1}{2}}$	**Series**	**Series** If frequency splitting is present; • optimize distance, capacitance and inductances. ***P-S is not suitable for WPT**

pseudocapacitance can be obtained using Equation (10.3) [9];

$$\omega_0 = \alpha + \sqrt{\frac{\sin\frac{\alpha\pi}{2}}{LC_\alpha \sin\frac{\pi}{2}}} \qquad (10.3)$$

where ω_0 is the angular frequency, α is the order in the range of 0 to 2, L is the inductance of the coil, and C_α is the pseudocapacitance value in Farad/s$^{(1-\alpha)}$. The angular frequency influences the pseudocapacitance value, as the relationship suggests. Equation (10.4) calculates the conventional capacitance (C) in Farads.

$$C = \frac{C_\alpha}{\omega^{(1-\alpha)}} \qquad (10.4)$$

Table 10.3 Comparison of CFE and Oustaloup approximations

Feature	Continued fractional expansion (CFE)	Oustaloup approximation
Method	Approximation by continued fraction	Approximation by integer-order transfer functions
Accuracy	High, but depends on the number of terms used in the continued fraction	High, but depends on the number of integer-order transfer functions used
Computational complexity	Medium to high, depending on the number of terms used in the continued fraction	Low to medium, depending on the number of integer order transfer functions used
Flexibility	Flexible, as the number of terms in the continued fraction can be adjusted to achieve the desired accuracy	Limited, as the approximation is based on a fixed number of integer-order transfer functions
Implementation	Requires numerical techniques for the computation of continued fraction terms	Requires the computation of fractional integration and differentiation by parts

The impedance of a FOC can be given as

$$Z_{CPE}(s) = \frac{1}{C_a s^\alpha} \qquad (10.5)$$

The transfer functions, which are derived from fractional derivative definitions like the Riemann–Liouville and Caputo definitions, have always been used to represent fractional-order components (with an order between 0 and 1). Converting the transfer functions into an equivalent electrical schematic necessitates the use of network synthesis approximations such as the continued fraction expansion (CFE), partial-fractions expansion (PFE) or Oustaloop approximations. A comparative analysis provided by Tsirimokou et al. [10] concludes that using the CFE approach allows for the approximation of fractional-order transfer functions using simple circuits with high phase accuracy. When compared to the CFE method, the Oustaloup method provides a higher level of magnitude accuracy. Table 10.3 contains a detailed comparison of the two approximation methods.

10.4 FRACTIONAL COMPONENTS AND WPT

Fractional calculus has traditionally been regarded as speculative mathematics due to a lack of progress in its research. Many electrical devices and systems have fractional-order properties, according to current research, which is why fractional calculus has gained prominence in electrical engineering [11]. Actual components such as capacitors and inductors can be more accurately modelled using fractional calculus. Most capacitor orders are close to one when fractional-order characteristics are ignored, so "1" was initially used to describe the basic model of a capacitor. Supercapacitors, for example, have been discovered to have strong fractional-order properties (its order is much smaller than 1). This characteristic of supercapacitors has been explored, analysed, and documented in reference [12], as supercapacitors were found to have a variable structure fractional model. The experiment was carried out with three different supercapacitors of varying sizes and manufacturers. The results revealed that the actual orders for supercapacitors varied depending on the manufacturer and were close to but not equal to one. The fractional orders of the Kyocera AVX supercapacitors were 0.93 and 0.92, respectively, whereas the fractional orders of the other two brands varied from 0.42 to 0.93 depending on the capacitance values. This experiment establishes the existence of supercapacitor fractional-order properties and provides a flexible supercapacitor model for realistic, accurate time domain modelling. Similarly, time-domain analysis of fractional-order circuits and comparison with the classical integer components are presented [13]. Fractional-order circuits exhibit characteristics of a fractional-order element (FOE), such as a FOC or a fractional-order inductor (FOI). FOCs can be of two types: the active capacitor $(1 < \alpha < 2)$ and the passive capacitor $(0 < \alpha < 1)$ [14]. It was demonstrated that the classical integer derivative was highly inaccurate and could not reflect the dynamic behaviour of the process by simulating the behaviour of a fractional-order derivative using ladder elements and comparing it to it. During the initial charging state, the ladder network was observed to support rapid voltage changes, indicating a more accurate and dynamic system. By establishing the circuit model of a FOC and FOI, Shu and Zhang [15] have analysed the influences of these FOEs on a WPT system. Theoretical analysis revealed that different orders of the FOC (α) and FOI (β) have different effects on transmission efficiency. However, the effect of fractional orders on output power was found to be proportional, meaning that the output power increased as the fractional orders of the elements increased. If the system is realized using physical components, such theoretical analysis can be used to find the optimum orders for each FOE in order to obtain better characteristics. In relation to realized fractional-order WPT (FOWPT) systems, Zhang et al. [16] proposed a FOE-based WPT system which can achieve a higher power efficiency and a lower resonant frequency when compared to using conventional integer order components. By designing a FOC in the Foster II RC canonical form and realizing it using the obtained parameters, the dynamic behaviour of a FOC was tested before it was implemented in a WPT system. Upon realization of the FOC and finding the phase difference, it was determined that the actual order was 0.54 instead of 0.5. This was due to discrepancies between the computed RC values

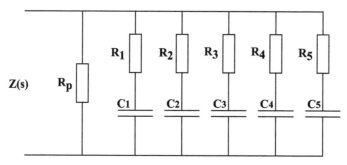

Figure 10.3 Fifth-order foster II RC network.

and the actual RC values used in the FOC realization. Nonetheless, at a transfer distance of 0.3 m, the FOC of order 0.54 was implemented in a WPT system and achieved a unity power factor. A power factor of one indicates greater energy efficiency and a successful MRC. While this experiment and analysis demonstrate the successful implementation of a FOC to achieve MRC and thus higher efficiency, it does not state the transfer efficiency, does not compare the results of the FOC WPT system to an equivalent integer order WPT system, and does not test the various fractional orders of a FOC in the WPT system to determine the best α. Jiang and Zhang [17] have developed a similar system, i.e., a WPT system that incorporates a FOC on the transmitting circuit, but with an α greater than 1. This system is proposed in the article as a solution to the unpredictable shifting of a WPT system's resonant frequency in the real world due to external disturbances in the environment. The results show that within the area of strong MRC, the WPT system with a FOC of order greater than one was insensitive to changes in the receiver's resonant frequency and transfer distance. Jiang et al. [18] proposed a FOWPT system based on MRC, which incorporates the use of FOCs. The system was modelled and theoretically examined to determine the effects of load and FOC order on the transfer characteristic of the system. The analysis revealed that the FOWPT can achieve a constant current output that is independent of the load if the appropriate FOC parameters, namely the fractional order (α) and pseudocapacitance ($C\alpha$), are chosen. A system prototype was also created, and the results matched the theoretical analysis. The system had one flaw: if the inductance and internal resistance of the coil change due to interferences from the surrounding environment, the required order of the FOC changes.

10.5 CASE STUDY

A data-driven approach was used to incorporate a FOC of order between 0 and 1 in a WPT system and analyse its effect on the system. An RC network representing a FOC was created for orders $0.05, 0.10, 0.15, \ldots, 0.95$ using

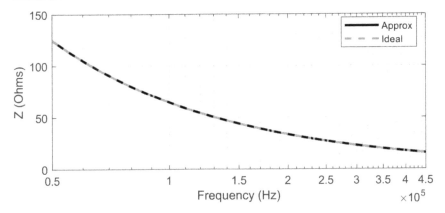

Figure 10.4 Magnitude response of FOC approximation.

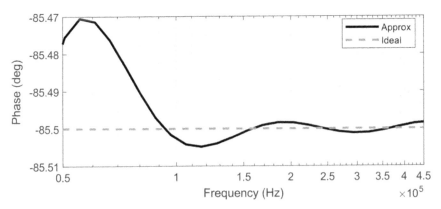

Figure 10.5 Phase response of FOC approximation.

the CFE approach and approximating the impedance (see Equation (10.5)) in the Foster II canonical form. The approximated structure of the FOC RC network is shown in Figure 10.3. The magnitude, frequency, and error plots for the CFE approximation of the 0.95 FOC in the Foster II RC network are shown in the figures below. The plots were created for frequencies ranging from 100 kHz to 400 kHz. Figure 10.4 depicts the approximation's magnitude response, which shows a nearly complete overlap between the "Approx" and "Ideal" responses. Figure 10.5 depicts the frequency response of the approximation, which deviates slightly from the ideal response. The deviation, however, is observed to be minimal at the resonant frequency of 300 kHz. The errors plot in Figure 10.6 shows that the approximated system has few errors (all errors are below 0.015% between 100 kHz and 400 kHz). The errors are smallest around 300 kHz because the approximation was computed with this frequency as the centre frequency.

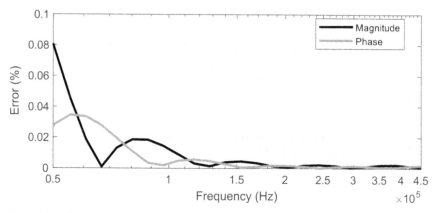

Figure 10.6 Error in FOC approximation.

Table 10.4 Simulation circuit parameters

Parameter	Value
U_s	200 V_p
f	250 kHz
R_1	1.3 Ω
R_2	1.3 Ω
L_1	159.2 μH
L_2	159.2 μH
R_L	10 Ω, 100 Ω, 1kΩ, 10kΩ

In Simulink®, a WPT system was designed for MRC at 250 kHz. In the simulation, an unconstrained power source was used to allow the system to draw the necessary power to achieve the best efficiency when subjected to a specific load resistance. Three cases were simulated to better understand how the inclusion of a FOC affects system performance.

10.5.1 Case 1: Classical wireless power transfer (CWPT)

To investigate the behaviour of the S–S and S–P WPT, the circuit parameters shown in Table 10.4 were used to create the simulation circuits for each topology composed of integer-order components. For data analysis, the input power, output power, and efficiencies were tabulated.

10.5.2 Case 2: Data-driven FOWPT design with fixed order FOC

To assess the impact of fractional–orders on the WPT circuit, a FOC with an order of 0.95 replaced the integer–order capacitor on the receiving side, followed by the transmitting side and both sides of the circuit. Through a data-driven approach, simulations were conducted for fractional-orders ranging from 0.1 to 0.9 to understand their effect on transmission efficiency. Performance metrics such as input and output powers, voltage, and currents were collected, serving as data points for evaluating efficiency under different fractional-order scenarios. The analysis revealed that orders below 0.95 resulted in poor efficiencies due to inadequate adaptation of circuit parameters. Consequently, these orders were eliminated from further testing, allowing a comprehensive understanding of how fractional–orders influence WPT circuit efficiency.

10.5.3 Case 3: Frequency decrease in CWPT and data-driven design of FOWPT

This case dealt with CWPT and FOWPT being subjected to a decrease of 100 kHz in the operating frequency in order to observe the behaviour of the circuits. The input power, output power, and efficiencies were obtained for analysis. The strategy used for simulating and extracting the data is given in the flowchart in Figure 10.7. To begin the process, a MATLAB® script was created, requiring the declaration of circuit parameters such as coil inductances, resonance frequency, fractional order, and compensation capacitance value. The script's responsibility was to compute the values of passive elements for the FOC, which would become part of the Foster II network. Moving forward, the next steps involved selecting the load resistance value and creating the desired topology and model of the case in Simulink®. With each increment of 0.1, the coupling coefficient, k, was increased from 0.1 to 0.9, while the simulation was run at each step. Extracting the input and output parameters (voltage and current), their respective values were multiplied to obtain the input and output powers. Subsequently, these results were tabulated, and graphs depicting efficiency versus k were plotted. Figures 10.8 and 10.9 show plots of the S–S and S–P topologies, respectively. The S–S topology achieved a peak efficiency of 97.37% with a load of 1 k, whereas the S–P topology only achieved a peak efficiency of 95.01% with the same load. The coupling coefficient (k) measures the strength of coupling between the Tx and Rx coils; values closer to 1 indicate strong coupling with the shortest distance. In the simulation, the coupling coefficient serves as a proxy for distance: the smaller the value, the greater the distance. While the S–S topology has a higher peak efficiency, the results also show that the S–P topology can maintain efficiency much better even at low coupling coefficient values (see Figure 10.9), indicating that transfer is possible over long distances. Figure 10.10 depicts the efficiency versus coupling coefficient curves for three different loads in the S–S topology at a frequency of 150 kHz. The results clearly show that the FOWPT efficiencies are significantly higher than the CWPT efficiencies for any given load. Similarly, Figure 10.11 shows the efficiency versus coupling coefficient

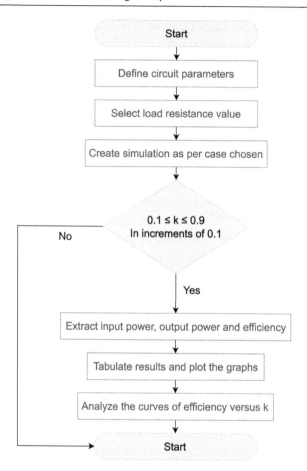

Figure 10.7 Procedure of data extraction

curves with varying loads in the S–P topology. Despite the topology change, the FOWPT system outperforms the CWPT for all simulated load values.

10.6 RESULT COMPARISON

To further validate the simulation findings, an experimental setup based on Table 10.5 specifications was created.

A data-driven procedure was used, with data tabulated for the S–P topology with operation at the resonant frequency and at a lower frequency. The resonant frequency of 300 kHz was chosen because the coil quality factor (Q) of the self-wound coils (see Figure 10.13) peaked around this frequency. The pseudocapacitance was calculated using the circuit parameters listed

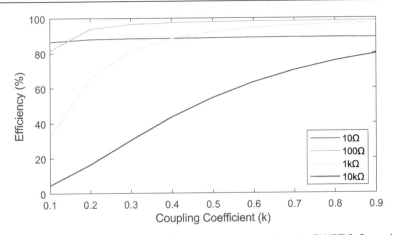

Figure 10.8 Efficiency vs coupling coefficient for varying loads in the CWPT S–S topology.

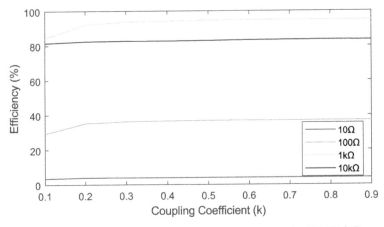

Figure 10.9 Efficiency vs coupling coefficient for varying loads in the CWPT S–P topology.

above by rearranging Equation (10.3) to get Equation (10.6).

$$C_{0.95} = \frac{\sin\left(\frac{0.95\pi}{2}\right)}{\omega^{1.95}\,(L_1)\sin\left(\frac{\pi}{2}\right)} \tag{10.6}$$

The pseudocapacitance was calculated to be approximately 48 $nF/s(1 - \alpha)$, and the approximation resulted in the passive component values in Table 10.6 and the experimental setup is shown in Figures 10.12 and 10.13. A function generator supplied a 20 V_{peak} signal to the transmission circuit, allowing for frequency adjustments.

While the current supplied by the function generator was insufficient to transfer large amounts of power, it was sufficient for result verification. The

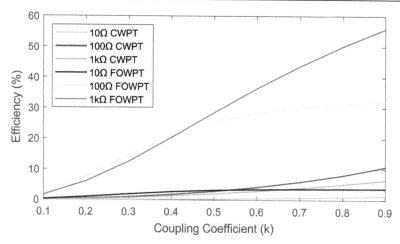

Figure 10.10 CWPT and FOWPT (FOC on Tx side only) in S–S topology at 150 kHz.

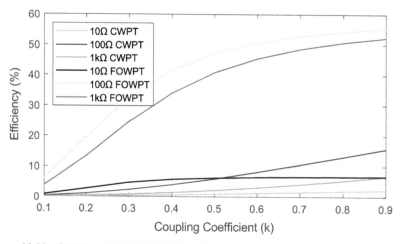

Figure 10.11 CWPT and FOWPT (FOC on Tx side only) in S–P topology at 150 kHz.

Table 10.5 Experimental setup circuit
parameters

Parameter	Value
U_s	21 V_{pp}
f	300 kHz
R_1	0.228 Ω
R_2	0.752 Ω
L_1	12 μH
L_2	49.17 μH
N_{TX}	5
N_{RX}	10

Table 10.6 RC values for FOC approximation in the Foster II form

R_p	R_1	R_2	R_3	R_4	R_5	C_1	C_2	C_3	C_4	C_5
11.46kΩ	45.28mΩ	39.64Ω	224.60Ω	677.60Ω	1.75kΩ	20nF	1.87nF	1.36nF	1.45nF	2.38nF

Figure 10.12 Experimental setup for result verification.

results of the experimental setup are shown in the figures. Figure 10.14 depicts the CWPT and FOWPT plots on the same pair of axes. The CWPT has a higher peak efficiency than the FOWPT, as seen in the simulation, but the efficiency loss with increasing distance is more gradual in the FOWPT. Both the CWPT and FOWPT were able to transmit power over a distance of 0.3m at the resonant frequency.

This nature of the FOWPT in comparison with CWPT is observed to hold true for any operating frequency within the system's natural frequency range. The FOWPT performs better when the system is forced to operate at the upper limits of this range, which is 180 kHz (see Figure 10.15). Because the power supplied to the transmission circuit is limited, these efficiencies are obtained over shorter distances.

10.7 CONCLUSION

It can be seen from the results that, at natural resonant frequencies (and in the natural frequency range), the CWPT system is more efficient than the FOWPT system. Deviating from this frequency range reduces the CWPT system's efficiency: the deviation occurs due to external disturbances caused by metal and impedance changes or by attempting to operate the system in a

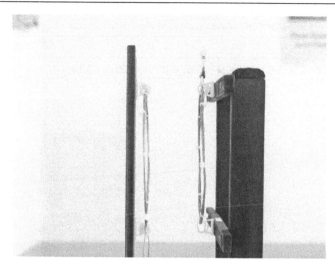

Figure 10.13 Transmitting and receiving coils with a distance of 0.1 m in between.

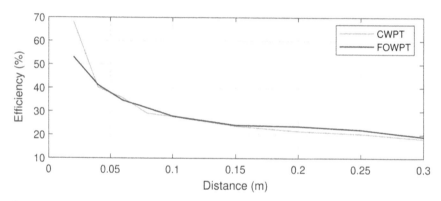

Figure 10.14 CWPT and FOWPT in the S–P topology at 300 kHz (experimental).

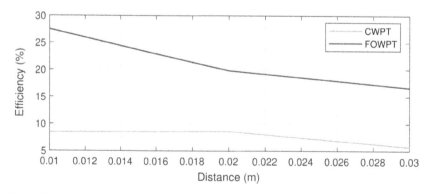

Figure 10.15 CWPT and FOWPT in the S–P topology at 180 kHz (experimental).

complex electromagnetic environment. With the FOWPT system, operating outside this range is possible with acceptable efficiency as the system is more robust and maintains efficiency better (in both topologies). The crucial characteristic is that high efficiency can be obtained even when there are variations in the system's operating frequency or if a lower frequency of operation is desired. For $\alpha < 1$, the resistance of the fractional order is present and is positive, resulting in additional losses, i.e., the lower the order, the greater the losses, and the lower the efficiency, hence only 0.95 was used in the simulation. Using the data-driven approach, the analysis identified the correct parameters for the physical realization of the schematic. Despite only being able to transfer a few milliwatts, the experimental setup employed in the study proved adequate for verifying the simulation results. The nature of the simulation and experimental results were consistent. For future work, it is suggested to design a medium power transmission circuit using power inverter topologies to increase current supply, generate a larger magnetic field for improved coupling, implement efficient switching techniques like zero voltage switching, and conduct ample research to enable the design of FOE greater than 1. These advancements would enhance power transfer capabilities, optimize system performance, and explore the potential of active components with negative resistance for reduced losses.

REFERENCES

1. Morris Brenna, Federica Foiadelli, Carola Leone, and Michela Longo. Electric Vehicles Charging Technology Review and Optimal Size Estimation. *Journal of Electrical Engineering & Technology*, 15(6):2539–2552, November 2020.
2. Ryosuke Ota, Dannisworo Sudarmo Nugroho, and Nobukazu Hoshi. A Consideration on Maximum Efficiency of Resonant Circuit of Inductive Power Transfer System with Soft-Switching Operation. *WEVJ*, 10(3):54, September 2019.
3. Nassim Iqteit, Khalid Yahya, and Sajjad Ahmad Khan. Wireless Power Charging in Electrical Vehicles. In Mohamed Zellagui, editor, *Wireless Power Transfer âŁ" Recent Development, Applications and New Perspectives*. IntechOpen, August 2021.
4. Xiao Lu, Ping Wang, Dusit Niyato, Dong In Kim, and Zhu Han. Wireless Charging Technologies: Fundamentals, Standards, and Network Applications. *IEEE Communications Surveys and tutorials*, 18(2):1413–1452, 2016.
5. Shalabh Gaur. A Research Paper on Wireless Charging. *JETIR* 6(5):648–655, 2019.
6. Mohamed Hassan and Amr El Zawawi. Wireless Power Transfer (Wireless lighting). In *2015 5th International Conference on Information & Communication Technology and Accessibility (ICTA)*, pages 1–4, December 2015. IEEE, Marrakech.
7. Jingchen Wang, Mark Leach, Eng Gee Lim, Zhao Wang, and Yi Huang. Investigation of Magnetic Resonance Coupling Circuit Topologies for Wireless Power Transmission. *Microwave and Optical Technology Letters*, 61(7):1755–1763, July 2019.

8. Runhong Huang, Bo Zhang, Dongyuan Qiu, and Yuqiu Zhang. Frequency Splitting Phenomena of Magnetic Resonant Coupling Wireless Power Transfer. *IEEE Transactions on Magnetics*, 50(11):1–4, November 2014.

9. Ravneel Prasad, Krishneel Sharma, Bhavish Gulabdas, and Utkal Mehta. Model of Fractional-Order Resonant Wireless Power Transfer System for Optimal Output. *Journal of Electrical Engineering*, 73(4):258–266, August 2022.

10. Georgia Tsirimokou, Aslihan Kartci, Jaroslav Koton, Norbert Herencsar, and Costas Psychalinos. Comparative Study of Discrete Component Realizations of Fractional-Order Capacitor and Inductor Active Emulators. *Journal of Circuits, Systems and Computers*, 27(11):1850170, October 2018.

11. Kajal Kothari, Utkal Mehta, Vineet Prasad, and Jito Vanualailai. Identification Scheme for Fractional Hammerstein Models with the Delayed Haar Wavelet. *IEEE/CAA Journal of Automatica Sinica*, 7(3):882–891, 2020.

12. Ravneel Prasad, Kajal Kothari, and Utkal Mehta. Flexible Fractional Super-capacitor Model Analyzed in Time Domain. *IEEE Access*, 7:122626–122633, 2019.

13. Ewa Piotrowska and Krzysztof Rogowski. Time-Domain Analysis of Fractional Electrical Circuit Containing Two Ladder Elements. *Electronics*, 10(4):475, February 2021.

14. Bo Zhang and Xujian Shu. *Fractional-Order Electrical Circuit Theory*. CPSS Power Electronics Series. Springer Singapore, Singapore, 2022.

15. Xujian Shu and Bo Zhang. The Effect of Fractional Orders on the Transmission Power and Efficiency of Fractional-Order Wireless Power Transmission System. *Energies*, 11(7):1774, July 2018.

16. Guidong Zhang, Zuhong Ou, and Lili Qu. A Fractional-Order Element (FOE)-Based Approach to Wireless Power Transmission for Frequency Reduction and Output Power Quality Improvement. *Electronics*, 8(9):1029, September 2019.

17. Yanwei Jiang and Bo Zhang. A Fractional-Order Wireless Power Transfer System Insensitive to Resonant Frequency. *IEEE Transactions on Power Electronics*, 35(5):5496–5505, May 2020.

18. Yanwei Jiang, Bo Zhang, and Jiali Zhou. A Fractional-Order Resonant Wireless Power Transfer System with Inherently Constant Current Output. *IEEE Access*, 8:23317–23323, 2020.

Index